THE NOVEL:

A Modern Guide to Fifteen English Masterpieces

By Elizabeth Drew

DISCOVERING POETRY

POETRY: A MODERN GUIDE

THE NOVEL: A MODERN GUIDE

THE NOVEL:

A Modern Guide to Fifteen English Masterpieces

BY ELIZABETH DREW

W · W · NORTON & COMPANY · INC ·
NEW YORK

ACKNOWLEDGMENTS:

Passages quoted from the following novels are reproduced with the permission of their publishers:

James Joyce, *A Portrait of The Artist as a Young Man*. The Viking Press, Inc.

D. H. Lawrence, *Women in Love*. The Viking Press, Inc.

Virginia Woolf, *To the Lighthouse*. Harcourt, Brace and World, Inc.

Contents

Preface

All kinds of creative artists flourish in the field of literature, but the only kind of criticism of literature which is of any value is that which makes us want to go and read or reread the books it discusses. This collection of essays is written in the hope that it will do that. Henry James describes the novel as "the most independent, the most elastic, the most prodigious of literary forms." It is all that. It is also the most popular of literary forms, which sometimes obscures the values it has beyond those of mere entertainment. We use the novel as "literature of escape," as something to remove us from the drabness and harshness of actuality to a fictional world of adventure and excitement, or emotional wish-fulfillment, or comic fantasy. We are all grateful for this kind of novel, since life has a way of being unintelligible and monotonous, human relationships are never completely satisfying and human experience is strictly circumscribed. Yet the novel can provide us not only with a temporary escape *out of* living, but escape *into* imaginative worlds where we find our own actual lives enhanced and vitalized by the company of created characters and events, and of the particular minds controlling them. These stimulate instead of lulling our own faculties; they make us more alive. These are the novels we read and reread, whatever age they are written in.

Reading novels, like reading any other literature, is a creative act, a collaboration between reader and writer. Our own minds and senses, emotional and moral feelings, have to be receptive, willing first to surrender to all that the writer can give. Having done that, we can then be alert to question, to argue, to disagree. For criticism, of course, is inevitably subjective and partial; even with the best efforts at objectivity, we respond to one novel and not to another; we admire one grudgingly and another wholeheartedly. Among the choice of English books here it will be clear that I have my own personal preferences and prejudices: I prefer *Emma,* for example, to *Women in Love,* and *To the Lighthouse* to *Clarissa,* and *Lord Jim* to *A Portrait of the Artist.* I banish Walter Scott and Charlotte Brontë altogether. But I could not exclude Henry James, who, though an American, is so international and so important.

All the books, however, are now "classics" and in a way they close a chapter in the history of the novel. For all of these writers, from the eighteenth to the early twentieth century, have one thing in common: they belong to what we may call the humanist tradition. However differently they view experience, and whatever different methods they use to give perspective to their view, basically they belong to the same cultural heritage, they hold the same intellectual, ethical and social standards. That tradition has been weakened by the contemporary world in revolutionary changes in the cultural climate, which in turn have affected the novel.

I analyze these changes briefly in the Epilogue, but within the tradition of the past, I have arranged the novels in some general categories, for purposes of discussion. There is nothing dogmatic about these. Works of art don't fit neatly into pigeonholes any more than human beings fit neatly into the types invented for them by psychologists and sociologists. Obviously certain books could be moved around: *Lord Jim* could go into the section "The Game of Art," or *Great Expectations* into Social Comedy, or *The Portrait of a Lady* into The Tragic Vision. The arrangement is simply a convenience for grouping books which have something in common, and to bring out distinctions within that common bond.

Henry James said that the house of fiction has the possibility of a million windows, any of which can be fashioned to open on the spreading field of the human scene by the pressure of an individual will and vision. The windows can be of any shape, "either broad or balconied or slit-like and low-browed." They represent the literary form the writer chooses. Yet in themselves, he says, the windows are as nothing without "the posted presence of the watcher . . . the consciousness of the author." The aim of this book is to look out of some of the windows, describe the view and suggest what it tells us about that posted watcher.

E.D.

*Although our productions have afforded more
extensive and unaffected pleasure than those of
any other literary corporation in the world, no
species of composition has been so much de-
cried. . . . "And what are you reading, Miss —?"
"Oh! it is only a novel!" replies the young lady
. . . It is . . . only some work in which the greatest powers of the mind are displayed, in which
the most thorough knowledge of human nature,
the happiest delineation of its varieties, the live-
liest effusions of wit and humour, are conveyed
to the world in the best-chosen language.*

JANE AUSTEN, *Northanger Abbey*

Life and Art in the Novel

Ever since the novel came into being as a literary form, in the first half of the eighteenth century, the reading public has delighted in it. But it has been one of the clichés of criticism for many years now that no serious examination of the *art* of the novel existed before Flaubert, and that Henry James alone among English-speaking artists followed in his footsteps. We have been told that earlier novelists regarded themselves as entertainers and that they and their public existed in a state of critical innocence.

This was true of the public, though never of the writers. Fielding pointed out that the whole flavor of a novel depended on "the cookery of the author." But it was true that critics did not bother themselves with much serious treatment of the form until the late nineteenth century. Then, recent research has proved, persistent discussion went on in reviews and essays. All the topics we examine now—structural unity, objective versus subjective presentation, the place of the didactic, the limits of naturalism—all were aired and argued. And, as in the eighteenth century, the novelists themselves knew very well what went into the creation of novels. Dickens was the greatest "entertainer" of them all, but listen to Dickens on the subject of his calling:

> I hold my inventive capacity on the stern condition that it must master my whole life, often have complete possession of me, make its own demands on me, and sometimes for months together put everything else away

from me. . . . Whoever is devoted to an Art must be content to deliver himself wholly up to it and to find his recompense in it.

It might almost be Flaubert speaking. Again, after Thackeray's death, Dickens commented: "He too much feigned a want of earnestness. . . . He made a pretence of undervaluing his art, which was not good for the art he held in trust."

There is no danger today of the serious modern novelist or his critics undervaluing the aesthetic elements in his work, but this has led to a dilemma which was unknown to writers of the past. In the introduction to a book on the modern novel, published a few years ago in England, the author says: "I have written as an intellectual addressing other intellectuals; one tract of fiction I have therefore omitted: the bestseller." Such a remark would have been inconceivable in the eighteenth or nineteenth century. Most great classics among our novels—*Robinson Crusoe, Tom Jones, Clarissa, Tristram Shandy, Vanity Fair, Jane Eyre, David Copperfield, The Mill on the Floss*—all these were best sellers in their own day. There existed no such separation as this division into the intellectual sheep and the best-selling goats.

Revolutionary changes have certainly taken place, but before discussing them further, perhaps we should go back to the beginning and ask: What is a novel?

Novels are generally lumped under the term "fiction," which is regarded in the library lists as the opposite of "nonfiction." This inevitably leaves fiction with a slightly disreputable flavor of falsity about it. That fact worried some nineteenth-century critics. One called Thackeray's *The Newcomes* "one of the masterpieces of English fiction, if fiction is the proper term for such a great work." Another pleaded: "George Eliot's novels are not fiction in the ordinary sense of the word, they are dramas."

We are not so squeamish now about refusing fiction an equality with drama. Nor do we accept the definition given by Miss Prism in Oscar Wilde's *The Importance of Being*

Earnest. She said of her novel: "The good ended happily, the bad unhappily, that is what fiction means." We don't require that particular falsity in our fiction, and moral questions do not have to come into our definitions— though they always come into the novels. But it is still difficult to find a good definition. It is easier to shift ground somewhat and quote Arnold Bennett's straightforward description of the novelist, not of the novel.

> The novelist is he who, having seen life, and being so excited by it that he absolutely must transmit his vision to others, chooses narrative fiction as the liveliest vehicle for the relief of his feelings.

"The novelist . . . having seen *life* . . ." Life, of course, is the basic raw material of all art, but no artist is so close to his raw material as the novelist. It's all around him all the time: people, incidents, scenes, sense impressions, conversations—anything can arouse his curiosity, his excitement, his compulsion to transmit it into language and thus relieve his own feelings and communicate them to others.

All literary art is, as we say, "impure" compared with the arts like painting or music; the latter are more removed from the actualities of human experience since they do not have to use speech as their sense medium— the medium in which we carry on our everyday living. But among all the impure literary arts, the novel is the most impure. It deals directly with the actions and passions of characters whom we inevitably come to think of as fellow human beings, with whom we identify ourselves; it usually tells us of moral and emotional crises, of incidents and situations within the observation of us all. The novel is bound to concern itself directly with the emotional and moral standards men live by, and all the problems of conduct which beset us every day. It's as impossible to keep such problems out of the discussion of novels as it is to keep them out of the living of life. As E. M. Forster says in his *Aspects of the Novel:*

The intensely, stiflingly human quality of the novel is not to be avoided; the novel is sogged with humanity; there is no escaping the uplift and the downpour, nor can they be kept out of criticism. We may hate humanity, but if it is exorcised or even purified, the novel wilts, little is left but a bunch of words.

But other critics nowadays insist on discussing the novel as "a bunch of words," since they point out that that is precisely what it is, and that to speak of content, as such, in a novel is not to speak of art at all, but simply of direct experience of life. Only, they say, when we tackle the content as revealed through the form and language can we speak as critics.

This again is only a half-truth, for novelists themselves differ so widely in what they ask of their readers, and in the value they set upon their own techniques. At one extreme we have Laurence Sterne in *Tristram Shandy* saying:

> I would go fifty miles on foot to kiss the hand of that man whose generous heart will give up the reins of his imagination into the author's hands—be pleased he knows not why, and cares not wherefore.

Or Samuel Butler declaring: "I cannot conceive how any man can take thought for his style without loss to himself and his readers." At the other extreme we have Flaubert, after completing twenty-five pages in six weeks:

> Sometimes I can't make out why my arms don't fall off my body with weariness, or why my brain doesn't turn to porridge. I have a harsh existence, devoid of all outward joy . . . I love my work with a frenzied, perverted passion, as an ascetic loves the hair shirt that scrapes his body.

Or Conrad, deploring his readers' unawareness of the pains of turning blood into ink, and telling of "the strain of a creative effort in which mind and will and conscience are engaged to the full hour after hour, day after day, to the exclusion of all that makes life lovable and gentle." The only material parallel he can think of is "the ever-lasting sombre stress of the westward winter passage round Cape Horn."

This inevitably prompts the question whether the novels that have provoked these appalling labor pains are neces-sarily better than the ones that achieve their form more easily. We think of Stendhal, for instance, confessing that to do any planning of a book freezes him stiff. His program was to dictate twenty-five or thirty pages a day and then go out in the evening for "violent distraction."

> It is necessary that by next morning I shall have for-gotten everything. When I read three or four pages of yesterday's chapter today's chapter comes to me.

Or Trollope, sitting with his watch in front of him, in the three hours before breakfast which he allowed for novel writing, determined to turn out a thousand words an hour—and doing it. No one would put Trollope among the giants, but nevertheless he remains entertaining and readable after a hundred years.

In fact, can we say that any one way of writing a novel is, in itself, better than any other way? It is the freest of all literary forms; the writer has only to please himself. He can tell the story in his own person, like Sterne, or dis-appear almost completely, like Jane Austen. He can com-bine a number of different points of view, like Richardson with his letter form, or as Conrad does in *Lord Jim,* so that the same characters and events are refracted through many personalities. He can interrupt his narrative con-stantly like Thackeray, always jogging the reader's elbow to remember this and not to miss that, or, like Joyce, he can make the form carry all interpretation dramatically. He can seem to be giving the facts and nothing but the facts, like Defoe, or spin endless filaments of feeling into a web which almost obscures the facts, like Henry James. He can, like Tolstoi, plunge us at once into action, with-

out any scaffolding to support it, or spend so long on the
foundations that we wonder, as we do with Balzac, when
the story is ever going to develop. He can tell a straightforward chain of events, like Fielding, or build intricate
symbolic patterns, like Virginia Woolf.

This complete freedom of form makes the novel very
slippery and elusive stuff to criticize. Where can we take
hold to make a start? The novelists themselves are helpful,
for many of them have had a taste for talking about their
art. Rather naturally, each usually comes out in favor of
his own method, but we can sort out from them at least
some of the elements that they feel basic to their enterprise, and that we must therefore look for in any novel.

> If there is one gift more essential to the novelist than
> another it is the power of combination—the single
> vision. The success of the masterpieces seems to lie not
> so much in their freedom from faults—indeed we toler-
> ate the grossest errors in them all—but in the immense
> persuasiveness of a mind which has completely mas-
> tered its perspective.

It is Virginia Woolf speaking, and saying something at
the heart of the matter. For the form of the novel is the
reflection of the vision of the individual artist; of his penetration, his sense of proportion, his emphases, in the
presentation of his human material. As we read, we become absorbed into the vision, and we have the *illusion*
that we are contemplating life itself. The surface aspects
may all be unfamiliar, but our own human experience
seems confirmed and freshened.

This is life, we say, as we read Jane Austen's *Emma*.
We don't have to spend our lives as women in Highbury;
thank heaven, we comment. But how familiar these social
situations are: the snobberies, the self-deceptions, the
petty humiliations, the scheming self-interest, the com-
placent humbug, the social cruelties and injustices. This
village chronicle of England in the early nineteenth century seems a complete view of common human nature.

Then maybe we take up *Vanity Fair,* and we think: Jane Austen was wonderful in that small sphere of ironic comedy; she kept everything so marvelously to scale that we were unaware of her limitations; but how small her scope is! This is life: this sweeping panoramic view of the social scale from highest to lowest. This wide variety of character and circumstance, this succession of vivid scenes in which they play out their destinies. And how true it is that life brings us all to that conclusion: "Which of us is happy in this world? Which of us has his desire? or, having it, is satisfied?" But then we may get absorbed in Virginia's Woolf's *To the Lighthouse,* and in a flash of revelation we exclaim: Why, none of the old traditional novelists had the secret after all! Life never builds itself into the convenient symmetry of a plot. Life is the quality of the immediate present as we live it from moment to moment. Experience is made from the silt of innumerable instants of consciousness, fusing the present with memories of the past; blending thought and action and sensation; expanding into the widest contemplation of the human situation in its universal aspects or contracting into the observation of some small objects around us, or into fragments of talk, gestures, some fleeting association. It's all discontinuous, inconclusive, fugitive, flickering. This, at last, is life!

So we could go on through hundreds of novels. But what we have been responding to is of course not life, but art. The life in the novel is distilled from the "single vision" of the author, from his intelligence, insight, subtlety, clarity of mind. It is the vitality of his expression, not that of the raw material expressed. Life remains life: it may be interesting and varied, or monotonous and dreary, pleasurable or painful. But books are exactly what their authors make them. We have the illusion that stories are in themselves delightful or dull, but it is not so. There are no dull stories, only dull people who write books (and, one must add, dull people who read them).

First, then, the novelist must have a "single vision"; we

must feel life filtered through a particular perception; seen
from a particular perspective. As Henry James puts it:

> When vigorous writers have reached maturity, we are
> at liberty to look in their works for some expression of
> a total view of the world they have been actively ob-
> serving. This is the most interesting thing their work
> offers us.

But what does "a total view of the world" imply? The
novelist's observation is far keener than that of the average man. We have only to read the *Notebooks* of Henry
James to see what trivialities of social exchange, or passing whiffs of psychological insight, served to arouse his
creative curiosity for fuller development. Yet this quality
of ultrasensitivity can be overplayed. Henry James said
he aimed to be "one of those on whom nothing is lost,"
and Virginia Woolf urged the writer to register the myriad
impressions that fall upon the mind in an incessant
shower.

> Let us record the atoms as they fall . . . in the order in
> which they fall, let us trace the pattern, however discon-
> nected and incoherent in appearance, which each sight
> or incident scores upon the consciousness.

But, really, could anything be more impossible—or
more useless? To be one of those on whom *nothing* is lost,
and who conserves every atom of consciousness, would be
to be mentally like those mad old misers who are finally
found dead in houses cluttered to the walls and roofs indiscriminately with riches and rubbish. We can have
many too many "atoms" in fiction: of sentiment in Richardson; of realistic detail in Zola; of undigested memory
in Joyce. Virginia Woolf recognizes this herself when she
is talking about the naturalistic novels she dislikes, and
all the "life" in them: "We have enough life on our hands
as it is, without reading all about it in prose."

A good novel is a selection of material by one individual
who has excluded everything irrelevant or superfluous to

his purpose, and has synthesized or slanted or distorted or adapted "life" to serve his own vision. Life stretches around the novelist in all its meaningless prodigality of relatedness, and, as Henry James again says: "really, universally, relations stop nowhere, and the exquisite problem of the artist is . . . to draw, by a geometry of his own, the circle within which they shall happily appear to do so."

Art is selection and symmetry: it creates the illusion of wholeness within its own strictly imposed outlines. But what the artist selects again depends on his personality. Like all other literary arts, the novel interprets life primarily through the emotions and the senses. André Gide said: "Never present ideas except in terms of character," yet we can think of many first-rate novels that are full of the authors' ideas: *Don Quixote* to start with; *Tom Jones; Candide; War and Peace* (though we may want to skip the historical theory); *Crime and Punishment; Middlemarch; The Magic Mountain.* George Eliot was criticized even in her own day for putting too many ideas into her books, but Leslie Stephen defended her:

> I confess that, for my part, I am rather glad to find ideas anywhere. They are not very common; and there are a vast number of excellent fictions which these sensitive critics may study without the least danger of a shock to their artistic sensibilities by anything of that kind.

Most readers, though, would probably agree that the presentation of personal relationships is the central interest of the novel, whether they are interpreted to us along with intellectual content, or projected dramatically in emotional and sensuous terms. In either form, the presentation is based on some pattern of interrelation between the events of a story and the characters who play it out. The traditional novel always emphasized action, but one of the new developments in the modern novel has been the tendency to turn away from any carefully worked out pat-

tern of events, and to prefer impressionistic incidents or
indirect approaches. The method aims at revealing a situation spatially, in depth, not in progression; constantly
expanding its themes out from a center rather than developing them lineally, in plot.

The methods of revealing character, as well as the types
of character revealed, mark the greatest changes in the
art of the novel from its beginnings to the present day.
We know Moll Flanders entirely from seeing her in so
many concrete situations, rattled off by Defoe with so
much realistic detail, while Virginia Woolf's Mrs. Ramsey,
whose life is so much more inward than outward, comes
to us through elaborate internal soliloquies and metaphorical parallels. Tom Jones is more type than individual,
surrounded by so much richness of social setting and interpreted to us so fully by his creator, while the heroes in
Conrad or Lawrence or Joyce are all isolated from their
fellows, struggling toward some individual self-fulfillment
outside their own society, and presented to us in some unfamiliar method of self-revelation.

The novel has always been able to reveal much more
about individuals than we know about our friends, for
characters in novels ultimately have no secrets from us,
whereas our friends all do, whether consciously or unconsciously. Nevertheless, the characterization in most novels
of the eighteenth or nineteenth century is very simple. In
spite of claims made for Richardson, George Eliot is the
first serious psychologist. Her analyses are accurate and
searching. But it was Henry James who first realized that
inward drama, all the unseen forces that motivate behavior, might be more absorbing than any overt action.
Proust again set the whole evocation of his world in the
associative processes of the memory, while Joyce and
Virginia Woolf practiced different varieties of the "stream
of consciousness" method to reveal inner realities.

Indeed "consciousness" rather than character in its
earlier sense became the center of many novels; the presentation of the vast unspoken experience that goes on in

us, both simultaneously with our outer life, and in solitude, became the great extension of fictional territory. Instead of mapping the social scene as the sole center, the novelists moved into the labyrinthine realms of inner being. Instead of observing only the *functioning* of the human organism in its social environment, they followed the psychologists into exploring the *nature* of the life processes going on beneath the surface. Just as modern experimenters in painting have tried to transcend the limitations of spatial art by conveying the illusion of movement and succession on canvas, so the experimenters in writing transcended its limitations as a temporal medium communicating succession only, to convey the illusion of a simultaneous creation of both sequence in time and expansion in depth. The temporal and the spatial strove to become coexistent in writing, and for a while experimental novels were as much dominated by patterns of "double time" as the Victorians were by patterns of morality.

It was these new revolutionary changes in technique, first set in motion by Henry James, which caused the rift between the "intellectuals" and the "best sellers." Henry James admired George Eliot very deeply, but he made one adverse criticism of her work: ". . . her conception of the novelist's task is never in the least as the game of art." This is true, but all it means is that her method of storytelling is simpler, more relaxed than that of James; that he was the first to explore individual psychology in a new way, and was the forerunner of later innovations in complexity. The "games of art" were the result of the need to find new methods for new insights. They contained their own dangers, however, as we shall see in later chapters. Elaboration of one kind of technique may illustrate great expansion of sensibility and subtlety and yet stifle the free creation of vital action and character. It remains deeply true, as Virginia Woolf said, that the success of a masterpiece is not necessarily the absence of faults, but the presence of a compelling creative intelligence. This is the real criterion, as James himself knew. He deplored the lack of economy, the "welter of helpless verbiage," which, to him, made the novels of Tolstoi and Dostoevski into "fluid puddings." At the same time he owns that "the amount of their own minds and souls in solution gives savour and flavour, thanks to the strong, rank quality of their genius and experience." The distinction is not really between "the game of art" and "fluid puddings"; it is in essence between one kind of art and another kind of art. Again the novel is so spacious a form that it has room for all varieties. If a writer creates a form and uses language so that he presents a convincing fictional world and carries his own mature knowledge and feeling into the mind of his reader, he is an artist, whether he is a best seller or an intellectual. Whether he has a perfect structural pattern or holds to a single "point of view" in his narrative or uses some new technical apparatus is irrelevant. His methods are effective for his own purpose. It may be, as Forster suggests, that the whole question of method comes down to "the power of the writer to bounce the reader into accepting what he says." The power must be there, but it may be used in many different ways as long as it carries the all-important "life." If it does that, any method is "art": it is the use of "a bunch of words" to create the illusion of significant human experience.

Nevertheless there is nothing to prevent us from imagining a dream novel, which shall somehow combine the vitality and abundance of humanity in Tolstoi and Dostoevski with the beautiful architecture of Henry James.

THE FORERUNNERS

DANIEL DEFOE
1660?–1731

Moll Flanders

We have said that the quality of a novel rests finally on the vision and vitality of its author. This is a basic truth, but no author writes in a vacuum. The novelist, like all of us, is a member of a specific society, in time and in place; any novel is, from one point of view, a social document. In fact, it was as an alleged social document, not claiming to be a work of art, that the novel came into being. We can trace poetry and drama to prehistoric roots in tribal magic or ritual, but the seeds of the novel as we recognize it are books written by an English middle-class, middle-aged tradesman and journalist in the early eighteenth century—Daniel Defoe.

Defoe did not call his books "novels." If, however, we take as a working definition of the novel that it is a prose work of a certain length and a certain artistic unity, which purports to be a story of "real life" and sets out to convince its readers that it is, then we may call Defoe the first novelist. In his journalistic writing he had chosen, as he said, "a downright plainness, and to speak home both in fact and in style." When he used this method for an autobiographical fiction of a narrator describing his or her life and hard times, he created the modern novel.

Storytelling must of course be as old as life itself. Clas-

sical epic, drama and pastoral are different forms of it,
and many kinds of stories in English existed before the
birth of the novel. Romances, chivalric or pastoral or
"heroic," in poetry and in prose, flourished from the Middle Ages to the seventeenth century. Collections of stories
were popular, serious and comic, moralistic or coarse, like
Boccaccio's *Decameron* and Chaucer's *Canterbury Tales*.
Lyly's *Euphues* created a short-lived Elizabethan fashion
for telling a moral tale in an absurd, stilted and orna-
mented prose. Nashe's *The Unfortunate Traveler, or The
Life of Jack Wilton* (1594) was the first "picaresque"
fiction in England. The *picaro* or rogue as hero originated
in Spain in the fifteenth century. He was an outcast from
society, often a bastard, living by his wits. Jack Wilton is
a rascally page of an aristocratic master who travels all
over Europe. His adventures make a small book, but the
individual episodes have no over-all theme or unity, and
the interest in character is almost nonexistent, so it
hardly qualifies as a novel. No evidence exists that Defoe
had ever read or heard of Nashe, though Defoe too is in
the picaresque tradition. He seems to have stumbled upon
his own new literary form quite by accident when he published *Robinson Crusoe* in 1719, in his late fifties. *Moll
Flanders* followed in 1722.

The immediate popularity of his stories showed how
ready the public was for them, and it is natural to ask
what it was in the social structure and environment of the
period that made the new form particularly welcome.
For one thing, the great popular entertainment in the
Elizabethan and Jacobean ages—the theatre—had decayed. It had dwindled into "heroic" romances and ultra-
sophisticated bawdy comedy entertaining to the Court,
whose taste no longer corresponded to that of the "people."
The epithet "middle class" nowadays gives us the feeling
of something conservative and stodgy. But if we go back
two hundred and fifty years, the middle class were the radi-
cals and rebels. Politically it was they who had beheaded
an English king, and who tolerated monarchy again only

if it was hedged about with safeguards against tyranny and feudal power. It was the middle class who built up the great English trading enterprises; who were pushing ahead in scientific discovery, and who brought about that revolution in the use of *language* which was essential for its new functions. The Royal Society, founded in 1662, demanded of its members "a close, naked, natural way of speaking; positive expressions, clear senses, a native easiness . . . preferring the language of artisans, country-men and merchants before that of wits and scholars."

Simple middle-class language was needed not only as the instrument for the fresh exploration of the nature of the universe, but also for the literary use of the new society that was coming into being. The philosopher John Locke had defined the function of language as "to convey knowledge of things." This was a new concept, for until then, narrative art had been in the tradition that literary treatment transformed "things" into some appropriate epic or romantic rhetoric. But "romance" in its old feudal trappings was in decay as much as the drama. The interminable fantasies of courtly and supernatural adventures, which Mrs. Pepys found so fascinating in the mid-seventeenth century, did not please the next generation of readers. They too sought, as readers have always sought, an escape from the monotony or hardship or emptiness of actual existence into another world; but the nature of that substitute world changed.

Various influences had worked toward the change of taste. The rise of journalism, for one thing, trained a new reading public in an interest in the history and manners going on around it. The writing of biography, diaries, memoirs, "characters," and sketches such as the Sir Roger de Coverley essays in *The Spectator* developed a fresh attitude toward the study of ordinary types and experiences. Then, the women of the new middle-class society had more time on their hands for reading than their mothers or grandmothers. A great increase in feminine leisure came about by the manufacture of many commodities formerly "homemade." Bread, beer, candles, soap, dress materials could all be bought in the shops and markets, thus releasing the housewife from many of her old duties. Education too was much more widespread. Moll Flanders, the bastard orphan, falls into the care of a village woman who keeps a little school; Richardson takes it for granted that Pamela, the young servant girl, can write and read as well as her employers. Twenty years after the publication of *Pamela,* the first circulating library was opened in London, to be followed shortly by many others. Books could be borrowed for a penny a volume, so that all classes could find "escape" in the novel, as they have continued to do ever since. Everything, in fact, was ready and waiting for the new kind of "romance"—the "realistic novel."

It was a small but a very important step when Defoe, taking advantage of all these new interests and mores, and using a gift very personal to himself, published stories about strongly individualized human beings, set in authentic contemporary environments, acting out their problems in a patterned though somewhat crude plot sequence, and using the language of ordinary speech. Very few writers have created both a new subject matter and a new form for its embodiment, but Defoe (though he seems to have been unaware of it) did both, and united the highly educated and the semieducated into a reading public for his innovations.

Virginia Woolf (in *The Common Reader*) said that *Moll Flanders* stands "among the few English novels which we can call indisputably great." At the other extreme, Mark Schorer (in *Forms of Modern Fiction*), denigrating Defoe and his values, has said that "the novel is not the true chronicle of a disreputable female, but the true allegory of an impoverished soul, the author's." Either statement has a touch of absurdity. The story, like Defoe himself, is much less than great and much more than sordid.

Defoe was as admirably fitted to tell the inside truth about human roguery and rascality as to illustrate the vigor and toughness of the human spirit. He wrote of his own life:

> No man has tasted differing fortunes more,
> And thirteen times I have been rich and poor.

Bred as a tradesman, his ventures in hosiery, brickmaking and other businesses always failed. He was in and out of bankruptcy all his life, and seems to have died in hiding, trying to escape a persistent creditor.

Defoe became an author, indeed, because he failed as a businessman. At the age of thirty-three, with a wife and seven children to support, he turned to journalism as a means of livelihood. Defoe is remembered now for a few stories written during five years late in his lifetime. It has been estimated that he published more than 350 political pamphlets, verse and prose satires, books on topical themes and manuals of domestic conduct, besides producing *The Weekly Review,* written entirely by himself, three times a week, for seven years. Some of this writing shows Defoe to have been a most progressive thinker for his time. He urged education for women, a university of London, a foundling hospital, religious tolerance, the same law for the rich and the poor, and he was full of practical schemes for the improvement of travel and trade. But his chief occupation was political pamphleteering—a risky business in the days of William III and Queen Anne. Defoe found himself in Newgate prison several times, and had the humiliation of standing in the pillory for three days after he had attacked the extreme Tory attitude toward the Dissenters. Born and brought up in a dissenting family, Defoe never changed his creed to suit his fortunes or pretended allegiance to the Church of England, though it would have been much to his advantage to have done so. His gift for ready and readable writing and his skill in undercover activities made him the perfect secret-service agent, and he appears to have traveled all over England and Europe on intelligence work for the government. Nor was he very particular about which government he served.

Late in his life he summed up his political observations:
"I have seen the bottom of all parties ... their interest
governs their principle." Perhaps the same could be said
of Defoe himself in the political though not in the religious
field. Defoe, like his Moll Flanders, was a wonderful mixture of hypocrisy and honesty, of inconsistency and courage. In the Preface to the book, with his tongue in his
cheek, he pretends that it tells a true story and that it
preaches a pious morality. Obviously it does neither, but
surely to see it as "the allegory of an impoverished soul"
is to falsify its flavor. However imperfectly worked out, Defoe's vision is of an individual pitted against a social system in which the scales of justice are weighted heavily
against her. Moll's innate tenacity of spirit and vigorous
intelligence alone save her personality from extinction by
poverty, by social injustice, and by misfortune; she survives and wins friends and fortune by her own courage
and vitality alone.

Moll is born in Newgate prison, the child of a mother
condemned to transportation for a petty theft, and a
chance father. She is adopted by a poor woman in Col-
chester, and sees no future for herself except to spend her
life as a servant, against which her independent spirit
rebels. This fate she escapes by being taken into the household of the mayoress and educated with her own daughters. She develops into a beauty, but soon realises the grim
truth of what one of her foster sisters says: "If a young
woman have beauty, birth, breeding, wit, sense, manners,
modesty, and all these to an extreme, yet if she have not
money, she's nobody, she had as good want them all."

She is seduced by the elder brother of the family, and
loves him truly, but he tires of her, and she is forced into
a marriage, loveless on her side, with his younger brother.
At his death five years later, Defoe gives us the first of the
many accountings she makes of her position. She has
about £1200, but "My two children were, indeed, taken
happily off my hands by my husband's father and
mother ..." She refuses to take a lover:

> I had money in my pocket . . . I had been tricked once
> by that cheat called love, but the game was over; I was
> resolved now to be married or nothing, and to be well
> married or not at all.

She chooses unwisely: her linen-draper husband spends
her money and disappears, and thenceforth she becomes
a lone adventuress, launching into "cumulative bigamy"
and a life of multiple hypocrisy and deceit. Yet we always
feel that her comment on her situation is perfectly valid:

> I wanted to be placed in a settled state of living, and
> had I happened to meet with a sober, good husband, I
> should have been as . . . true a wife to him as virtue it-
> self could have formed. If I have been otherwise, the
> vice came in always at the door of necessity, not at the
> door of inclination . . .

When she thinks she has found a sober, good husband,
and goes with him to the plantations in Virginia where he
has estates, it is only to find that his mother is also her
own mother, and that he is her half-brother. Horrified at
her incestuous relationship, she leaves him and her children, and after various other unlucky "marriages" and
the desertion of a few more children, she turns thief. Here
necessity and inclination become somewhat confused, for
though pushed into thievery by poverty, she soon makes
enough money to have retired virtuously. But by that time
the addiction proves too strong: "as poverty brought me
in, so avarice kept me in . . . [and] I had not so much as
the least inclination to leave off."

After twelve years of successful pilfering, she is caught
stealing "two pieces of brocaded silk," imprisoned and
condemned to be hanged. She then repents of all her
former misdeeds, though repentance does not apparently
demand giving up any of her savings. In addition, it
brings a practical reward—the minister who has converted
her wins her a reprieve, and she is shipped off to "the
plantations" with her favorite "husband," whom she has
met again in prison. In Virginia she meets her son, and

discovers that she is part-heiress to her mother's estate. Her half-brother-"husband" dies, leaving the way open to a full explanation of the past to her current "husband," and of the present to her newly discovered son. "Thus all these difficulties were made easy, and we lived together with the greatest kindness and comfort imaginable." We leave them in old age, back in England, peaceful and prosperous, and resolved "to spend the remainder of our years in sincere penitence for the wicked lives we have lived."

What can we say of Defoe's moral pretentions? He declares in the Preface that there is not a wicked action in any part of the book but is "first or last rendered unhappy and unfortunate." This of course is nonsense, and it is difficult not to believe that the whole Preface is intended ironically. Plenty of Moll's escapades bring her unhappiness, but her fortunes steadily improve from the time she turns thief. Her repentance saves her life, but it is no change of heart that alters her behavior afterward, merely the fact that she is happy with the man of her choice, and is in comfortable financial circumstances.

Some critics think Defoe is practicing an elaborate irony not only in the Preface but throughout the story, obliquely criticizing Moll's morality by showing the difference between her pretenses and her practice. Some, like Dorothy van Ghent, are outraged at Moll's sanctimonious humbug (or that of her creator), and declare that "she has no moral being, nor has the book any moral life." This is only too true. Moll's conscience is here today and gone tomorrow throughout. When she seduces and robs a rich and drunken young man, relieving him of "a gold watch, a silk purse of gold, his fine full-bottom periwig and silver-fringed gloves, his sword and fine snuff-box," she professes herself full of sorrow for his wife and children; when she tricks a child and steals a necklace from her, she manufactures a righteous reason for it: "I only thought I had given the parents a just reproof for their negligence, in leaving the poor lamb to come home by itself, and it would teach them to take more care another time."

As for her own children, it is difficult to keep track of the number she abandons. She does take steps to have one illegitimate child adopted by a foster-mother; she is duly shocked to discover how many such children are born and how cruel their fate usually is, while the baby-farmers rake in the profits. (We remember Defoe's arguments for the building of a foundling hospital.) But Moll never concerns herself in the least for the fate of all the other children she has left. When she meets her son in Virginia, however, she is overwhelmed by a rush of maternal emotions, and we are quite ready to believe in them. Moll indeed, like her creator probably, ignores the gap between her professions and her practice. Outside of Defoe's stubborn loyalty to the faith he was born in, at real cost to his prospects, his preoccupation was to keep financially afloat and support his family, and he was not too particular about the ways he did it. In the same way Moll confronts the conventional code of morals with the primary need to survive, and by the real actions and passions of human beings engaged in the process of successful survival. She is at least honest about her motives. When a friend of hers is arrested for a theft of which Moll herself is really guilty, she is "troubled exceedingly" at her own responsibility for the disaster: "But my own life, which was so evidently in danger, took off my tenderness; and seeing she was not put to death, I was easy at her transportation, because she was then out of the way of doing me any mischief, whatever should happen."

It is difficult to believe that Defoe is being ironical here and elsewhere when Moll is frequently driven to follow the same instinct of self-preservation at the cost of others. As he makes her say of one such disreputable episode: "I am giving an account of what was, not of what ought or ought not to be." There is nothing in the book to suggest that Defoe sees the situations any differently from his heroine. If any satire is suggested, is it not rather against the society in which Moll has to function than against Moll herself? In spite of her often shocking actions, if that society were allowed to judge her and bring her to ruin, would we not feel dismayed and outraged? Moll lives by expediency, not principle, because it proves the only way in which she can develop an identity and assert its vitality. That she is determined to do. She will *not* be snuffed out by "that worst of devils, poverty."

It is quite true that the book has no moral life, but it is nevertheless bursting with *life,* and with the energy and determination to make life worth living. Listen to Moll, at the age of forty-two, abandoned by her latest lover, and, as usual, reckoning up her assets: about £500 in cash, some silver and linen, and a supply of clothes:

> With this stock I had the world to begin again; but you are to consider I was not now the same woman as when I lived at Rotherhithe; for first of all I was nearly twenty years older, and did not look the better for my age, nor for my rambles to Virginia and back again; and though I omitted nothing that might set me out to advantage, except painting, for that I never stooped to . . . yet there would always be some difference between five-and-twenty and two-and-forty.

But as she says, she will be "discouraged at nothing," she will "stand her ground," and she sets out dauntlessly.

It has been said by an unsympathetic critic that Moll has only two motivating forces: money and fear. This is a harsh judgment. Money plays a large part in her life, since her life depends on a supply of it, and at every turn she tells us about it and its equivalent in material possessions in terms of exact costs and values. It is supremely important because only through its possession can she fulfill herself in that life of middle-class comfort which is her ideal, and essential to her self-respect and dignity. Sometimes we feel that the only thing Moll really dislikes about the life of a thief is that it brings her into contact with such a low class of person! She always dissociates herself from the "hardened wretches" who are following the same profession. It is always "they," not "we." She re-

mains a "gentlewoman" through it all, and indeed she
has a soft spot toward a husband or lover who cheats
her, provided he does it in style. Her second husband
apologizes very courteously to her when he explains that
he has spent all her money and is about to leave her: "He
said some very handsome things to me indeed at parting;
for I told you he was a gentleman, [though] that was all
the benefit I had of his being so." In the same way, when
her Lancashire lover reveals his trickery, her comment is:
" 'Tis something of relief even to be undone by a man of
honour rather than by a scoundrel."

In her early days as an adventuress she is haunted by
the fear of poverty, then by the fear of arrest, and finally
in Newgate by the fear of death, yet it gives no sense of
her real impact on readers to picture her as a woman
driven only by greed and fear. Moll never loses her humanity or her courage; warmth and a good heart go along
with her toughness and sharp practice. She accepts her
own moral shortcomings and therefore can be tolerant of
those of others. She and her Lancashire "husband" (who
turns out to be a highwayman) have mutually tricked
each other by pretending to wealth. When they discover
the truth, instead of heaping reproaches on one another,
they sit down to a good talk, which concludes:

> "But, my dear," said I, "what can we do now? We are
> both undone. . . ." We proposed a great many things, but
> nothing could offer where there was nothing to begin
> with. He begged me at last to talk no more of it, for, he
> said, I would break his heart. So we talked of other
> things a little, till at last he took a husband's leave of
> me, and so went to sleep.

Moll is certainly not heartless, but no one could claim
that the book has any psychological depth. As long as Moll
is comfortably provided for she is happy and gives happiness to others, but we never have any true sense of her
sufferings at other times. After her first theft, she longs

to know whether the things in the bundle "were a poor body's goods, or a rich."

> Perhaps, said I, it may be some poor widow like me, that had packed up these goods to sell them for a little bread for herself and a poor child, and are now starving and breaking their hearts for want of that little they would have fetched. And this thought tormented me worse than all the rest for three or four days' time.

Once she laments her loneliness in the necessity of playing a part. She needed, she says, "to make the world take me for something more than I was," but "the consequence of that was that I had nobody to whom I could in confidence commit the secret of my circumstances; and I found by experience, that to be friendless is the worst of conditions, next to being in want, that a woman can be reduced to." Moll, like Mr. Prufrock, laments the need to "prepare a face to meet the faces that I meet," but in her it produces no neurosis. The need for action soon extinguishes the emotional introspection. When she is imprisoned in Newgate she is struck dumb: "It is not to be expressed how I was harassed." Her loneliness throws her into "fits and swooning several times a day," and when some of her fellow prisoners are led off to be hanged, she falls into a fit of crying: "nor could I stop or put a check to it, no, not with all the strength and courage I had." But again we never get below the surface of her situation; Moll's emotions are as evanescent and inconsistent as her morals. We can justifiably question the possibility of the coexistence of so much good nature and so much guilt. Could her basically honest and generous traits have survived the long habits of time-serving and double-dealing, of deserting children and cheating her fellow men and women? Would her "governess," who trains her in thieving and who is besides baby-farmer, abortionist and "fence," be as amiable and kindly as Moll herself, and completely loyal to Moll's financial interests while she is in Virginia? It all seems most unlikely.

It is a tribute to Defoe's creative skill and zest that such problems intrude so seldom. Moll's periodic bursts of pious humbug become comic rather than nauseating, and are so obviously "planted" to support the assurances in the Preface that the book will prove both ethical and entertaining. It is difficult to believe that intelligent readers of Defoe's day were any more convinced than ourselves of its valuable moral lessons and its power for good. They may have been more inclined to believe in the factual truth of the story, but what must have captivated them as it continues to captivate readers today is Defoe's extraordinary immediacy and vividness of presentation.

The structural defects of the book are as obvious as its emotional and moral ones. The story has no organic plot. It is full of unrelated episodes and loose ends. Since, however, the story is an alleged autobiography, that is excuse enough for its lack of architecture. All the episodes happen to Moll, and that unites them sufficiently. The repetitions, the long-winded commentaries, the casual transitions, can all be forgiven, provided each episode lives and carries us smoothly to the next, so that our interest in the heroine never dies. It never does, so long as Moll is in action, and we have scene after scene rendered with an extraordinary exactness of physical detail.

We watch one of her lovers telling her to fetch him all the money she has. She fetches a little private drawer and throws out six guineas and some silver on the bed

> ... then reaching his pocket, [he] pulled out a key and bade me open a little walnut-tree box he had upon the table, and bring him such a drawer, which I did. In this drawer there was a great deal of money in gold ... but I knew not how much. He took the drawer, and taking me by the hand, made me put it in and take a whole handful. I was backward at that, but he held my hand hard in his hand, and put it into the drawer, and made me take out as many guineas as I could well take up at once.

When I had done so, he made me put them into my
lap . . . and poured out all my own money among his,
and bade me get me gone and carry it all into my own
chamber.

She relates this, she says, "because of the good humour
of it," and a good contrast to it is the scene of her first
robbery, where the atmosphere is that of near horror, but
the use of physical detail equally telling.

Wandering thus about, I knew not whither, I passed by
an apothecary's shop . . . where I saw lie on a stool just
before the counter a little bundle wrapped in a white
cloth; beyond it stood a maid-servant with her back to
it, looking up towards the top of the shop where the
apothecary's apprentice, as I suppose, was standing
upon the counter . . . a candle in his hand, looking and
reaching up to the upper shelf. . . .

This was the bait; and the devil, who laid the snare,
prompted me as if he spoke, for I remember, and shall
never forget it, 'twas like a voice spoken over my shoul-
der, take the bundle; be quick; do it this moment. It was
no sooner said but I stepped into the shop, and with my
back to the wench . . . I put my hand behind me and
took the bundle and went off with it.

She can laugh at herself too, as when, instinctively, she
makes off with a horse which has been left unattended,
and is then completely at a loss to know how to dispose
of it. She can even temper her sentimental account of her
reunion with her son by a touch of wry cynicism.

I made him one present, and that was one of the gold
watches . . . I happened to have with me, and gave it
to him at his third visit. I told him I had nothing of any
value to bestow but that, and I desired that he would
now and then kiss it for my sake. I did not indeed tell
him that I stole it from a gentlewoman's side at a meet-
ing-house in London. That's by the way.

And so we go along with her from her childhood, where her taste for "genteel living" asserts itself, through her many adulterous relations, which, however, never coarsen or destroy her instinct for "quality." (Whatever attacks can be made on Defoe for his materialistic ethic, no one can accuse him of exploiting sex in any prurient way.) The scenes are even more vivid in her later life of crime since in the nature of them the suspense and excitement are greater. When she is falsely accused of stealing a piece of satin, she carries the situation off with great haughtiness, and threatens to bring suit for assault. Her attorney advises her to meet with the mercer and settle out of court, and to impress him with her appearance. As she has claimed to be a widow, she dresses in black, but in a new suit. "My governess also furnished me with a good pearl necklace that shut in behind with a locket of diamonds, which she had in pawn, and I had a gold watch by my side; so that I made a very good figure." The mercer becomes "mighty humble" and she gets £150 and a suit of black silk clothes, as well as her attorney's charges and "a good supper into the bargain." Taking a gold watch off a child in St. James's Park, as she lifts her up to see the king go by to the Parliament House, is easy, while a complicated "prank" between Harwich and London, involving the contents of a Dutch gentleman's portmanteau, is safely brought off before the final catastrophe. The final pictures in America, are all of quiet happiness, first with her son, and then with her ex-highwayman, who loves his new role of country squire. Moll takes especial care to buy him all the trappings:

... two silver hilted swords, three or four fine fowlingpieces, a fine saddle with holsters and pistols very handsome, with a scarlet cloak; and, in a word, everything I could think of to oblige him, and to make him appear, as he really was, a very fine gentleman. ... And indeed we used to look at one another sometimes with a great deal of pleasure, reflecting how much better that was, not than Newgate only, but than the most

prosperous of our circumstances in the wicked trade
we had been both carrying on.

The only bad mark we must give to Defoe for his narrative style is its monotony. In spite of the clarity and liveli-
ness of the scenes, he creates no perspective, no changes
of emphasis or lighting or speed; an unsuccessful effort
at shoplifting has the same importance as the discovery
of incest; a night of love is no more exciting than a visit
to Oxford.

In spite of the fact that Defoe was pioneering in new
territory, neither he nor the contemporary reading public
seem to have been aware he was, or to have made any
claim for him. By hindsight we hail him as the inventor
of the first realistic novel, but it seems that he himself
regarded his stories as variants of his other journalistic
ventures. He denied specifically that they were "fictions."
The "I" of the Preface to *Moll Flanders* is an editor who
has expurgated the text of Moll's memoirs, and toned down
her vocabulary, but he insists that the story is a "true
confession." Richardson, Fielding and Sterne were to get
all the credit and renown for developing new literary
forms, while Defoe—in the strange company of Bunyan—
is dismissed as a "best seller" catering to a low audience.
A Letter to the Society of Booksellers, published in 1738,
has this to say:

> It is certain, that the sale of a book chiefly depends on
> the universality of the subject . . . and accordingly we
> find that *Robinson Crusoe* sells quicker than Locke on
> Human Understanding . . . nay, it is not sufficiently
> known that some have acquired estates by printing
> Tom Thumb, Riddles, Songs, Fables, The Pilgrim's
> Progress, and such like common trumpery.

It was not until two years later that *Pamela* was to make
the novel a respectable new genre in the eyes of the contemporary critics.

SAMUEL RICHARDSON

1689–1761

Clarissa

Desmond MacCarthy, in an essay published in 1932, declared that Samuel Richardson in his day performed much the same service for his contemporaries and successors as Proust has done for us: he fixed attention on the immediate texture of social living and of inner emotional reaction to it, while at the same time extracting from the material a scale of values which were acceptable and welcome to contemporary sensitivities.

Both writers discovered a new method of writing—detailed, long-winded, exact. The picture of life is in each case all foreground; both dwell continually upon trifles because these are significant and important feelings they desire to communicate.... Both novelists confirmed and directed the sensibility of their day. That this sensibility was, in 1740, emotionally lachrymose and sentimentally moral, and in 1920 was predominantly skeptical, esthetic and amoral—this fact does not affect the relationship in which, with their preternaturally minute imaginative faculties, they stood to their times, though it does alter, of course, their comparative value for us.

Both writers were the victims of nervous disabilities and withdrew from society in general to be the center of a coterie of admiring friends, and to spin, spiderlike, their creative intricacies from their own inner consciousness. It is difficult to push the comparison much further, since Richardson lacks the complex aesthetic gifts and

sensibilities which gave richness to both the life and the
work of Proust, and he wrote deliberately for a bourgeois
audience while Proust aimed at the intelligentsia. The
comparison has the point, however, that it forces us to
look at *Clarissa* in an *historical* perspective, and it is really
only in such a framework that the book comes alive. Perhaps that is a rash statement, though, for some modern
critics are almost as enthusiastic about it in its own right
as were its earlier admirers. The book is one of the curi-
osities of literature indeed, because of the violently opposing opinions it has produced ever since its publication. We
should expect it to be popular with the women readers
who went into ecstasies over *Pamela*, the book that made
Richardson's reputation and was published seven years
before. But then we find Rousseau declaring that "no one,
in any language, has ever written a novel that equals or
even approaches *Clarissa*." Diderot says he will put it on
the same shelf with Homer and Euripides; Alfred de Mus-
set thought it "the first novel in the world"; Balzac and
George Sand joined in the chorus of praise. Among modern critics of the novel, Dorothy van Ghent calls Clarissa
"a fabulous creature of epic stature, clothed with the ideals
of a culture and of a race"; Arnold Kettle names Richardson the first truly *tragic* novelist, for he sees Clarissa
placed in a dilemma from which—in the terms of her
own society—there is no escape; Leslie Fiedler too finds
the characters raised from particular to universal significance.

It is for its psychological insights that it has been most
extravagantly praised, ever since Dr. Johnson pronounced
it "the first book in the world for the knowledge it displays
of the human heart." Its insights were indeed remarkable
if again we look at the book historically, for Richardson
invented the method of psychological analysis. His technique of telling the story in personal letters opened up intimate private experience for literary exploration and the
reader becomes infected with the atmosphere of doubts,

hopes, terror, disappointment, indecision, in which the characters are suspended. As Richardson said himself in the Preface:

> All the letters are written while the hearts of the writers must be supposed to be wholly engaged in their subjects (the events at the time generally dubious): so that they abound not only in critical situations, but with what may be called *instantaneous* descriptions and reflections.

But what manner of man was it who produced the book, and how did he view his larger aims and accomplishments?

Like Defoe, Richardson was middle-aged before he made his name as a novelist, and he was the last person in the world who would be suspected of creating a taste for stories of sexual intrigue. As a youth his father destined him for the church, but shortage of funds led to his apprenticeship to a printer and bookseller. In the pattern of the industrious apprentice, he married his master's daughter and opened a business of his own. Six children by his first wife all died in infancy, but four of the six by his second wife, all daughters, survived him. His business prospered, but his health was poor. By his own description he was short, and "rather plump than emaciated, notwithstanding his complaints." He was afraid of altercations, so avoided going among his workmen; he was afraid of riding, so exercised himself upon a "chamber-horse." He was "very shy of obtruding himself on persons of condition" and was silent and ill at ease in company—in masculine company, that is, for this tremulous, obsequious, fussy little man was completely at home among the ladies.

In a memoir of his own life, Richardson gives details of this trait in his personality. "As a bashful and not forward boy, I was an early favorite with all the young women of taste and reading in the neighbourhood." He would read aloud to them and comment on the books, but his attraction went beyond that:

> I was not more than thirteen when three of these young women, unknown to each other, having a high opinion of my taciturnity, revealed to me their love secrets, in order to induce me to give them copies to write after, or correct, for answers to their lovers' letters.

In this way he early became acquainted with the feminine heart and all through his life (in the most decorous way, needless to say), his first interest was in women, "his eye always upon the ladies," as he said of himself.

When he was near fifty, he rented a house in the London suburb of North End (now Fulham), where he spent more and more of his time, especially in the "grotto," or garden house, attached to it. There, when fame had come to him, he entertained the circle of admiring young women who called him their dear papa, and admiring older women who sustained his vanity with the incense of admiration and flattery. And there he wrote the books "to exalt the sex" that brought him their homage. He does not seem to have sought any masculine literary society, and he consistently belittled his fellow writers of fiction, sneering at the "lowness" of Fielding and saying of Sterne that the only extenuating circumstance about his books was "that they are too gross to be inflaming."

His success burst upon him with the publication in 1740 of *Pamela, or Virtue Rewarded*. A bookseller friend had asked him to write a small book "of familiar letters on the useful concerns in common life." While he was compiling these models, he remembered a story told him by a friend, of a young servant girl, daughter of honest and pious parents, who worked for a wealthy family. The young son of the house tried to seduce her, but she resisted him with such moral nobility that finally he married her. This story gave him the idea of including a few letters "to young folks circumstanced as Pamela was." His imagination seems to have been set ablaze. The volume of general letters was put aside, and in two months the novel was completed.

Quite aware that he had invented "a new species of writing," Richardson hoped that it "might possibly turn young people into a course of reading different from the pomp and parade of romance writing . . . and might tend to promote the cause of religion and virtue." *Pamela* had an immense success, and ran through six editions in a year. Pope is reported to have said: ". . . it will do more good than many volumes of sermons." The clergy recommended it from their pulpits, and at Slough, where the local blacksmith had been reading it aloud to the villagers, his audience rushed to ring the churchbells at the point where Pamela succeeds at last in bringing Mr. B—— to his knees with a proposal of marriage.

All readers of the book, however, were not so simple-minded. A boisterous parody called *Shamela* was almost certainly written by Fielding, and other critics pointed out that several of the episodes where Mr. B—— attacks Pamela's virtue were in themselves inflammatory, while it was possible to regard her actions as a kind of sexual blackmail. Richardson, in fact, was the first novelist to discover that a mixture of religion and sex is the best recipe for a best seller. A modern critic has said that the book "gratified the reading public with the combined attractions of a sermon and a striptease." This could be said of much of *Clarissa* too, where the slow unfolding of the story in letters from the principals in the action and their friends gives us a succession of keyhole views of the earlier efforts at seduction, leading up to the central episode of the rape itself, which is hinted at, half-revealed, advanced toward and retreated from, with a wealth of erotic suggestion, before it comes out in the open in plain terms. Its long aftermath of preparations for death plays on an allied morbid curiosity.

The original title (all in italics and capital letters) professes that the book is about personal and social situations:

> Clarissa: or the history of a young lady:
> Comprehending the most important concerns
> of private life, and particularly showing the
> distresses that may attend the misconduct both
> of parents and children in relation to marriage.

Elsewhere, however, Richardson declared that his central aim was to teach "the highest and most important doctrines of Christianity."

This is a rough outline of the story, which in the original appeared in seven volumes, though it has now been condensed into one. Mr. Robert Lovelace, a young gentleman with aristocratic connections but a reputation for "faulty morals," has been courting a Miss Arabella Harlowe, daughter of a wealthy middle-class country family. He finds himself more attracted to her young sister, Clarissa, and this transference of his attentions offends Arabella and sets the rest of the family—in particular her authoritarian father and her mean-spirited brother—against the match. They determine that Clarissa shall marry a suitor she detests, Roger Solmes. Lovelace continues to correspond secretly with Clarissa, and driven to desperation by the persecution of her family she arranges a meeting with him. By a trick he turns this into an elopement, and she is in his power.

Lovelace is now torn between his genuine admiration for Clarissa and his longing to humiliate the Harlowes. Moreover, he is a practiced rake, and though he professes his intentions are honorable, he wants Clarissa as mistress before marriage, or better still, without marriage. Clarissa longs to believe in his good faith, and she allows him to find lodgings for her in London. The lodgings, however, are really a brothel kept by a Mrs. Sinclair. After a determined but unsuccessful attempt to seduce her during an alarm of fire, Lovelace rapes her when she has been drugged by Mrs. Sinclair.

The remaining two thirds of the book is taken up with Clarissa's determination to die and her preparations for doing so. Lovelace, remorseful, now offers immediate marriage, and his family all urge it, but Clarissa, with great dignity, refuses it absolutely: "The man who has been the villain to me that you have been shall never make me his wife." Her father puts his curse upon her and refuses her a home, so she moves into rooms in London under the devoted protection of Lovelace's former friend, Jack Belford. After her death, her cousin and the trustee of her private fortune, Colonel Morden, challenges Lovelace to a duel in Italy, and mortally wounds him. In a postscript, Belford tells the reader of the suitable punishments inflicted by a just Providence on the evil doers.

Nothing could be more unlike Defoe's simple world and underworld of competing egos. Here we move in a variety of worlds. Partially we are in a fairy-tale existence of tyrannous parents, and a cruel brother and sister; Mrs. Sinclair, the keeper of the brothel that Clarissa mistakes for respectable lodgings, is a witchlike figure of evil. Then we pass into melodrama, with a plan for forced marriage, abduction, complicated machinations, impersonations, forged letters, false arrest, the spotless heroine and the wicked villain. But the pervasive faintings and weepings, the upraised eyes, the long prosings about virtue and "delicacy," and the final death are in another convention—the cult of "sentiment"—which seems particularly alien to the modern reader. From the time of its publication the conclusion was hotly debated, but for four volumes in the original edition Richardson pandered to the taste of his sentimental readers for scenes of sickness, death and burial. With a fascinated morbidity Clarissa declares: "I have more pleasure in thinking of death than of a husband"; we see her subsisting on water gruel and weak tea, developing trembling hands, misty eyes and panting breaths—which, however, seem to enhance her charms to her attendants. Gruesomely she insists on keeping her coffin in her bedroom and using it as a writing desk, and the final death scene, the description of the "lovely corpse" and its disposal, introduce an orgy of sob stuff.

The plot itself is utterly incredible by any rational

standards. It has often been pointed out that short work
would have been made of Lovelace if Clarissa had made
a deposition in court before her neighbor in Bow Street,
Mr. Henry Fielding, Justice of the Peace. Richardson has
the greatest difficulty in persuading us that Clarissa could
not have escaped to, or been rescued by, friends. As for
her fiendish family, a very young friend of Richardson,
Sally Wescomb, pricked the bubble of any social realism
there by writing: "Permit me to say that it seems a little
unnatural that so general an infatuation should run
through Clarissa's whole family . . . to bring about the ruin
of this admirable young creature."

But in spite of all the naturalistic detail, Richardson
is not too much concerned with social realism. *Clarissa*
runs to about a million words, yet it is true, as Richardson said, that "there is not one digression, not one episode,
not one reflection, but what arises naturally from the subject . . . and carries it on." The subject, on the face of it,
in spite of his announced intentions, seems to be a mixture of the sensational, the sordid and the sentimental.
How does it nevertheless transcend this rubbish and take
on any dignity and interest?

It is fashionable nowadays to label any serious emotional or social pattern which emerges in a work of art as
an archetype or myth. In these terms, Dorothy van Ghent,
in her book *The English Novel,* and Leslie Fiedler in *Love
and Death in the American Novel,* have given most interesting discussions of *Clarissa.* My own feeling is that
the themes or patterns do not have sufficient force to be
honored with so much distinction, though that is not to
say that Richardson was not convinced that he wrote out
of powerful religious and moral convictions.

The patterns, religious, moral and social, emerge from
the relationships of the heroine to the other main characters. The conflict starts on the social level, with the or-
ganization of the family versus the rights of the individual, and that persists all through the book. A bequest from
her grandfather has made Clarissa financially independ-

ent, but this has caused such jealousy in her father that she has dutifully put her estate into his hands. When, however, he takes the attitude that she too is a piece of property to be disposed of in marriage as he wishes, Clarissa rebels. It is here that Richardson seems somewhat to blur his theme and to have a foot in each camp. We cannot of course suppose that he means us to think that Clarissa should have married the odious Solmes, but at the same time he deliberately puts her in the situation when to appeal for help to Lovelace is her only chance of escape. Yet he commented later on the episode which leads to her flight with Lovelace: "I did not want her to be wholly blameless." This, in fact, was to be Clarissa's "tragic flaw": "Going off with a Man is the thing I wanted most to make inexcusable." But yet again we are not of course to suppose her family are right in regarding it as inexcusable, and that she deserves the fate that it brings upon her. Her groveling penitence toward her father after the shocking outrage seems most unnecessary. His curse seems to crush her even more than Lovelace's crime. She turns from rebel to guilt-ridden sinner in her own estimation. Her friend Miss Howe writes sensibly: "Why this pining solicitude after a reconciliation with relations as unworthy as implacable?" But Clarissa declares that they are "filled with *just* resentments against me (just to them, if they think them just)"; that is, she is willing now to accept their code, their standards of greed, hatred and revenge, which really makes nonsense of her original admirable rebellion.

Clarissa's final attitude of course is of the transcendence of an earthly father by a heavenly one, who alone can combine justice with mercy. Nor is society at large made as charitable as Clarissa herself in not holding her family to blame. All Lovelace's relations and friends take Miss Howe's view, and we find Mrs. Harlowe complaining of "the general cry against us . . . as if she were innocent, we all in fault." Jack Belford sums up the matter best as he reports his conversation with Colonel Morden:

> Good God! How could your accursed friend—
> And how could her cruel parents? interrupted I.
> We may as easily account for *him* as for *them*.

It is indeed difficult to account for either outside Richardson's conventions, and his imposed patterns of religious and moral truth, which come down to "the doctrine of future rewards," and in which Clarissa plays the part of Christian saint. She rises above all earthly judgments by her forgiveness of her cruel parents, and in the same way she defeats Belford's accursed friend, Lovelace, who plays the part of devil.

On the moral plane, the sex duel becomes that between virtue and vice, but only in its narrow sense of chastity versus lust. Richardson's moral attitude is the unlovely Puritan obsession of equating frigidity with purity and sexuality with sin. Clarissa is the modest, chilly, chaste virgin, "this charming frost-piece," and Lovelace the profligate, remorseless, scheming villain, whose only aim is to violate her. She is sexless, he is the embodiment of lust.

He starts as the fascinating but heartless rake of Restoration comedy. Among men, he can be honorable and generous; he is a complete cad only where women are concerned. Women are his natural prey, and the game of amorous pursuit is one in which no "gentlemen's agreements" exist. Some "sportive cruelty" may be necessary, but "consent in struggle . . . yielding in resistance" will follow. It is a battle of wits and wills, with the catch as final triumph. Lovelace commiserates with the more sober Belford on his lack of the true gift for the chase:

> Thou knowest nothing, Jack, of the delicacies of intrigue; nothing of the glory of outwitting the witty and the watchful; of the joys that fill the mind of the inventive or contriving genius, ruminating which to use of the different webs that offer to him for the entanglement of a haughty charmer.

Belford objects that the conflict is not a fair one:

Thou, a man born for intrigue, full of invention, intrepid, remorseless, able patiently to watch for thy opportunity, not hurried as most men by gusts of violent passion ... the lady scrupulously strict to *her* word, incapable of art or design, apt therefore to believe well of others.

But Lovelace is implacable. "Mine is the most plotting heart in the world," he asserts, and under a mask of tender gallantry and integrity he hides his true nature.

Poor Clarissa is of course no match for him at all on his own ground of "sportive cruelty." By a trick she finds herself in his power, but at first, in her innocence, she thinks *she* holds the trumps and that she will make marriage contingent on his reformation and on his reconciliation with her family. She totally misreads his real intentions, which are to bring her to heel "without conditions, without reformation promises. ... Then shall I have the rascals and rascalesses of the family come creeping to me."

Lovelace's plottings and trickeries, however, founder against the rock of Clarissa's invincible chastity. The total failure of his determined effort to seduce her proves her "purity" to Lovelace, but it has the unforeseen result of convincing Clarissa that she will never marry him. She sees him for what he is and cries out in words that remind us of Jane Eyre, a century later, scorning Mr. Rochester:

Leave me! My soul is above thee, man! Urge me not to tell thee, how sincerely I think my soul above thee! ... Thou hast a proud heart to contend with!

Having therefore failed in what Belford calls "fair seduction," his mingled rage and lust and revenge drive Lovelace to his foul rape. Again Clarissa's will triumphs. No threats of her family, no pleadings from Lovelace's aristocratic relations, no grovelings from the penitent Lovelace himself will budge her. She *chooses* to die of grief, and divine grace permits her to do so. This conclusion really defeats Richardson's intention that she should be regarded as a *tragic* figure, since the tragic hero is always *defeated* in his efforts to impose his will on events and mold them as he sets out to do. Instead of failure and defeat, Clarissa by her death asserts her triumph: not only her personal triumph over Lovelace, but the triumph of all the values her creator wishes to emphasize; love of God transcends love of man, divine justice transcends human justice, chastity triumphs over sexuality, the heart over the head, spirit over sense, principle over expediency.

Yet who reads *Clarissa* now to enjoy these conclusions? The solutions are too facile, and arrived at by too much absurdity of action and intrigue. Yet we can become absorbed in the book. What keeps our attention and imaginative participation?

Partially, no doubt, it is the "period" quality. To see the manners and morals of a different era and to find oneself in a strange world so far removed from our own bring their own brand of interest. The spectacle of this universe of "sentiment" and prudery, which became so widespread a vogue in life and letters for almost a hundred and fifty years, and is now so completely obliterated, brings home to us that perhaps our modern vogue, at the opposite extreme of violence and depravity, may equally pass into historical memory.

But the period interest is in any case minor. It cannot compete with Richardson's major theme and major gift. For all the values we have described as emerging in the pattern of the story are interesting only as they are bound up with the central concern—the struggle and the triumph of the individual consciousness against conventional social codes. Moll Flanders, too, insisted on her identity and her right to assert it by any means in her power. Clarissa is a very different type, but her positive affirmation of her own personal will is equally her supreme value. The superiority of Richardson as a literary artist is in his psychological subtlety, his knowledge of the conflicts hidden in

the heart. Defoe spends very little time on the inner life
of Moll Flanders. She is driven perpetually by the necessity of *action* to keep herself afloat. Her emotional processes are of the simplest: she is lonely, fearful, disillusioned or in need of money, but it is what she *does* to escape these plights that we hear about. But Richardson is
far more interested in the conflicting motives that lead to
action, and the conflicting emotions that are its results,
than in the actions themselves. The skeleton of the plot
is ridiculous and gives us no idea of the varieties of tone
and the sharp insights into character that emerge from
this flood of correspondence. Again, Richardson is not a
complex psychologist. I cannot agree with one critic who
claims that he reveals "the frightening reality of the unconscious life which lies hidden in the most virtuous
heart." Since the publication of *Clarissa* we have had the
opportunity to read books such as *The Mill on the Floss,
Madame Bovary, Anna Karenina* or *The Portrait of a
Lady.* All of these contain much more impressive studies
of young women than Richardson was capable of, just as
Lovelace seems crude beside the great masculine figures
of the French and Russian novels of the nineteenth century. Yet Richardson started the whole thing. He is the
pioneer in the analytical study of individual behavior in
conflict with an oppressive social code, and also in the
analytical study of the conflict within the individual consciousness itself. While the religious and sexual ideals and
patterns that emerge from the whole structure are evasive,
stale and artificial, the studies of the individuals within
them are often refreshingly genuine.

Richardson organized the whole novel as a "dramatic
narrative" worked out "in a double yet separate correspondence between two young ladies of virtue . . . and two
gentlemen of free lives." Though numbers of other characters write letters later in the book, all the main part if it
is reported by these four correspondents, and Richardson
contrives to make the two women and the two men excellent foils to one another. Clarissa is all emotion and

fine-spun feelings, with her heart always ruling her head; Anna Howe is witty and worldly, full of good sense as well as good feeling. It is she who counsels Clarissa to keep control of her own estate; who sees that she is being "over-nice, over-delicate" when she finds herself compromised, and bursts out: "Were it *me* . . . I do assure you, I would in a quarter of an hour know what he drives at"; and who urges her friend to live and not to die.

> Comfort yourself . . . in the triumphs of a virtue un-sullied; a will wholly faultless. . . . Many happy days may you yet see; and much good may you still do, if you will not heighten unavoidable accidents into guilty despondency.

In the same way Lovelace, unstable, cruel, intriguing, is matched with Belford, steady, sound and sympathetic. To Lovelace's ruthless plans he answers: "Why should'st thou tempt her virtue? Why should'st thou wish to try when there is no reason to doubt? . . . I join *her* sake, *honour's* sake, motives of justice, generosity, gratitude and humanity, which are all concerned with the preservation of so fine a woman." Lovelace heeds him as little as Clarissa heeds Anna Howe, for they are both driven by compulsions which good sense cannot satisfy.

Naturally the central conflict and contrast is between Clarissa and Lovelace. It is Shaw's *Man and Superman* in reverse. All John Tanner's struggles to escape are doomed to fail against the force of Ann Whitefield's mating instinct, while all Lovelace's struggles to possess are doomed to fail against Clarissa's invincible chastity. In the large religious pattern Clarissa is saint and Lovelace devil; but in human terms both are incomplete creatures in whom spirit and flesh cannot harmonize. In the course of the day-by-day living described in the letters they become a woman and a man full of common human inconsistencies and self-deceptions. As Lovelace says of her: "Flying from friends she was resolved not to abandon, to

the man she was determined not to go off with. *The Sex
all over!*" Yet he is no more all of a piece than she is, and
can confess himself, after the failure of his deliberate
plot to seduce her, "puzzled, confounded and ashamed of
myself."

Indeed each shifts by almost imperceptible changes
into a position in flat contradiction to that at the opening
of the book. Clarissa starts as a healthy country girl, with
an exaggeraed view of family authority, but with plenty
of spirit and determination to have her own way. She is
quite sure she can manage things for herself, and in spite
of Miss Howe's insight, refuses to accept that she is at all
in love with Lovelace. Her bitter discovery of her own mistakes, and the puncturing of her vanity, remind us of
Jane Austen's Emma Woodhouse some seventy years later.

> I thought I could *proceed* or *stop* as I pleased. . . . And
> what vexes me more is, that it is plain to me now, by
> all this behaviour, that he had as great a confidence in
> my weakness as I had in my own strength. And so . . .
> he has triumphed; for he has not been mistaken in me,
> while I have in myself.

Yet Lovelace attracts her powerfully, though she distrusts
him, and just when he has been writing to Belford of his
plots to ruin her she is telling Miss Howe about his "natural dignity . . . an open and I think an honest countenance." But she sees how skillfully he extricates himself
from any promise of marriage, and comments miserably:
"But surely this cannot be his design. . . . So much passionate love, *lip-deep*." "We are both great watchers of
each other's eyes," she reports, but though she will describe herself storming at him in vigorous fury, a few
minutes later she will be confessing her utter defenseless-
ness, "unable to look backward without reproach or forward without terror."

We see her calm and tempestuous, dignified, tender,
pleading, arguing rationally or sick with fright, and she is

convincing in all these moods. When the worst has happened and Lovelace offers immediate marriage, her scorn is red-hot: "Was it necessary to humble me down to the low level of thy baseness before I could be a wife meet for thee?" Even in her shock and confusion she has wits and spirit enough to think up a plan of escape from the brothel, and put it successfully into action. We lose interest in her only when she starts the long-drawn-out self-dramatization of her will to die.

Our interest in Lovelace holds up longer than our interest in Clarissa since he remains more acceptable all through—that is, if we can accept him at all. In many ways he is a "constructed" more than a created character. To the Puritan imagination he is planned as the embodiment of evil: a dissolute nobleman, wealthy, idle, vain, revengeful, and altogether diabolical in his intricate plotting to ruin a defenseless young girl. He is absurd: we don't believe in him for a moment—yet he insists on coming alive in spite of the part he is made to play. He is full of sparkle and vitality; he writes such witty, lively letters, and finds it so hard really, in spite of his deviltry, to sustain his wickedness in the face of Clarissa's innocence and charm.

> Every time I attend her, I find that she is less in *my* power; I more in *hers*.
>
> Yet a foolish little rogue! To forbid me to think of marriage till I am a reformed man! Till the implacables of her family change their nature and become placable!
>
> How it swells my pride to have been able to outwit such a vigilant charmer!

But his masculinity demands more satisfaction. To Belford's protests he replies:

> Wilt thou not thyself allow me to try if I cannot awaken the *woman* in her? To try if she, with all that glowing symmetry of parts, and that full bloom of vernal graces ... be really inflexible as to the grand article?

As repulse follows repulse in that field, Lovelace recognizes that this is not really a struggle for Clarissa's honor so much as a battle of the sexes itself.

> This sweet creature is able to make a man forego every purpose of his heart that is not favorable to her. And I verily think I should be inclined to spare her all further trial ... were it not for the contention that her vigilance has set on foot, *which* shall overcome the *other?*

No sooner has he committed the unforgivable outrage than he realizes that his apparent victory is defeat. He tries to rationalize what has happened, in the terms of his own philosophy, and is forced to answer his own logic.

> When all's done, Miss Clarissa Harlowe has but run the fate of a thousand others of her sex—only they did not set such a romantic value upon what they call their *honour;* that's all.
>
> And yet I will allow this—that if a person sets a high value upon anything, be it ever such a trifle in itself, or in the eye of others, the robbery of that person of it is *not* a trifle to *him*— Take the matter in that light, I own I have done wrong, great wrong, to this admirable creature.

Yet Richardson is skillful in revealing Lovelace's very gradual recognition of his failure. Vanity such as his can undergo no sudden conversion. He can be bitter enough about the general social view that marriage will set all to rights: "Can there be much harm done if it can be so easily repaired by a few magical words: as *I, Robert, take thee, Clarissa....*" But he himself believes frequently that Clarissa will finally accept this reparation, though he still dreads marriage itself.

> But here is the curse—she despises me, Jack! What man ... can bear to be despised, especially by his wife? O Lord, what a cursed hand have I made of this plot.

He knows himself worsted: "I am over-matched, egre-
giously over-matched, by this woman. What to do with her,
or without her, I know not." One day he is afraid she may
ruin her constitution by playing at being sick, though on
another he is in hopes she may be pregnant. (Lovelace
is the only person in the book who delights in Clarissa's
health and her potentialities for *life*.) In one letter he is
planning to resume his "usual gaiety of heart" if she rejects him, in another he is crying: "Having lost her, my
whole soul is a blank," in another he is declaring that she
is dying simply to revenge herself on him, "and still *more*
to be revenged, puts on the Christian and forgives me."

His final realization that by death she is escaping him,
and making his guilt ineradicable, is a fine stroke: "No
power left me to repair her wrongs! No alleviation to my
self-reproach! No dividing of blame with her!" His reaction to the news of Clarissa's actual death is subtly managed by Richardson. His wild ravings and physical violence are described to Belford with great scorn and contempt by a mutual friend who disapproves of them
heartily. Lovelace's letter to Belford a few days later is
very vivid in its mad and macabre logic. He insists that
the body of his "ever-dear and beloved lady" be embalmed
and put in *his* family vault.

> Surely nobody will dispute my right to her. Whose was
> she living?—Whose is she dead, but mine? Her cursed
> parents, whose barbarity to her, no doubt, was the *true*
> cause of her death, have long since renounced her. She
> left *them* for *me*. She *chose* me therefore: and I was her
> husband. What though I treated her like a villain. Do
> I not pay for it now? Would she have been mine had I
> not? And has she not forgiven me? I am then in *statu
> quo prius* with her—am I not?—as if I had never of-
> fended? Whose then can she be but mine?

Matching the psychological notation is a series of pictures in which we follow the drama visually: Clarissa de-
fying her parents, her uncles and aunt and brother and

sister and the pitiful Solmes, "bowing and cringing" although his waistcoat is "standing on end with lace"; Clarissa in a tigerish rage pushing Lovelace away "as if I had been nothing," as he tries to snatch a letter from her; Clarissa running to Lovelace's room "with a face of sweet concern" when she is told he is sick; Clarissa at the alarm of fire "with nothing on but an underpetticoat, her lovely bosom half-open," snatching up a pair of scissors to defend herself; or weeping at his feet, pleading to be released; or sinking her head on her bosom "like a half-broken stalked lily, top-heavy with the overcharging dews of the morning." Clarissa dying elegantly in a white satin nightgown, while Lovelace rides crazily back and forth between Piccadilly and Kensington, waiting for news.

Richardson can command comedy too, even in the midst of a scene of highly charged emotion and pathos. Clarissa is storming at Lovelace to release her from the brothel after the rape:

> Begone, devil! Officious devil, begone! Startled the dear creature; who, snatching up hastily her head from the chair, and as hastily popping it down again in terror, hit her nose, I suppose, against the edge of the chair; and it gushed out with blood, running in a stream down her bosom.
>
> Never was mortal man in such terror and agitation as I; for I instantly concluded that she had stabbed herself with some concealed instrument.
>
> I ran to her in wild agony. What have you done! O what have you done! . . . Sweet injured innocence, look up to me! Long will I not survive you! And I was on the point of drawing my sword to dispatch myself, when I discovered . . . that all I apprehended was a bloody nose, which, as far as I know . . . may have saved her head and her intellects.

We have to own that the prim, genteel, prudish little bookseller adds an immense territory to the art of the novel. It is true, as has been said, that the letter form is both the most natural and the least probable way of telling a story. It has certain advantages of immediacy and variety, and it opens the way for the revelation of the inner life. On the other hand, it is implausible and wasteful; repetitions slow the narrative to a snail's pace, while every situation is commented on from various points of view. Richardson did nothing to help. He was naturally prolix, and he made a virtue of it, saying "there was frequently a necessity to be very circumstantial and minute, in order to maintain that air of probability which is necessary . . . in a story designed to represent real life." It has remained for later critics to calculate that the chief characters must often have written letters for around eight hours a day to cover the ground. Richardson undertook once to try some cutting for a reprint, but he reports: "I am such a sorry pruner . . . that I am apt to add three pages for one I take away."

Later editors have performed the task for him, and nowadays we are less likely to quarrel with the length than to deplore the influence of Richardson's attitudes on the taste of his age. Perhaps, though, we should deplore simply the taste of an age whose puritanical view of sexual morals and general propriety is reflected more truly in *Clarissa* than in the more masculine and vigorous creations of Defoe, Fielding and Sterne. For a hundred and fifty years after Richardson the English novel became more and more shackled by rigid conventions about sexual topics. Any open challenge to these led to a ban by the circulating libraries, and the novelists depended on sales there for a living. It is ironical but quite logical that soon one of the books considered below the standard of decency was *Clarissa*. Lovelace was too full-blooded and the descriptions of Clarissa in distress too provocative for the super-prudish Victorians. So we find Thackeray lamenting: "O my faithful, good old Samuel Richardson! Hath the news yet reached thee in Hades that thy sublime novels are huddled away in corners, and that our daughters may no more read *Clarissa* than *Tom Jones?*"

HENRY FIELDING

1707–1754

Tom Jones

Lady Mary Wortley Montagu, on hearing the news of Fielding's death in 1754, at the age of forty-seven, wrote in a letter to her daughter: "He was so formed for happiness, it is a pity he was not immortal." This sounds as if his life had been particularly happy, which it was not, but Fielding had a tremendous zest for living and the world of his books is a happy one. His attitude toward life is that of the writer of comedy, who manipulates his material so that whatever the trials of the hero and heroine and whatever the quality of the society in which they have to function, the final outcome is that of reconciliation.

The names of Richardson and Fielding are always coupled in any discussion of the novel, and with good reason. They were contemporaries, writing in the same cultural climate (*Tom Jones* was published in 1749, a year after *Clarissa*). Both had genius and both were widely recognized immediately. Yet they are utterly different in their tastes and temperaments, and therefore in their visions of city and country, of men and women, and even of good and evil.

Their lives too were very different. Richardson was born and bred in the middle class and never moved out of it, except to create a few imaginary characters of high and low life. Fielding was an aristocrat by birth, educated at Eton and the University of Leyden, familiar with life in large country houses, mixing freely in "high life" in London, though he declared he found it much the dullest of all classes of society. Richardson was always comfortably

off, with a solid business behind him; Fielding for many
years lived from hand to mouth, making a living by his
pen. He spent ten years writing for the theatre—comedies,
farces, social and political satires. This career was cut
short by the Licensing Act of 1737, which imposed a strict
censorship on plays. The work in the theatre proved useful
to Fielding, however, as a training in the techniques of
dramatic situation, action and dialogue. But before turning to novel writing he spent three years in political
journalism and in training as a lawyer. After he was appointed Justice of the Peace for Westminster, he and his
half-brother John spent their time trying to control
brothels and gambling houses, to curb robbery and murder, to better prison conditions and to reform the graft
and corruption in the London police force. As a result of
his writings on these subjects, Parliament appointed an
investigating committee which led to a radical overhaul of
the laws and their administration.

Before the publication of *Tom Jones,* Fielding had written *Joseph Andrews,* which was perhaps begun, though not
continued, as a parody of *Pamela. Tom Jones* was created
out of his experience in the theatre, as a social satirist, as a
theorist and practitioner of the art of fiction, and out of a
life lived richly in both action and thought. Fielding was
proud of his aristocratic birth, but he was no social snob.
Tom Jones remains a bastard even when his parents are
discovered. He gains his position by merit, not marriage
lines. Fielding declares, however, that a novelist must be
acquainted "with all ranks and degrees of men," and gain
knowledge of human nature from conversation with both
low and high. From low life, he says, he will easily find examples of plainness, honesty and sincerity; in the other,
refinement, elegance and "a liberality of spirits, which
last quality I myself have scarce ever seen in men of low
birth and education."

Fielding does not define what he means by "liberality
of spirits," but we suspect that he means that easy assurance of values and wide sweep of experience that distin-

guishes his own work from that of Richardson—what one critic describes as "that freedom from strain that makes Fielding an easier novelist to live with than Richardson." Though Fielding ridiculed *Pamela,* he twice expressed, in print, high admiration of *Clarissa.* Richardson, however, had no corresponding "liberality of spirits." He never forgave Fielding's laughter. He pretended that he would not read *Tom Jones,* though giving adverse opinions about it freely, and labeling it "a dissolute book," "a profligate performance," and an attempt "to whiten a vicious character."

Readers and critics too have usually taken sides. Dr. Johnson, favoring Richardson, saw in the two "all the difference between a man who knew how a watch was made, and a man who could tell the hour by looking on the dial plate." We might argue that the whole purpose of a watch is to tell the hour, but though it is difficult to see how anyone could prefer the *personality* of Richardson to that of Fielding, it is really fruitless to argue about the two men in terms of comparative creative merit. They aimed at quite different effects, and fathered respectively two different traditions in the history of the novel—that of psychological exploration and that of the broad social panorama. Each declared he was concerned with universal truth and not with mere individuals, but Richardson focussed his attention on a particular personality, on motives and reactions, whereas Fielding said in *Joseph Andrews* that he was portraying "not man but manners, not an individual but a species." His characters, he said, are taken from life, but adds that a particular lawyer was "not only alive, but hath been so this four thousand years."

Fielding called himself "historian" rather than writer of novels or romances, declaring that the requirements of his calling are invention and "judgment," by which he means the creative faculty plus "a quick and sagacious penetration, and the gift of learning from both books and men." His penetration is "quick," it does not have the patient unraveling of Richardson. The difference is between

depth and width. Richardson concentrates on a central
figure who usurps more and more of the picture and finally transcends society and purely social values. In *Tom
Jones* the individual finds fulfillment and harmony within
the accepted social pattern. The foreground is so crowded
with figures that character development or the exploration of personal relationships in depth cannot expand. We
are to suppose that Tom adds prudence to his other excellent qualities when he is safely married to Sophia and
settled at Paradise Hall, but it is not illustrated in any of
his later actions in the book. In fact, no one changes at
all. The little incidents surrounding Sophia's pet bird,
which take place when she is thirteen and Tom two years
older, really reveal the character of all the main figures.
Tom has given the bird to Sophia, who loves it and has
tamed it, though she keeps a light string on its leg to prevent it from flying away. Young Blifil, jealous of Tom, per-
suades Sophia to let him hold her pet, and then at once
slips the string off and tosses the bird into the air. Tom,
impulsive and thoughtless of self, climbs into a tree after
it, but the branch breaks and he falls into the canal, while
the bird flies off and is caught by a hawk. Blifil declares
hypocritically that he freed it because he thought it cruel
to keep it in captivity. Mr. Allworthy, full of rather obtuse
good will to all, promises Sophia a much finer bird, and
finally Squire Western "chid her for crying so for a foolish bird; but could not help telling young Blifil, if he was
a son of his, his backside should be well flayed."

Characters are simple and are revealed dramatically by
their actions and speech. Fielding builds a most intricate
and complicated plot which really forbids any psychological revelation, since if we were allowed into the minds of
the characters, the accidents and coincidences, the igno-
rances and surprises, on which the secret of Tom's birth
depend, could not develop. Fielding's subject and the
source of his characters is, as he tells us repeatedly, "the
vast authentic Doomsday-Book of Nature." His model is
Don Quixote, and his aim is to present a "prose epic,"

which shall create a panorama of society seen through the vision of ironic and satiric comedy, and framed in a personal critical commentary in which he tells us his theories of human nature and of literary art.

In line with the tastes and expectations of his day, Fielding announces at once in the dedication that his purpose is moral. Not only is there nothing in the book "prejudicial to the cause of religion and virtue," but on the positive side, "to recommend goodness and innocence hath been my sincere endeavour." His aim, though, is not narrowly didactic, but broadly humane. In the Invocation to his Inspiration (love of fame and of "that jolly substance," money), which prefaces Book XIII, he prays to his genius: "Teach me . . . to know mankind better than they know themselves," and to bring to his aid not only Learning and Experience, but Humanity, with "all those strong energies of a good mind, which . . . swell the heart with tides of grief, joy, and benevolence."

We could wish that Fielding had allowed his story, with all its skillful ironic juxtapositions, to tell itself dramatically, or with the minimum of comment; but that is not his way. His ethic is full of wisdom and insight, his critical positions sound and sensible, but the perpetual overflow into lecture and commentary is a trial for the modern reader. Standing always at our elbow, the author will not leave us alone. He must interpret it all for us, with his "sagacious penetration"; he must direct our attention where he wants it, and control our reactions, and even deliberately mislead us if it suits his purpose.

Apart from the constant intrusion of this ubiquitous Chorus, a huge cast of characters is woven into an organically interlocking pattern of action. It is not true to say that everything in the plot contributes to the main outline of the story. The episodes of Tom and Partridge among the gypsies and at the puppet show are offshoots, and the stories of the Old Man of the Hill and of Mrs. Fitzpatrick are unnecessarily long. But we never lose sight of the theme, which is the discovery of Tom's origins, and, more important, the reader's discovery of Tom's character. During the course of these revelations we spend one third of our time in the country, one third on the road and one third in London. The first six books sketch the background of the households of Mr. Allworthy and Squire Western; we are told of Tom's supposed parents and of the events that lead up to his banishment and the flight of Sophia from a forced marriage with Blifil. In the next six books the old device of flight and pursuit doubles and redoubles. Tom flees from his home, Sophia sets out to reach London, Mr. Western pursues Sophia. At the inn at Upton, when she learns that Tom is there and has been unfaithful to her, she flies from *him*. She finds herself sharing a coach with her cousin from Ireland, Mrs. Fitzpatrick, whose husband is pursuing *her*. Tom, returning from a night spent with Mrs. Waters, finds Sophia's muff in his empty bed, put there by her maid, Mrs. Honour, and, full of remorse, sets out to pursue Sophia.

The books telling of London life have less humor and more satire, and it is impossible not to find the conclusion artificial. After Tom's fortunes have gone from bad to worse and he believes himself to be guilty of both murder and incest, suddenly, within the space of a couple of days, revelation after revelation triumphantly establish his innocence and his respectable parentage; all his difficulties melt away into final reconciliation with both Mr. Allworthy and Sophia.

Coincidence plays too large a part in the denouement, and for modern readers other aspects of the book may seem wearisome. Fielding said that he introduced the "mock-heroic" parodies and burlesque imitations of epic rhetoric for "the entertainment of the classical reader." The ignorant reader tires very quickly of the device, and also of the number of "violent uproars," the amount of knockabout farce, and all the fisticuffs, bloody noses, battered heads and scratched faces encountered on the way. Squire Western's tantrums are apt to turn him into a stock comedy figure, and the same applies to Partridge's cowardice and superstitious terrors. "Every book ought to be read with the same spirit and in the same manner as it was writ," Fielding says, but unfortunately this is impossible. The passage of time and the changes of fashion take their toll, and it becomes in spite of, rather than because of, certain elements that the book remains immortal.

For it surely does. Fielding's "sagacious penetration" of the human scene is everywhere, colored by the humor, and above all by the irony which is his hallmark.

Irony depends on contrast. It inheres in the opposition between appearance and reality, between the *ought* and the *is*, the expected and the unforeseen. Fielding delights in this principle of contrast, "which runs through all the works of creation, and may be the basis of all beauty." Certainly it is the basis of much of his characterization and his satiric method.

In its crudest form we see it in the contrast between Tom and Blifill, between good and evil as Fielding sees them. Fielding was roundly attacked in his own day and all through the nineteenth century for allowing his good man several sexual lapses. Dr. Johnson announced firmly that he "scarcely knew a more corrupt work than *Tom Jones*"—an extraordinary remark for a person of Johnson's wisdom and knowledge of the world. But his views of sexual morality were puritanical, and it can be only from that standpoint that he could make such a comment. Even then it shows careless reading of the book, for in spite of the number of embarrassing situations into which Tom's "violent animal spirits" land him, Fielding is very careful to keep the sympathy of the reader on his side. Lack of prudence and judgment are always responsible, never real vice. Women (including Sophia herself) always take the initiative, and Tom never corrupts innocence in the unmarried, or virtue in the married. He is simple-minded enough to believe that he is the father of Molly Seagrim's child, and is prepared to marry her until he has proof that she is cheating him. When a similar situation arises in London, and the trusting but foolish little Nancy Miller is pregnant as a result of being seduced by young Night-ingale under promise of marriage, Tom gives his ethic of sexual behavior.

"Lookee, Mr. Nightingale," said Jones, "I am no cant-ing hypocrite, nor do I pretend to the gift of chastity more than my neighbours. I have been guilty with women, I own it; but am not conscious that I have ever injured any. Nor would I, to procure pleasure to myself, be knowingly the cause of misery to any human being."

When Nightingale, finding his father demands his mar-riage to an heiress, informs Nancy that he is forced to desert her, Tom bursts out at the dishonor of his action.

"Can you, with honour, be guilty of having under false pretences deceived a young woman and her family, and of having by these means treacherously robbed her of her innocence?"

Nightingale replies that the world will think he is dis-honoring himself if he marries a whore, even his own.

"Fie upon it, Mr. Nightingale!" said Jones; "do not call her by so ungenerous a name: when you promised to marry her she became your wife; and she hath sinned more against prudence than virtue. And what is this world which you would be ashamed to face but the vile, the foolish, and the profligate?"

Tom himself at this time, having arrived in London penniless, and being immediately pursued amorously by Lady Bellaston, is in "the ignominious circumstance" of being her gigolo. But he is not permitted to gain any satis-faction from this indignity. She insists on coming to his rooms in Mrs. Miller's house, which leads Mrs. Miller to ask him to leave. Moreover, Sophia herself, in ignorance of Lady Bellaston's reputation, has taken refuge with her, which makes the situation impossible. In desperation, Tom allows himself to be persuaded by young Nightingale to bring the affair to an end by proposing marriage. He

knows that Lady Bellaston will certainly refuse, because
to consent would be to put her fortune in his hands. Re-
luctantly Tom writes to her, though the whole scheme is
repugnant to "one who utterly detested every species of
falsehood or dishonesty." And of course it backfires: Tom
does not foresee that Lady Bellaston, already furiously
jealous, will show the letter to Sophia to prove Tom's faithlessness. If, however, Sophia could finally forgive him, it is
hardly the place of the reader to condemn!

Sophia, indeed, is as goodhearted and as generous in
spirit as Tom. Fielding tells us that she is a portrait of his
first wife, Charlotte Cradock, with whom he made a run-
away match in 1734, and who died ten years later. Sophia
falls in love with Tom from natural attraction and pro-
pinquity, encouraged by Mrs. Honour's story of seeing
Tom kissing her muff. Tom's affections are fanned when
he is told that on hearing of this, Sophia retrieved the
muff, which she had given to Mrs. Honour, and presented
the maid with a new one in its place. When Tom is exiled
and she hears that her father and her aunt plan an immediate marriage for her with Blifil, whom she hates, her
resolution is taken immediately: "I am determined to leave
my father's house this very night." Mrs. Honour argues the
difficulties of getting horses or a conveyance, but Sophia
replies intrepidly: "I thank Heaven my legs are very able
to carry me." To Mrs. Honour's fear of a chill, she retorts:
"a good brisk pace will preserve us from the cold." Again
when she believes Tom has betrayed her at the inn at
Upton, she decides immediately to continue her journey
without seeing him. She explains later that it was not his
acceptance of the favors of Mrs. Waters that she resented,
since at this point in the story Tom thinks he has said
good-bye to her forever, but her erroneous belief that he
dishonored her by gossiping about her with the servants. It
is really Partridge who has done this, and Tom is shocked
when he discovers it.

Fielding contrasts the standards of honor in sexual
matters, exemplified in the true affection of Tom and

Sophia, with a host of descriptions and direct dramatic presentations of opposing attitudes and situations. Tom's opposite, Blifil, gloats in a sadistic way over possessing Sophia against her will: "this served rather to heighten the pleasure he proposed in rifling her charms, as it added triumph to lust." The description of Mr. Western's dead wife, also married unwillingly, is a bitter picture.

> The squire, to whom that poor woman had been a faithful upper servant all the time of their marriage, had returned that behaviour by making what the world calls a good husband. He very seldom swore at her . . . and never beat her: she had not the least occasion for jealousy, and was perfect mistress of her time; for she was never interrupted by her husband, who was engaged all the morning in his field exercises, and all the evening with bottle companions.

Mr. Western combines this with being jealous of Sophia because she preferred her mother to him. Indeed perhaps our chief challenge to the "realism" of the novel is the repeated assertion of Sophia's affection for her brutal boor of a father. Fielding's way of describing his feeling for her is to say: "Mr. Western grew every day fonder and fonder of Sophia insomuch that his beloved dogs almost gave way to her in his affections." Is it possible that she could sustain a devotion to a parent whose immediate response to his sister's suggestion that his child is in love with Blifil is to say: "I was never more rejoiced in my life; for nothing can be so handy together as our two estates," and who is perfectly willing to sell her into slavery for life to a man she detests in order that the bargain can be struck? His wild fury against his daughter when she refuses is meant, presumably, to be a comedy parallel to the more measured cruelty of Mr. Harlowe against Clarissa, but Fielding in his own person comments grimly on the habit of parents in persisting in this pattern. Thus on Mr. Western's treatment of his orphan niece, who has eloped with the heartless fortune-hunter Fitzpatrick, the author is uncompromising:

> This being a stolen match, and consequently an unnatural one in the opinion of the good Squire, he had, from the time of her committing it, abandoned the poor young creature, who was then no more than eighteen, as a monster.

The Quaker, whom Tom meets on his travels, has behaved in the same way to his daughter, and old Mr. Nightingale is following the same pattern in planning a marriage for his son with a silly, ill-natured but wealthy girl. Though his brother urges him to let his son choose for himself, the brother's behavior is not much better. When he learns that young Nightingale is not actually married to Nancy Miller, but plans to go through the ceremony on the following day, he does his best to make his nephew give up the idea.

> ... you well know how trivial these breaches of contract are thought ... Is there a man who afterwards will be more backward in giving you his sister or daughter? ... Honour is not concerned in these engagements.

But if Fielding gives us plenty of illustrations of women as victims in a predatory masculine world, he holds the balance even with plenty of light ladies and the portrait of one really vicious woman, Lady Bellaston. Tom speaks of the "wickedness and folly" of his relations with her, but it is she who has snared him into them. With the laws of property what they were, her wish to avoid remarriage is natural, but when we find that out of pique and revenge she is arranging for Sophia to be raped by Lord Fellamar, and arguing that "neither law nor conscience" forbids a plan to have Tom kidnaped by a press gang, she becomes devilish. Nor is Mr. Western's sister much better. With all her claims to education and sophistication, she is willing to believe that Fitzpatrick is courting *her,* when he is really plotting to get the fortune of her niece, who is supposed to be under her protection. She too abandons the orphan girl after her elopment. Nor has she any sympathy for Sophia: she is quite willing to concur in the plan to marry her by force to Blifil. Indeed a reading of *Tom Jones* makes us suspect that the world of *Clarissa*, with its blackguardly villain, inhuman parents, raped virgin and false arrest, is perhaps not melodrama at all, but an accurate picture of what went on in mid-eighteenth-century England.

Against all this Fielding can present only that generosity, that "benevolence," which seems to have been the ruling principle in his own nature. There it was matched by intelligence and shrewd knowledge of the world, but in the book its embodiments are the credulous Mr. Allworthy and the brave but too simple-minded Tom. Fielding sees "benevolence" as that "active principle" in some men whose use is not so much "to distinguish right from wrong, as to prompt and incite them to the former and to restrain and withhold them from the latter." It is a spontaneous impulse to help others, as opposed to the careful calculations of self-interest, which he sees as the active principle in evil. Yet by itself it appears as of little value in the action. Mr. Allworthy proves an easy dupe of his sister, the Blifil brothers and the Blifil son, and of Thwackum and Square; and this gullibility leads to active injustice to others; not only to Tom, but to poor Partridge as well. Finally Tom himself triumphs not by his good qualities but by the intervention of carefully manipulated good fortune.

Yet this attitude is at the center of the moral pattern of the book. The disillusionments of the Old Man of the Hill have driven him to cynicism. He goes through Europe "holding my nose with one hand and defending my pockets with the other," and finally retires to a worship of Nature and the God of Nature, and an abhorrence of the human race. Tom, however, holds firmly to his belief that "nothing should be esteemed characteristic of a species, but what is to be found among the best and most perfect individuals of that species."

Tom's actions are always inspired by spontaneous generosity. He practices mercy instead of justice toward the "highwayman" who tries to rob him. When he finds that the man's story of a starving wife and children is true, he immediately gives him what money he has. Later, in ignorance that Mr. Anderson, Mrs. Miller's unfortunate cousin, is the same man, he urges Mrs. Miller to take the whole £50 Lady Bellaston has just given him, and to spend it for the family. When Anderson comes to the house, he recognizes Tom as the man he tried to rob—an incident he has not confided to Mrs. Miller. Tom keeps silent on that aspect of their earlier meeting, and puts aside Anderson's protestations of gratitude for the fresh gift.

> If there are men who cannot feel the delight of giving happiness to others, I sincerely pity them, as they are incapable of tasting what is, in my opinion, a greater honour, a higher interest, and a sweeter pleasure than the ambitious, the avaricious, or the voluptuous man can ever obtain.

Fielding's quiet irony is well illustrated in the ensuing scene between Anderson and Mrs. Miller, when Tom has left them. Anderson is tempted to confess to the attempted robbery and to tell how Tom's generosity went beyond mere money and saved him from arrest, but "luckily recollected" that it might lower him in Mrs. Miller's opinion.

> Yet such was his gratitude, that it had almost got the better of discretion and shame, and made him publish that which would have defamed his own character, rather than omit any circumstance which might do fullest honour to his benefactor.

Tom possesses in abundance this quality of loyalty which is so easily conquered by self-interest in Anderson. His earliest scrape arises from a refusal to own that Black

George has in fact shot the partridge in Squire Western's property, for which he is blamed. Black George has successfully hidden himself, and Tom "stoutly persisted in asserting that he was alone," for he knows that the gamekeeper will lose his job if he is convicted of poaching. Tom gets a thrashing as the result, but Mr. Allworthy, suspecting that his motive for lying is but "a mistaken point of honour," gives him a little horse to make up for the pain of the whipping. This causes Tom acute embarrassment, for "he could more easily bear the lashes of Thwackum than the generosity of Allworthy." He almost blurts out the truth, but remembers in time the consequences to Black George if he does. Tom's loyalty is wasted. Blifil betrays him to Thwackum and Mr. Allworthy dismisses Black George as a result. Things are not made better when Tom then sells the horse, as well as his Bible, to help the gamekeeper's starving family. Sophia too has the same instinctive goodness of heart, but no one else in the book possesses it, I think, except little Mrs. Miller. When Mr. Allworthy has come to London and is lodging with her, Blifil comes in when they are at breakfast, bursting with the news that Tom is in prison for attempted murder, and opens the subject by declaring that he is one of the greatest villains on earth. Before Mr. Allworthy can say anything, Mrs. Miller cries:

> By all that's sacred, 'tis false. . . . Mr. Jones is no villain. He is one of the worthiest creatures breathing; and if any other person had called him villain, I would have thrown all this boiling water in his face.

For the rest, self-interest, greed, hypocrisy and snobbery rule supreme. Partridge pleads to be let into a country cottage on the grounds of cold, hunger and darkness: "he made use of every argument, save one, which Jones effectively added; and this was, the promise of half-a-crown." The Quaker treats Tom with all respect and sympathy until he hears that he is a bastard, and then "all compassion for him vanished." The doctor is very careful to keep Tom sick until he finds he has no money, when he at once declares him cured. Since well-to-do parents openly want the best price for their daughters, and young men go around fortune hunting for rich wives, it is no wonder that the acceptance of bribes is universal in all classes and that money is the general language of intercourse. Mrs. Honour and Black George carefully calculate where their loyalty will pay best, and the landlady at Upton instructs the chambermaid that she could not have seen Tom in Mrs. Waters' bed because they are good customers, which is all that matters.

> I have not had a better supper ordered this half-year than they ordered last night; and so easy and good-humoured were they, that they found no fault with my Worcestershire perry, which I sold them for champagne . . .

Tom and Sophia alone, among the young people in the book, give away money to others, and here again, the episode of Mr. Anderson is used to illustrate another ironic contrast. Young Nightingale, ignorant that Tom has at once offered his £50, is loud in protestation about Anderson's misfortunes, and offers to subscribe a guinea. The Millers are embarrassed at the difference in generosity between the two young men, but Fielding's comment is:

> If either of them was angry with Nightingale it was surely without reason. For the liberality of Jones, if he had known it, was not an example which he had any obligation to follow, and there are thousands who would not have contributed a single halfpenny, as indeed he did not in effect, for he made no tender of anything, and therefore as the others thought proper to make no demand, he kept his money in his pocket.

Although the plot of the novel is concerned with *who* Tom is, Fielding makes it very clear that his theme is *what* Tom is. This is no doubt why, contrary to convention, his birth is left illegitimate. Given the picture of society in the book, it is of no consequence whether Tom is acceptable by its standards and conventions. Tom is human nature as Fielding would have it be, seen against a panorama of the follies, vices and hypocrisies of the world as it is. It is true that Tom himself has a limited consciousness and a limited experience, though his good heart is in itself a form of instinctive intelligence; but his maker can supply to the book all that its hero lacks. He offers his readers a mature presentation and criticism of almost every topic of general human interest: religion, sex, love, war, the nature of man, the nature of woman, and the nature of the institutions they have evolved, all seen through a satiric yet tolerant pair of eyes. When we have read *Tom Jones* we have been in close companionship with one of the most generous and vigorous spirits in English literature, as well as one of the wisest and wittiest. This is the greatness of Fielding: that his book creates and controls for us a great perspective of the human scene, never achieved in the novel before; a spaciousness of vision, together with a warmth and humor totally missing in both Defoe and Richardson.

LAURENCE STERNE

1713–1768

Tristram Shandy

By the mid-eighteenth century the novel had been established as the most popular literary form, and the seeds of all its later developments had been planted. Defoe and Fielding stressed realistic social satire and comedy; Richardson reveled in sensation, sentiment, psychological revelation and, as he saw it, tragedy. Sterne is the forerunner of all the later novelists who have created worlds of their own; have exploited the interplay of external and internal time and have played "the game of art" with their material and their medium. He was unique in his own day and unlike any other major novelist since in making no pretensions to be doing anything but enjoy himself and entertain his readers.

Anyone unaware of Sterne's biographical circumstances could hardly guess them from his novel, or that until the publication of the first two volumes of *The Life and Opinions of Tristram Shandy,* when he was forty-seven, he was entirely unknown to the literary world. A country clergyman with a shrewish wife and a teen-age daughter, stricken himself with tuberculosis, he had written nothing but sermons. He discovered his vein of humorous raillery in writing a pamphlet against an attorney who was troublesome to the Dean of York Minster, where Sterne himself was prebendary. Turning this gift for comic extravagance to the creation of fiction, he dashed off the volumes in six months in his country vicarage and borrowed money to pay for their publication in York. They appeared in January, 1760, and the story of how they took the reading public by storm is one of the fairy tales of

literary history. Sterne went to London in March to ar-
range for a second edition, and was lionized by ministers
of state, bishops, the aristocracy and the stage. An earl
presented him with a rich living, and the second edition
of the book came out with engravings by Hogarth and a
dedication to William Pitt, Secretary of State. By May he
was perhaps the most famous man in England, christened
the English Rabelais, and he returned to York riding in
his own carriage, driving his own horses.

Yet already other voices were heard: Horace Walpole
panned the book as "a very insipid, tedious performance";
Dr. Johnson refused to meet the author after one encounter; divines christened him "shameless Shandy" or
even "Antichrist himself"; a friendly fellow clergyman ad-
vised him against continuing the book until he had got
preferment in the church.

Sterne paid no attention. "I wrote not to be fed, but to
be famous," he declared. He knew he could not live long,
but the years were going to be filled with Shandyism. He
published another four volumes, his health steadily deteri-
orating, and in 1762 set out for France in the hope of improvement, though his "spider legs" could scarce carry
him, his voice was a whisper and his face the color of a
dishcloth. He found he was as famous in Paris as in
London and basked again in the sunshine of admiration.
He returned home the following year, but his wife and
daughter settled in France, their extravagance keeping
him in financial difficulties. He himself was always in the
midst of some amorous relationship. "It harmonizes the
soul," he declared, then added, "but I carry on my affairs
quite in the French way, sentimentally" (which we can
interpret as we wish). He wrote three more volumes of
Tristram Shandy, and *A Sentimental Journey,* which was
published in February, 1768. It too was a triumphant success, but Sterne did not live to enjoy much of it.

He died the following month, at the age of fifty-five,
"a wretched worn-out old scamp," according to Thackeray.
Thackeray's opinion, publicized in his lectures on "The

English Humourists of the Eighteenth Century" (1851),
set the tone for Sterne's reputation among the Victorians
—"a dabbler in filth," "a mere mountebank," vain, dirty-
minded, blasphemous; excused only because he wrote
some beautiful prose passages, and created Uncle Toby.
Sterne came to be remembered for his inability to resist
a witty indecency, a bawdy story or a double meaning,
though Sir Walter Scott had said very sensibly that
Sterne's licentiousness "is not of the kind which applies itself to the passions, or is calculated to corrupt society." It
is only one aspect of his humor, though it is all-pervasive.
Perhaps it is so because Sterne knew very well that the
flesh unites us all, and that the average man or woman
never seems to tire of jokes on the subject. For modern
tastes, however, many of Sterne's stories are coarse without
being very funny, and they take much too long in the telling. Many of his double meanings are obsolete, and a pun
that must be explained in a footnote ceases to amuse.

Possibly, however, the sexual tinge is so pervasive because in a sense the whole book is about the paradoxical
creativeness and helplessness of man, and obviously sex
is a central symbol for that. The whole thing starts with
a joke about a begetting and ends with one about impo-
tence, and the material enclosed within that frame is a riot
of creative fantasy about the comic and pathetic frustrations of the writing of books and the living of lives.

Sterne is one of the great comic writers, in the tradition
of Rabelais and Cervantes and Swift. In spite of all that
has been written about it, by psychologists and critics,
laughter remains somewhat of a mystery. It has so many
forms, from the most primitive to the most sophisticated.
Freud tells us it is the free discharge of repressed psychic
energy, and it is certain that it has that element of *release* in it. Comedy asserts the vitality and resilience of the
flesh; it is play, in actions and in words. It is irreverent; it
asks awkward questions about appearance and reality and
truth and convention. It puts on masks of innocence, per-
plexity, ribaldry; it mocks at the rational and the orderly,

at any effort to confine life in systems or knowledge in books. At the same time it can be sympathetic, and often close to tears. It can present scenes that are both ridiculous *and* moving. In fact, it is what Sterne creates in *Tristram Shandy*. He called himself Yorick, the jester whose skull sets Hamlet commenting on the mystery of life and death and time and laughter. In his portrait by Reynolds, he *looks* the jester: the deep-set eyes, the long nose, the wide, full-lipped, humorous mouth, tilting up at the corners.

He said of *A Sentimental Journey* that his design was "to teach us to love the world and our fellow-creatures better than we do," and indeed both his books and his sermons do have that aim. He is entirely without malice. Like Fielding, Sterne was a scholar and a wit, but his comedy has no satiric social intent. The comedy of manners sets out to expose the weaknesses and hypocrisies of both the standards of society itself and of human behavior in the social framework. It reveals vulgarity, greed, vanity, stinginess, snobbery or cowardice, and punctures their pretensions. But no such qualities *exist* in *Tristram Shandy*. Sterne does not attack moral or social abuses because he does not portray them. As he says, he has neither anger nor zeal, and hates disputes. His book "is wrote against nothing but the spleen." It is fabricated "for the laughing part of the world." He wrote it listening to Death clattering at his heels, but determined to "lead him a dance he little thinks of." It "springs from that great and elastic power within us of counter-balancing evil," which so astonished Mr. Shandy himself.

When one runs over the catalogue of all the cross reckonings and sorrowful items with which the heart of man is over-charged, 'tis wonderful by what hidden resources the mind is enabled to stand it out and bear itself up, as it does against the impositions laid upon our nature.

Or turning it into the concrete picture, as Sterne loves to do, it is Tristram's hobbyhorse, "the sportive little filly-folly which carries you out for the present hour . . . which a man makes a shift to get astride on, to canter it away from the cares and solicitudes of life." It carries us to a world very different from that of Defoe or Richardson or Fielding, a world where birth and death and love and war and learning are all alike comic material. Again, in spite of the fun, the modern reader has to be prepared for a good deal of tedium. The tradition of Rabelais, Cervantes and Sterne's other masters is now dead for the common reader: all the learned lumber becomes wearisome, and Tristram's own breathless antics with language and composition can pall. Yet to read the book is an adventure; to puzzle about it is an exercise for the wits, and to laugh with it a most refreshing experience. Dr. Johnson declared after Sterne's death, when his writings went into an inevitable slump: "Nothing odd will do long: *Tristram Shandy* did not last." But it has proved singularly resilient to attack. Nowadays indeed it has had far more serious criticism as a work of art than ever before. Sterne said he wanted an uncritical reader who would "be pleased he knows not why, and cares not wherefore." His early readers did just that: they accepted the book as a whimsical chaos and took Tristram's own remarks at their face value: "I begin with the first sentence,—and trusting to Almighty God for the second;" or "Ask my pen,—it governs me,—I govern not it." Now it is argued about lengthily, yet few people seem agreed about its plan, if it has one, and any new reader finds himself in very peculiar surroundings.

Someone is setting out to write an autobiography, which starts with his begetting, but does not reach his birth until the end of the third volume, or his christening until the fourth, and then leaves his story altogether while he is between the age of five and the period at which he is writing. The first volume wanders on with some information about the midwife and a discussion of hobbyhorses;

interrupted by a mock dedication, it goes on to a sketch
of the parson of the parish; this is followed by a digression on digressions, by a burlesque legal document which
purports to be Mrs. Shandy's marriage settlement, an
account of Mr. Shandy's hatred of the name Tristram, and
a legal memoir, in French, on the subject of baptism before birth. We are introduced to Great Aunt Dinah, who
married the coachman, to Tristram's dear, dear Jenny,
whose relationship to him is discussed but left uncertain,
and finally to his uncle Toby, who had been invalided
out of the army after receiving a wound in his groin at
the siege of Namur. Tristram, with Dr. Slop's hindrance,
is born in 1718 and we leave the story at the end of the
ninth volume in 1713, having meanwhile traveled ahead
as far as 1766, and backward to the reign of Henry VIII.

And the writing! It is strewn with dashes, asterisks,
apostrophes, parentheses, catalogues, misplaced chapters,
odd typography, blank pages. One chapter takes sixty
pages, another four lines. The one on Whiskers, frequently mentioned, never materializes. Meanwhile the
author is pretending that he hasn't the slightest idea
what is going on, or how he got into this tangle, or how
he can possibly get out of it.

> —in order to conceive the probability of this error in
> my uncle Toby aright, I must give you some account of
> an adventure of Trim's, though much against my will.
> I say much against my will, only because the story, in
> one sense, is certainly out of its place here; for by right
> it should come in, either amongst the anecdotes of my
> uncle Toby's amours with widow Wadman, in which
> corporal Trim was no mean actor,—or else in the mid-
> dle of his and my uncle Toby's campaigns on the bowl-
> ing green,—for it will do very well in either place;—but
> then if I reserve it for either of those parts of my story,
> —I ruin the story I'm upon,—and if I tell it here—I
> anticipate matters, and ruin it there.

He must throw himself on the mercy of the reader:

> —bear with me—and let me go on, and tell my story
> my own way ... don't fly off,—but rather courteously
> give me credit for a little more wisdom than appears
> upon my outside;—and as we jog on, either laugh with
> me, or at me, or in short, do anything,—only keep your
> temper.

Fielding promised the reader that he would digress whenever he felt inclined. He has his planned introductory chapters, and he chats over his characters a good deal with the reader. But Sterne's method is all his own. He does not break the illusion of the fiction to play the part of chorus in his own person. We cannot really speak of the *intrusion* of the narrator because he is never absent. *The narrator and his mind are the subject of the book.* Nothing has any existence except in the medium of Tristram's rambling talk ("writing, when properly managed ... is but a different name for conversation") as he skips from narrative, to discussion, to soliloquy, to dialogue. Sterne wrote: "The world has imagined because I wrote *Tristram Shandy* that I was myself more Shandean than I really ever was." Tristram is Sterne's mask, his escape from life into art. As for personality, he has really split his own personality between Yorick and Tristram. He gives Yorick his own long, lean appearance, and his calling as country clergyman, while Tristram has his bad health, his fondness for painting and music and women. Both are scholars and wits, full of gaiety and good humor; both write—Yorick his sermons, and Tristram his life and opinions.

Nietzsche said that Sterne was the freest writer of all time. This is true in the sense that the world he creates is not tethered to any ordinary laws of place or time. All its unity arises from the fact that it takes place in Tristram's mind. It is a highly original mind. Because Sterne himself said he was steeped in the writings of John

Locke, critics have made much of Locke's influence on
him. But he disagrees as often as he agrees with Locke's
philosophy. What he particularly liked about him was
that he made no effort to explain "the miracle of sensation," but left it in the hands of God, and rested in what
was Sterne's own position: "We live among riddles and
mysteries; . . . and even the clearest and most exalted
understanding amongst us find ourselves puzzled and at
a loss in almost every cranny of nature's works." *Tristram
Shandy* is really Sterne's Essay Concerning Human Understanding, and it poses the question whether our beliefs
in a rational world of controlled cause and effect, or free
will, or steady human identity, are perhaps fantasies con-
tradicted continually by the facts.

—My good friend, quoth I—as sure as I am I—and
you are you—
—And who are you? said he.—Don't puzzle me; said I.

Moll Flanders, or Clarissa, or Tom Jones, make moral
choices which illustrate their characters and affect their
destinies. In *Tristram Shandy* it seems as if no one can
control events: fate always foils them. "Sport of small accidents Tristram Shandy! that thou art, and ever will be!"
tied and cross-tied and knotted by unlucky circumstances
and coincidences as fast as the instruments in Dr. Slop's
obstetrical bag. However carefully Mr. Shandy plans for
his son's virility, he is defeated by fortune. Tristram's
prenatal influences are hopelessly jarred by Mrs. Shandy's
ill-timed question at his conception, and the consequent
wrong dispersion of the "animal spirits"; his chance of a
well-formed nose is destroyed by Dr. Slop's forceps; instead of being called Trismegistus he is mistakenly called
Tristram, a name which Mr. Shandy is convinced could
produce "nothing but what was extremely mean and pitiful"; and when Mr. Shandy takes the opinion of the
learned clerics on altering the name, they work around
to a convincing logical proof that it cannot be done be-

cause the parents are of no kin to their own child.

Every incident breaks up unfinished; facts bounce off one another at unlikely tangents into new paths; communication continually breaks down; it is all a vast game of cross purposes. Man, in fact, is a flawed and impotent creature, floundering among petty frustrations. The author and his characters are the sport of unhappy interruptions, physical accidents and the betrayals of language. We can never foresee the actions of either the writer or the writing. This is Tristram's form of dramatic suspense: "If I thought you was able to form the least judgment or probable conjecture to yourself, of what was to come on the next page,—I would tear it out of my book." His trick of "eternal scampering of discourse from one thing to another" was not all brought out of a hat by Sterne; nor did it arise only, as is so often stated, from Locke's doctrine of the association of ideas. Sterne's wandering method is an old comic device used before him by Rabelais, Burton in his *Anatomy of Melancholy*, Marivaux, Swift and his club friends in *The Memoirs of Martinus Scriblerus*, and in our own day, James Joyce. It is Sterne's *use* of it which is new, the way in which its dartings backward and forward in time, its hoverings and swoopings and circlings gradually outline the picture of a group of personalities and their creator.

The outlines are not complete. Critics sometimes speak as if Sterne invented both the Proustian method of exploring memory and the "stream of consciousness" method of Joyce and Virginia Woolf, which then lay unused until our own century. But Tristram's use of memory and consciousness is very limited. He is neither reporter nor analyst of the inner psychic life of emotional associations in himself or in others. He never uses the present to *interpret* the past, and though his mental activity is unflagging, it never explores inward or downward into unfamiliar territory. All his digressions and expansions do is to emphasize the simultaneity in the mind of the present with the memory of the past, and the coexistence

of competing memories clamoring for expression. He is
starting on an episode—

> But I have fifty things more necessary to let you know
> first,—and I have a hundred difficulties which I have
> promised to clear up, and a thousand distresses and
> domestic misadventures crowding in upon me thick
> and three-fold, one upon the neck of another,—a cow
> broke in (tomorrow morning) to my uncle Toby's for-
> tifications . . . Trim insists upon being tried by a court-
> martial,—the cow to be shot . . . myself to be *tristram'd,*
> and at my very baptism made a martyr of . . . I have
> left my father lying across his bed, and my uncle Toby
> in his old fringed chair sitting beside him, and promised
> I would go back to them in half-an-hour, and five and
> thirty minutes are lapsed already.

We do not get back to that scene for another forty pages,
and this confusion of clock time and mental time is a
comic device throughout.

> It is about an hour and a half's tolerable good reading
> since my uncle Toby rung the bell, when Obadiah was
> order'd to saddle a horse and go for Dr. Slop the man
> midwife; so that no one can say, with reason, that I
> have not allowed Obadiah time enough . . . both to go
> and come . . .

He tells us that the ride is eight miles each way, and then
boasts proudly that:

> I have brought my uncle Toby from Namur, quite
> across all Flanders into England—That I have had him
> ill upon my hands near four years;—and have since
> travelled him and corporal Trim in a chariot and four,
> a journey of near two hundred miles down into York-
> shire;—all which put together must have prepared the
> reader's imagination for the entrance of Dr. Slop . . .

We then find that Dr. Slop had been by chance coming in
at the gate as Obadiah set out, so that in the main narra-

tive line, only a few minutes have elapsed since the ring-
ing of the bell.

On another occasion Mr. Shandy and Uncle Toby con-
verse as they go downstairs, and the comment is:

> Is it not a shame to make two chapters of what passed
> in going down one pair of stairs? for we are got no
> farther yet than to the first landing, and there are
> fifteen more steps down to the bottom; and for aught
> I know, as my father and my uncle Toby are in a talking
> humour, there may be as many chapters as steps . . .

Critics disagree whether the book is finished or whether
Sterne planned to continue it had he not died, but obviously whenever it had ended everything would still have
been in flux. As he says himself in the fourteenth chapter,
speaking of it in terms of a journey: "In short, there is no
end of it;—for my own part, I declare I have been at it
these six weeks, making all the speed I possible could,—
and am not yet born . . ."

Later he explains the complete hopelessness of his undertaking:

> I am this month one whole year older than I was this
> time twelve-month [when the first two volumes had
> been published]; and having got, as you perceive, al-
> most into the middle of my fourth volume—and no
> farther than to my first day's life—'tis demonstrative
> that I have three hundred and sixty-four days more
> life to write just now, than when I first set out; so that
> instead of advancing, as a common writer . . . on the
> contrary, I am just thrown so many volumes back—
> was every day of my life to be as busy a day as this—
> And why not?

The progression can never catch up with the digressions;
we can never reach any new perspective from which we
can look back and survey the way we and the characters
have come; nothing can ever be finally resolved and con-

cluded, and the time is an eternal dramatic present which
blots out all sense of past or future.

Indeed this world and its inhabitants are timeless and
almost placeless. They float in an ether of their own, and
though we are told that the setting is a Yorkshire village,
we meet no village folk. Tristram's group of characters
do not exist *in* a society: they *are* a society. They play a
series of scenes in the theatre of Tristram's mind, isolated
from contact with the mundane world of the audience. He
issues stage directions to himself—"drop the curtain,"
"shift the scene," "clear the theatre"—and we move, in
Shandyland, from the parlor, to the bedroom, to the
kitchen, to the staircase, to the bowling green, to the
house of the widow Wadman, or with Tristram on his
travels in France. In these scenes we watch his characters
play their parts, for they are not rounded, realistic figures, but carefully constructed to support and contrast
with one another in comedy situations. It is a strange
fact too that though some of the subject matter would
be very distressing in actuality—Mrs. Shandy's difficult
confinement, Bobby's death, Uncle Toby's wound, Tristram's accidental circumcision from the window sash,
his race with Death—we never become involved in any
painful feelings about them. They all occur offstage, as
it were, and our attention is fixed on the reactions of
others to these experiences, not on their actuality.

As no progressive line is sustained, to build a unified
plot and the development of character in a time sequence,
all the interest must center in spatial composition. Very
large claims are now made for width and depth in Tristram's vision. Alan D. McKillop, in *The Early Masters of
English Fiction*, states:

> Reality is not simply built up out of single units; it is
> contained in the given unit. The individual experience
> somehow images in little and simultaneously a moral
> order and a cosmic order, the world of conscience and
> consciousness and the world of microscope and tele-
> scope.

I do not myself feel this sweep of significance in Sterne's episodic method. It is Walter Shandy who expounds the doctrine of the interdependence of all knowledge, which Mr. McKillop quotes:

> Knowledge, like matter, he would affirm, was divisible *in infinitum;* that the grams and scruples were as much a part of it, as the gravitation of the whole world.— In a word, he would say, error was error,—'twas alike fatal to truth, and she was kept down at the bottom of her well as inevitably by a mistake in the dust of a butterfly's wing, as in the disc of the sun, the moon, and all the stars of heaven put together.

But Mr. Shandy's opinions are not to be taken very seriously and Tristram later comments on his father's passion for speculation: "He would move both heaven and earth, and twist and torture everything in nature to support his hypothesis.... By which means, never man crucified Truth at the rate he did." Whatever Sterne's own beliefs may have been, it seems difficult to find moral, intellectual and spiritual order in Tristram's consciousness. His ethic is a simple Christian one, and he has great fun laughing at all systematized inquiry.

Locke saw the senses as the entrances for all exploration of the mind, and Tristram follows him. The book is full of tableaux famous for a most precise use of physical detail: Mr. Shandy throwing himself on his bed when he hears the news of his son's squashed nose; Mrs. Shandy listening at the parlor door; Trim's stance as he reads Yorick's sermon, or takes off his Montero cap. But these are set pieces, physical counterparts to the various rhetorical figures of speech which Sterne is constantly using for comic effects. The same criticism applies to the worked-up scenes of broad comedy such as Dr. Slop's fall into the mud, the incident of where the hot chestnut fell, the description of the clerics at the Visitation dinner. In Sterne's finest dramatic scenes, however, the physical and the emotional melt into one another and are indivisible. The effect may be one of primitive comedy, as when the widow Wadman makes love to Uncle Toby by coming to visit him in his sentry box in the bowling green, and getting him to put aside his pipe and trace out the plan of attack with his forefinger, puts her own by it

> ... close thro' all the little turns and indentings of his works. ... This, tho' slight skirmishing, and at a distance from the main body, yet drew on the rest ... how could she forget to make him sensible that it was her leg (and no one's else) at the bottom of the sentry-box, which slightly pressed against the calf of his— So that my uncle Toby being thus attacked and sore push'd on both his wings—was it a wonder if now and then it put his center into disorder?

Or the result may be a scene of pure pathos, like the famous one of LeFever's death, or when Tristram looks forward to the scene of Uncle Toby's funeral, with Trim laying the sword and scabbard on the coffin and returning to lead the mourning horse by the bridle:

> ... where all my father's systems shall be baffled by his sorrows. ... When I see him cast in the rosemary with an air of disconsolation, which cries through my ears,—O Toby! in what corner of the world shall I seek thy fellow?

Sterne's best-known scenes of pathos—the incident of mad Maria and her goat, and his conversation with the ass in the gateway at Lyons—deliberately end with a comic twist. And in the famous scenes of the various reactions to the news of Bobby's death, he mingles both elements and presents a skillful grouping and contrasting of a larger cast of characters. Mr. Shandy finds consolation in quoting a string of classical literary sources, telling of the ways in which death has come and the reactions of others to it. But while he is pouring out his rhetoric in the parlor, each of the servants in the kitchen is giving his or her individual response. When Obadiah announces, "My young master . . . is dead!," Susannah's mind jumps first to a green satin nightgown of Mrs. Shandy's. "We must all go into mourning," she says. But in spite of the word "mourning:"

> it excited not one single idea, tinged either with grey or black,—all was green. . . .
>
> —O! 'twill be the death of my poor mistress, cried Susannah.—My mother's whole wardrobe followed.— What a procession! her red damask,—her orange-tawny,—her white and yellow lutestrings,—her brown taffeta,—her bone-laced caps, her bed-gowns, and comfortable under-petticoats.—Not a rag was left behind.— "No,—she will never look up again," said Susannah.
>
> We had a fat foolish scullion . . . she had been all autumn struggling with a dropsy.—He is dead! said Obadiah. . . . So am not I, said the foolish scullion. . . .
>
> —He was alive last Whitsuntide, said the coachman. —Whitsuntide! alas! cried Trim . . . Are we not here now . . . (striking the end of his stick perpendicularly upon the floor, so as to give an idea of health and stability)— and are we not—(dropping his hat upon the ground) gone! in a moment! . . . The descent of the hat was as if a heavy lump of clay had been kneaded into the crown of it.—Nothing could have expressed the sentiment of mortality, of which it was the type and forerunner, like it . . . it fell dead.

The scene is cut, but there is enough to show how vividly Sterne uses physical detail to carry emotional values, though the psychology is very simple; Susannah, whatever her lips are saying, thinking of nothing but inheriting her mistress' wardrobe; the dropsical scullion still feeling herself alive; Trim illustrating his eloquence with telling gestures.

This scene is Sterne's most ambitious dramatic presentation, and in general the incidents are limited to two actors at a time, though many other figures enter into the interpolated stories. Tristram declares:

> The hand of the Supreme Maker and First Designer of all things, never made or put a family together ... where the characters of it were cast or contrasted with so dramatic a felicity as ours was ...

Perhaps we may credit Sterne rather than the Supreme Maker with this creative felicity, but it is certainly there. The members of the Shandy family are carefully cast and contrasted so that each shall exist fully only in the context of the others. Mrs. Shandy plays only a small part, since her complete passivity is the essence of her character. Her conversation with her husband in "the bed of justice," as they discuss putting Tristram into breeches, is typical: she duly echoes every opinion he puts forward. But this is not what Mr. Shandy wants: "It was a consuming vexation of my father that my mother never asked the meaning of a thing she did not understand." As he says of her: "That she is not a woman of science ... is her misfortune,—but she might ask a question." Since Mr. Shandy's joy in life is to air his knowledge, his irritation is natural. But she does not want to understand his arguments, and Uncle Toby cannot follow them, and Parson Yorick, who understands them, does not agree with them; so that Mr. Shandy exists in a state of almost perpetual frustration. The frustration indeed is double; not only can he not communicate freely with his family in words, but the facts of life have a devilish way of tripping up his theories. Much of the comedy in the earlier volumes arises from the conflict between Mr. Shandy's world of obsolete speculation and the world of actual events: his theories of geniture and of the importance of names and of noses all founder on the rocks of evil chance or human error.

But this does not interfere with the enormous amount of Mr. Shandy's talk that we listen to. When Sterne wrote, the methods of prescientific scholars were not as far out of date as they are now, and there was no doubt more point to the humorous satire. Mr. Shandy's thinking is along "scholastic" lines. He starts with abstract premises in philosophy, law, psychology and philology, and his "proofs" are to list all the real and imaginary authorities on the subject. With immense care for logical accuracy, and a lavish display of formal rhetoric, and a blithe disregard for common sense, he sets out his hypotheses. Critics have traced all the "borrowings" from Rabelais, Montaigne, Cervantes, Burton and so on, but it is certainly unnecessary to know them. The point is always the comic disproportion between the huge paraphernalia of erudition and the small issue at stake if stated in simple language. Mr. Shandy's very elaborate researches into the nature and amount and regulation of "the radical heat and moisture" necessary to preserve health, ends: "If a child, as he grows up, can be taught to avoid running into fire or water . . . 'twill be all that is needful to be done on that head."

But it is not Mr. Shandy's tortuous speculations in themselves that supply the main human comedy, but the dramatic interrelation between him and Uncle Toby. One illustrates the eccentric flights of complicated theory defeated continually by the simplicity of facts; the other the limitations of simplicity of mind in the face of the complexities of experience. Uncle Toby has collected as many volumes on military science as Don Quixote had on chivalry, but outside his hobby his brain is like wet tinder which cannot be sparked. He and Corporal Trim spend as much time as possible in the bowling green, where they can play at sieges without interruption, making cannon out of Mr. Shandy's top boots and ammunition out of the weights from the nursery sash window. They are convinced that it is "for the good of the nation" that they should reconstruct the Duke of Marlborough's campaigns and that though they are peace-loving people, they are "answering the great ends of our creation" by devoting themselves to military affairs.

For what is war? . . . what is it but the getting together of quiet and harmless people, with their swords in their hands, to keep the ambitious and the turbulent within bounds.

In the evenings the brothers sit on either side of the fireplace smoking, napping or talking at cross purposes. Mr. Shandy is translating his favorite author, Slawkenbergius:

'Tis a pity, cried my father one winter's night ... that truth, brother Toby, should shut herself up in such impregnable fastnesses, and be so obstinate as not to surrender herself sometimes upon the closest siege.

Uncle Toby is innocent of all philosophy, but instantly pricks up his ears at the word "siege." Mr. Shandy notes it and hastens "to keep clear of some dangers ... apprehended from it."

'Tis a pity, said my father, that truth can only be on one side, brother Toby,—considering what ingenuity these learned men have all shewn in their solutions of noses.—Can noses be dissolved? replied my uncle Toby.

Mr. Shandy flies into a passion, strides about the room, bites Mrs. Shandy's pincushion in two, chokes on the bran and takes five minutes and thirty-five seconds to recover. Meanwhile Uncle Toby imperturbably smokes his pipe and whistles *Lillibullero*, which is his form of escape from his brother's talk and his tantrums.

But though Walter Shandy responds with a "witty kind of peevishness" at Toby's simplicity, he truly loves his brother, and all their intellectual misapprehensions are harmonized in a perfect emotional understanding. A *gesture* will instantly heal a wounding insult. "I wish the whole science of fortification ... at the devil;—it has been the death of thousands,—and it will be mine," shouts Walter, as Toby is monopolizing the attention of Dr. Slop. But Toby

look'd up into my father's face, with a countenance

spread over with so much good nature;—so placid;—
so fraternal . . . it penetrated my father to his heart:
He rose up hastily from his chair and seizing hold of
both my uncle Toby's hands as he spoke:—Brother
Toby, said he,—I beg thy pardon;—forgive, I pray thee,
this rash humour which my mother gave me . . . 'tis
ungenerous . . . to hurt any man;—a brother worse;—
but to hurt a brother of such gentle manners,—so un-
provoking,—and so unresenting;—'tis base . . .

The book has no resolution, but scattered through it are
scenes like this, where, instead of the usual dislocation—
sudden shift of subject—or switch to a staccato monologue by Tristram, we are allowed to feel communication
instead of confusion, peace instead of flurry, and harmony instead of unfulfillment. This never happens in the
sexual relations in the book, but between Toby and
Walter, between Toby and the faithful Trim, and in the
episode of the Gascoigne roundelay danced by Tristram
and Nanette (if only he could forget the slit in her petti-
coat!) we can enjoy moments of happy concord.

We want a cavalier, said she, holding out both her
hands, as if to offer them—And a cavalier ye shall
have; said I, taking hold of both of them. . . .
A lame youth, whom Apollo had recompensed with a
pipe and to which he had added a tambourin of his
own accord, ran sweetly over the prelude, as he sat
upon the bank . . . off we bounded . . .
The sister of the youth, who had stolen her voice
from heaven, sung alternately with her brother . . .
Viva la joia!
The nymphs join'd in unison, and their swains an
octave below them . . . why could not a man sit down
in the lap of content here—and dance, and sing, and
say his prayers, and go to heaven with this nut brown
maid?

The book gets nowhere, but that, after all, seems to be

Sterne's comment on the human condition. Life fulfills itself in moments of concrete experience, and the book fulfills itself in the creation of such moments, and the author fulfills himself in all his extraordinary fertility of verbal sense and nonsense. His writing, he says, is "two parts jest and one part earnest." Its wisdom is that of the acceptance of an existence at the best paradoxical and frustrating, yet shot through with the humor of the flesh and the humor of the mind, and with kindness, and with ultimate compassion for all. But it is as comedian that Sterne will always be read; for his zest and gusto in raillery; and for the exhilaration and enjoyment with which he pursues his dedication to mirth, "being firmly persuaded that every time a man smiles,—but much more so when he laughs, that it adds something to this fragment of life."

SOCIAL COMEDY AND SATIRE

JANE AUSTEN
1775–1817

Emma

Jane Austen's limitations are accepted as much by her admirers as by her detractors. Those who are bored point to her very narrow scope, and those who adore her extravagantly excuse her limitations as imposed on her by the circumstances of her life. Indeed these "Janeites" don't really *excuse* them, because the smallness and remoteness of her field, her "period" charm, is an aspect of her art which they love. To them she is the perfect "escape" novelist, taking them out of the complicated modern world into a haven of peace and primness and simple values. Her world, they say, is trivial and ladylike, but she adorns it with a wealth of sly satire and comic observation which are ample compensation for the narrowness of her experience and her material.

Even if our admiration for Jane Austen is not based on these arguments, it still remains true that limitations of material are the most striking and obvious characteristic of the novels. Not only does she not concern herself with the whole range of the great passions—spiritual aspiration, or passionate love, or ambition, or greed, or patri-

otism; she ignores also all the public affairs that filled
men's minds during her lifetime—the French Revolution,
the Napoleonic Wars, the vast social, political and economic changes which were being brought about by the ad-
vance of the industrial revolution. When she was urged to
try some more ambitious setting, she declared herself to
be "the most unlearned and uninformed female who ever
dared to be an authoress," and clinched the matter by
saying: "I must go on in my own way—I deal in pictures
of domestic life in country villages."

It is a deceptively innocent remark, and perhaps it is
natural that it has been taken rather too literally. It has
been interpreted to mean that Jane Austen wisely decided
to write only of what she knew, and that domestic life in
country villages was the extent of her knowledge; that
she was, after all, the unmarried daughter of a country
clergyman, so that it was natural that her standards
should be those of her genteel, limited and sheltered surroundings.

Reading her biography and letters, however, we lose
very easily the delusion of her sheltered existence. Though
she spent most of her life in the country, and much preferred it to the city, she lived four years in Bath, then a
considerable social center, and two years in Southampton,
a naval station. Her five brothers all married, four of
them twice, and produced thirty-four children, and Jane
paid frequent visits to them in London and elsewhere. Her
letters reveal plenty of sensational material: blackmail,
theft, accidents, lawsuits and tragic deaths. Moreover, she
is completely uninhibited in writing to her sister or her
nieces about social scandals, and will joke about mis-
tresses and natural children, amorous intrigues and
drunken husbands and wives. She knew as much of sophisticated social life as most of us, but she preferred
her family circle. She writes from London of her longing
to get back to "Candour and Comfort, Coffee and Crib-
bage," and to "the pleasures of friendship, of unreserved
conversation, of similarity of taste and opinion." The

Austens seem to have been a very self-sufficient group, both intellectually and emotionally. Their taste for satiric comedy we can guess from Jane's *juvenilia*, and from all the sketches and burlesques which she wrote for the family entertainment, and their warmth of feeling from a letter she wrote shortly before her death at the age of forty-one: "If I live to be an old woman, I must expect to wish that I had died now, blessed in the tenderness of such a family, and before I had survived either them or their affection."

Clearly, the world that Jane Austen creates in her novels is as it is because she chose to make it so; the restrictions of scope are self-imposed. She narrowed her field to domestic life in country villages not because she knew of nothing else, but because she felt that this setting was what she needed for concentrating the essentials of her vision.

Her world of comedy is rooted in the social order as it is. It deals with the relationships in a group and between particular individuals within the group. On the one hand we are shown the self-deceptions, the misreading of motives, the confusions of reality and illusion, the frailties and follies common to any social group and the sufferings these cause; on the other hand we see equally clearly the standards of good feeling, good sense and good taste which can make for full and fruitful living in this society, narrow though it seems. Evil in any serious sense does not exist in Jane Austen's world. There are no villains: no Lovelace or Blifil or Lady Bellaston. Socially harmful and mischievous qualities and persons take the place of evil. These are exposed for what they are, they are not allowed to inflict any lasting injury upon society or upon an innocent individual. But they are not punished: they survive as an ineradicable element in the social scene. Mrs. Elton, the most unpleasant character in *Emma*, goes out of the story in the last paragraph, still as snobbish and malicious as ever, commenting acidly on the wedding of the hero and heroine as "extremely shabby ... Very little white

satin, very few lace veils: a most pitiful business." Jane
Austen indeed has no illusions, though she is neither
cynical nor bitter. She is not blinded by any romantic
complacencies and refuses all sentimentality. Her positive values are assured and convincing but she does not
mask any of the triviality or the boredom or the unattrac-
tiveness of existence in country villages, or any of the difficulties of attaining the good life in such surroundings. It
is part of the maturing process in all her heroines, and
particularly in Emma, that they must learn to accept their
world as it is, and develop the necessary self-knowledge
and humility and generosity of spirit to achieve serenity.
The attitude of the heroine toward her world changes, the
world itself remains as it was.

The world of Emma is very small. It contains a group
of people in Highbury, sixteen miles from London. Emma
Woodhouse and her father live at Hartfield, one of the
large houses, Mr. Knightley at Donwell Abbey, an ad-
joining estate. At the opening of the book, Emma's ex-
governess has just married a neighboring widower, Mr.
Weston, at Randalls. In the village live Mr. Elton, the
vicar, old Mrs. Bates and her middle-aged voluble daughter, and the illegitimate Harriet Smith, a "parlour-boarder"
at Mrs. Goddard's school. Robert Martin, who owns a
nearby farm, wants to marry Harriet, but Emma inter-
feres. Indeed Emma's interferences produce most of the
troubles in Highbury. In addition to the permanent resi-
dents are Emma's elder sister and her husband, John,
Mr. Knightley's brother, who pay occasional visits, and
Jane Fairfax, Miss Bates's niece. New arrivals who play
important parts are Frank Churchill, Mr. Weston's
nephew, and the bride whom Mr. Elton brings home
from Bath. The warp and woof of the comedy is woven
from the relationships of these men and women in their
humdrum day-to-day doings. Emma herself is determined
to find romance if she can. She is sure, for instance, that
Harriet Smith's parentage is really aristocratic, or even
that she will prove to be the legitimate offspring of a secret

marriage. Or again Harriet's mild encounter with the gypsies and her "rescue" by Frank Churchill sets Emma's imagination racing: "Such an adventure as this,—a fine young man and a lovely young woman thrown together in such a way, could hardly fail of suggesting certain ideas to the coldest heart and the steadiest brain." But in each case Emma's romantic-fantasy solutions are exploded by prosaic facts. There are no real surprises in the plot, for every turn of events is prepared for. Of course the news of the secret engagement between Jane Fairfax and Frank Churchill is a terrible shock to Emma and to Highbury in general, but not to the *reader*. We have already seen Mr. Knightley's suspicion's aroused, and questions about Frank Churchill's sincerity in wooing Emma have been planted all along. She has not been allowed to become emotionally involved, and indeed has destined Frank for Harriet long before the news breaks. Jane Fairfax appears in the early part of the book as a Cinderella in a realistic setting, and it is obvious that her beauty and talents and goodness and suffering will lead to a happy issue. The clever twist there, as one critic has pointed out, is in making Emma play the part of an ugly stepsister, and having her realize how cruelly she has done so.

The limits of place are as strict as those of action. The scene never moves from Highbury, and though some of the characters come and go, Emma never leaves her home for more than a few hours. The important things are not what happen *to* her, but what happens *in* her.

The class structure is a little wider in range than in the other novels. Instead of everybody being more or less well-to-do members of the "gentry," some different gradations of the bourgeoisie appear in the Coles and Mr. Perry, the apothecary. Mrs. Goddard, who keeps the school at which Harriet Smith is a boarder, is admitted to Highbury society, but Robert Martin, the young farmer, though sympathetically described, is not. We never see or hear of any village activities except those of social life and personal gossip, and we never hear men talking except in the

company of women. The women, with the exception of
Mrs. Weston and Jane Fairfax, have no intelligent interests. Emma draws and sings in an amateur way, and is
always intending to improve her mind, but has never got
beyond making lists of books to read. In the action of
the story her interests are identified with those of Harriet,
and we are told: "The only literary pursuit which engaged
Harriet at present, the only mental provision she was
making for the evening of life, was the collecting and
transcribing of all the riddles of every sort she could meet
with." The same total mental vacuity affects Mr. Woodhouse and Miss Bates and Isabella Knightley. Events are
equally circumscribed: a couple of picnics, a dance and
a few small dinner parties are the extent of the "social
occasions." Around them we listen to the buzz of gossip
about the arrival of Mrs. Elton; the visit of the fashionable
young man Frank Churchill; the mysterious gift of the
pianoforte to Jane Fairfax; the scandal of the secret
engagement.

This society would be restricted enough anyhow, but
Emma makes things much worse for herself by her appalling snobbery. Her mind is obsessed with degrees of
rank and importance. She dislikes visiting at the sociable
Bateses and facing "all the horror of being in danger of
falling in with the second rate and third rate of Highbury,
who were calling on them for ever." She is convinced it
would degrade Harriet to marry Robert Martin, but thinks
it is quite suitable for her to aspire to the vicar, Mr.
Elton. But when Mr. Elton presumes to propose to Emma
herself she is horrified "that he . . . should suppose himself
her equal in connection and mind . . . look down upon
her friend, so well understanding the gradations of rank
below him, and be so blind to what rose above." When
the new Mrs. Elton arrives from Bath, Emma dismisses
her; she has brought "no name, no blood, no alliance,"
and has a father in trade! That is the trouble with the
Coles too. When she hears they are giving a party, her first
reaction is that certainly they would not presume to invite

"the regular and best families—Donwell or Hartfield or Randalls. . . . The Coles . . . were very good sort of people—friendly, liberal and unpretending, but on the other hand, they were of low origin, in trade, and only moderately genteel." She then hears that her friends from Donwell and Randalls have been invited and are going. Mrs. Weston says: "I suppose they will not take the liberty with you." But that does not satisfy her now: "She felt she should like to have the power of refusal." The invitation does come, she decides to go, and is pleased to meet Mr. Knightley arriving at the same time in a carriage, instead of walking as he usually does. "This is coming as you should, like a gentleman," she exclaims, and is not put down by his dry reply: "How lucky we should arrive at the same moment, for if we had met first in the drawing room, I doubt whether you would have discerned me to be more of a gentleman than usual." And anxious though Emma is to think well of Frank Churchill, she has to confess that "his indifference to a confusion of rank bordered too much on inelegance of mind."

Jane Austen said herself that in *Emma* she had chosen a heroine "whom nobody but myself will much like," and in the moral and emotional pattern of the book she did something new. Usually she works with two groups of characters, representing roughly the good and the bad. She embodies the vices in figures such as Mrs. Bennet, Mrs. Norris or Miss Eliot, who have something in common with Mrs. Elton in *Emma.* The other group always include the heroines. They have faults, but never faults of feeling or of taste, merely errors arising from lack of judgment and maturity. They are themselves the *victims* of snobbery or malice or interference from others, but they are not snobbish or unkind or meddling themselves.

But the portrait of Emma is more penetrating and subtler because in most of the book, Jane Austen's satire and irony are directed as much at Emma as at Mrs. Elton. Mrs. Elton seems to be a symbol of many of the elements that Jane Austen sees as a threat to civilized society.

Emma describes her as "self-important, presuming, familiar, ignorant and ill-bred," and in the structure of the novel, Jane Austen devises a series of scenes of ironic parallel and contrast, where, without any direct comment from herself, she illustrates her theme. The danger of Emma's total ignorance of her own nature is emphasized by showing us how much she has in common with this unattractive newcomer. Emma dislikes Mrs. Elton so much that she can hardly be civil to her, while at the same time she is shown to be infected with many of the same traits, though not in so crude a form. What Mrs. Elton does in a vulgar, loud way, Emma does in a more refined and ladylike way. Emma too is snobbish, self-complacent, presuming and malicious. And perhaps a further satiric subtlety is that whereas Mrs. Elton does nobody any active harm, Emma does.

Compare the scene in Chapter 3, where Harriet Smith is introduced to Hartfield, with Mrs. Elton's first call there, in Chapter 32. In the first, Emma is delighted and flattered by Harriet's "deference" to her. She feels at once what a pleasure it will be to detach her from her low friends the Martins: "*She* would notice her; she would improve her ... and introduce her into good society. ... It would be an interesting and certainly a very kind undertaking." At once we sense Emma's complete complacency about her own standards, and her love of interfering and managing other people's affairs. The first time she meets Mrs. Elton she sums her up in words which might almost be an unkind description of herself. She is convinced that Mrs. Elton is

> ... a vain woman, extremely well satisfied with herself, and thinking much of her own importance; that she meant to shine and be very superior ... that her notions were all drawn from one set of people, and one style of living; that if not foolish she was ignorant.

When Mrs. Elton returns her call, she boasts of her sister at Maple Grove; of what valuable introductions she could give Emma in Bath; of how she and Emma might form a musical club in Highbury; of how ladylike Mrs. Weston is even though she had been Emma's governess; and that "Knightley is quite the gentleman." She leaves, and Emma explodes: "Insufferable woman! . . . I could not have believed it. . . . I never met her equal." But everything that has aroused Emma's fury here she has already been guilty of herself: patronizing Harriet and planning to introduce her to better society, talking about who is and who is not a gentleman or a lady; basking in self-approbation. And by this time Emma has already revealed her own lapse of taste by discussing Jane Fairfax with Frank Churchill, and has been guilty, on no grounds whatever, of the mischievous and ill-bred suspicion that Jane and her friend's husband, Mr. Dixon, are in love.

That too is an illustration, not only that Emma can be guilty of bad taste, but of the streak of cruelty in her. She is unfair and unkind both to Jane and about her. She knows it, but will not analyze it honestly. She pretends it is because of Jane's coldness and reserve, and will not accept Mr. Knightley's diagnosis, which is that "she saw in her the really accomplished young woman, which she wanted to be thought herself." A further irony in the parallel between her and Mrs. Elton is that Mrs. Elton "takes up" Jane in exactly the same way in which Emma had "taken up" Harriet. But Mrs. Elton's instinct in choosing Jane for her patronage is a good deal better grounded than Emma's in choosing Harriet.

Another pair of scenes which add to the ironic comparison between Emma and the Eltons are the two most crucial ones in the book's whole moral and social design. One is an incident at the ball at the Crown Inn in Chapter 38. It is going well, when Emma, who is dancing with Frank Churchill, sees Harriet has no partner, and also that Mr. Elton is disengaged. Mrs. Weston asks him if he will dance and he says: "Most readily, if you will dance with me." She refuses and brings Harriet forward, upon which Mr. Elton gives her the snub direct, declares his dancing days are over and leaves her to go and speak to Mr. Knightley, "while smiles of high glee passed between him and his wife."

The Eltons have exposed themselves for what they are by their enjoyment of this public humiliation of the harmless Harriet, but again Jane Austen makes Emma guilty of the same kind of thing. The Box Hill picnic in Chapter 43 presents Emma at her worst. She allows Frank Churchill to monopolize her and to go to extreme lengths in his gallantries. She then falls in with his silly suggestion of how to make the party "go."

> "I am ordered by Miss Woodhouse to say . . . that she only demands from each of you either one thing very clever . . . or two things moderately clever, or three things very dull indeed . . ."
>
> "Oh!" exclaimed Miss Bates, "then I need not be uneasy. 'Three things very dull indeed.' That will just do for me, you know. . . ."
>
> Emma could not resist.
>
> "Ah! ma'am, but there may be a difficulty. Pardon me—but you will be limited as to number—only three at once."
>
> Miss Bates . . . did not immediately catch her meaning, but when it burst on her, it could not anger, though a slight blush showed that it could pain her.
>
> "Ah!—well—to be sure. Yes, I see what she means, (turning to Mr. Knightley,) and I will try to hold my tongue. I must make myself very disagreeable, or she would not have said such a thing to an old friend."

Jane Austen's economy of craftsmanship is so skillful that she makes both these little scenes crucial in the emotional pattern, as well as in the moral and social one. Indeed they finally become indivisible. The episode at the ball, by revealing Mr. Elton in his true colors, gives the first jolt to Emma's certainty about her own judgment, and we are shown that she can own herself in the wrong. Mr. Knightley's chivalrous rescue of Harriet from her embarrassment, and their dancing together, gives her the first illusion that he might marry her; but the conclusion of the chapter is one of the first hints that Mr. Knightley thinks of Emma in more than a friendly way. He asks her to dance:

> "Indeed I will . . . you know we are not really so much brother and sister as to make it at all improper."
> "Brother and sister! No, indeed!"

In the Box Hill incident, the behavior of Frank Churchill toward Emma brings Jane to the breaking point, and turns her from a passive to an active character in the emotional relationships. It also convinces Mr. Knightley that Frank and Emma are in love. But the most important thing in both scenes, besides revealing the lack of charity in both the Eltons and Emma, is to emphasize the opposite quality in Mr. Knightley. It is he who saves Harriet from her social humiliation, and it is he who, by the way he remonstrates with her, makes Emma recognize her own inhumanity. Her reaction is so immediate—"She felt it in her heart. How could she have been so brutal, so cruel to Miss Bates"—that we have no fears that she is not truly repentant, and her further comment gives a hint of her unrecognized feeling for Mr. Knightley:

> How could she have exposed herself to such ill opinion in one she valued! And how suffer him to leave her without saying one word of gratitude, of concurrence, of common kindness!

Mr. Knightley, in fact, is the measuring rod of Jane Austen's own moral, social and emotional standards. We realize it at once when he discusses Emma's weaknesses with Mrs. Weston in Chapter 5. He likes and respects Robert Martin, and he "looked red with surprise and displeasure" when he hears from Emma that she has persuaded Harriet to refuse Martin's offer of marriage. Standing up "in tall indignation," he tells her "loudly and

warmly" what will happen: "You will puff her up with
such ideas of her own beauty and of what she has a
claim to, that in a little while, nobody within reach will
be good enough for her. Vanity working on a weak head,
produces every sort of mischief." A few months later,
Emma, sick at heart, hears Harriet say of herself and Mr.
Knightley: "Now I seem to feel I may deserve him; and
that if he does choose me, it will not be anything so very
wonderful." He is the only person who quite firmly puts
Mrs. Elton in her place, though without rudeness. She
tries to play hostess and issue the invitations for the
strawberry party at Donwell. He defeats her civilly in this,
but she is irrepressible:

> "I shall wear a large bonnet, and bring one of my little
> baskets hanging on my arm. . . . We are to walk about
> your gardens and gather the strawberries ourselves, and
> sit under trees . . . it is all to be out of doors—a table
> spread in the shade, you know. Everything as simple
> and natural as possible. Is not that your idea?"
>
> "Not quite. My idea of the simple and natural will
> be to have the table spread in the dining room."

Mr. Knightley distrusts Frank Churchill from the start,
and when he suspects an understanding between him and
Jane Fairfax, his first thought is to warn Emma, for he is
afraid, of course, that she is falling in love with Frank.
She sweeps the idea aside with complete scorn, absolutely
sure, as usual, that she knows best.

It is part of Jane Austen's psychological insight that
she is aware that no amount of kindly wisdom or even
stern criticism from Mr. Knightley will open Emma's eyes
to the full truth about herself. She must learn by bitter
personal experience. Her first shock is to discover that
Frank Churchill had never cared anything about her at
all, and had simply used her to blind others to his real
relationship with Jane. It is a blow to her vanity. "A very

abominable sort of proceeding," she calls it, but she can still protect herself by blaming him: "Frank Churchill had behaved very ill by herself . . . but it was not so much his behaviour as her *own*, which made her so angry with him." From this point, however, step by step, humiliations fall upon her one after another. Her world of illusions comes tumbling about her, and she realizes her "false and insolent estimate" of her own merits.

> With insufferable vanity had she believed herself in the secret of everybody's feelings; with unpardonable arrogance proposed to arrange everybody's destiny. She was proved to have been universally mistaken; and she had not quite done nothing—for she had done mischief.

She has to recognize how those she has snubbed and patronized are her moral superiors. Jane bears her no ill will, and Miss Bates's ready forgiveness makes her see how much more largehearted is that despised little chatterer than herself.

Mr. Knightley has said to Mrs. Weston: "I should like to see Emma in love, and in some doubt of a return." This is the nadir of her suffering, with the added bitterness of knowing that if Mr. Knightley cares for Harriet, no one is to blame but herself. "O God! that I had never seen her!" she cries helplessly. Her searching self-analysis, and final full acceptance of her own responsibility, whatever it may cost, is most true and moving. As usual, Jane Austen evades the direct love scene in the garden which brings the reconciliation of comedy. But it is not needed, for she has fully communicated that "this one half-hour had given to each the precious certainty of being beloved," and that Emma went into the house "in an exquisite flutter of happiness—and such happiness, moreover, as she believed must still be greater when the flutter should have passed away."

On the first page of the book we are told that "the real

evils of Emma's situation were the power of having rather
too much her own way, and a disposition to think a little
too well of herself," and that the *danger* that threatened
her from these traits was at present "unperceived" by her.
Those "evils" and their "danger" are the moral and emotional substance of the story, and the development of
"perception" the solution. That is Jane Austen's theme,
and every action and character in the book supports it in
some way, illustrating the ironic contrasts between what
Emma believes herself to be, what others believe her to
be, and what she really is.

Jane Austen's method of social comedy, like that of
Fielding, centers in these contrasts. We have seen how
she plans this in the crucial scenes of the book, making
one emphasize another. She uses the same methods in
character groupings. Emma's good fortune in having two
such friends and advisers as Mrs. Weston and Mr. Knightley, and yet obstinately choosing Harriet as her intimate,
is set against Jane Fairfax, who has no one to turn to except Miss Bates on the one hand and Mrs. Elton on the
other, and yet keeps her dignity throughout. In individual
portraits she puts the quiet, courteous Mrs. Weston opposite the vulgar Mrs. Elton; the indiscriminately sociable
Mr. Weston against the taciturn Mr. John Knightley; the
lightweight but charming Frank Churchill against the
solid integrity of Mr. George Knightley; Mrs. Elton's kind
of egotistical babble against Miss Bates's silly but good-
natured garrulity. Finally, the whole situation of Miss
Bates and her poor old deaf mother in their extreme
"genteel" poverty is contrasted with the luxurious in-
validism of Mr. Woodhouse and his "habits of gentle
selfishness." His semi-imbecility of mind and his refusal
to let any thought for others interfere with his ideas of
diet and liking for hot rooms make much comedy, but the
implications are surely satiric also. Emma shows her own
essential shrewdness when she remarks to Mr. Knightley:
"Nobody who has not been in the interior of a family,

can say what the difficulties of any individual of that
family may be." Her own home situation illustrates this.
Mr. Woodhouse claims, and gets, the attention of everyone. Emma's tireless devotion to him is her one good
point in the first part of the book, but everyone has to
inconvenience himself to make him happy; Mr. Knightley
even abdicates his rights by going to live at Hartfield. (We
can be thankful that Jane Austen told her family that he
lived only two years after the marriage!)

Jane Austen undoubtedly learned much from her fore-
runners. Emma confronting her own vanity and self-deception reminds us of Clarissa doing the same thing, and
Fielding's mixture of sanity and sympathy and irony is
everywhere in her work. But while she has none of his
panoramic sweep or vigor of mind, she is a much more
penetrating psychologist and a much more finished and
subtle artist. The plot of *Tom Jones* is immensely ingenious, but it lacks any character development, and the range
of personalities in *Emma* is much richer than Fielding's
huge collection of simple types. Jane Austen's formal
design, too, is much more exacting. Her critical and in-
terpretive attitudes are almost entirely absorbed in her
narrative and dramatic presentation. She allows herself a
few discerning general comments, comic or serious:
"Human nature is so well disposed towards those who
are in interesting situations, that a young person, who
either marries or dies, is sure of being kindly spoken of."
"Seldom, very seldom, does complete truth belong to any
human disclosure..." "Perfect happiness, even in memory, is not common." But in general she keeps her de-
tachment and finds it unnecessary to intrude or explain.
The reader has only to watch what the characters do and
to listen carefully to what they say. Unlike Richardson
and Fielding she never insists on her moral purpose, nor
is there any need that she should. Her standards are implicit in the pattern of the work. Moreover, there is nothing "period" about these standards and ideals. They re-

main the basis for successful personal and communal relationships now, as they did in English country villages a
hundred and fifty years ago, just as the objects of her
satire remain the disruptive influences in such relations.
She chose to reveal her vision through the mode of social
comedy in a very small setting, but her depth and preci-
sion of observation make that vision universal. As we
shall see, it is the lack of a similar clarity, the uncertainty
of assured values, that mar the otherwise brilliant comedy
in *Vanity Fair*.

WILLIAM MAKEPEACE THACKERAY
1811–1863

Vanity Fair

That the idols of one age often become the tenpins of another is nowhere better illustrated than by the fortunes of Thackeray. Anthony Trollope, summing up the figures of the Victorian age in his *Autobiography* in 1883, says: "I do not hesitate to name Thackeray the first." W. C. Brownell, twenty years later, speaks of him as "one of the few great novelists of the world." But today, Walter Allen in *The English Novel* comments: "No novelist of genius has given us an analysis of man in society based on so trivial a view of life." Arnold Kettle in *An Introduction to the English Novel* quotes the famous ending of *Vanity Fair:*

> Ah! *Vanitas Vanitatum!* Which of us is happy in this world? Which of us has his desire? or, having it, is satisfied?

Kettle's comment is: "It is the feeblest of endings, the flattest of statements of faith. And one doesn't even feel that Thackeray means it."

The objection to that is that the words do not pretend to be a statement of faith but of disillusionment, and that since the whole of the rest of the book support them, there seems no reason to doubt Thackeray's sincerity. Nor does the epithet "trivial" seem a just one for Thackeray's view of life, though it is quite true that he is an ambiguous and somewhat evasive writer. His own age felt this too. Many of the contradictory elements in his personality felt by modern readers were pointed out in a letter from Carlyle to Emerson in 1854.

He is a big fellow, soul and body; of many gifts and qualities (particularly in the Hogarth line, with a dash of Sterne superadded), of enormous *appetite* withal, and very uncertain and chaotic in all points except his *outer* breeding, which is fixed enough . . . a big, fierce, weeping, hungry man; not a strong one.

This suggests his creative vitality, his satiric vigor, his emotional sensitivity, and at the same time a basic insecurity of outlook, an acceptance of convention, and the lack of those large qualities of intellectual energy and stability and full-blooded enjoyment of life that characterized his avowed model, Fielding. Thackeray professed to admire and envy the freedoms of the eighteenth century, and in the preface to *Pendennis* he attacks Victorian prudery:

Since the author of *Tom Jones* was buried, no writer of fiction among us has been permitted to depict to his utmost power a Man. We must drape him, and give a certain conventional simper . . . You will not hear what moves in the real world, what passes in society, in the clubs, colleges, mess-rooms—what is the life and talk of your sons.

But in spite of this protest, Thackeray savagely assailed the writings of Swift, called Sterne "an impure presence," and declared that Fielding's moral sense was blunted.

We can find reason enough for his emotional insecurities in the facts of his life. The only child of an official in the East India Company, he lost his father when he was four, and two years later his mother sent him back to England. Then, at the age of six, he was put in a school where his miseries seem to have matched those of Dickens in the blacking factory. Thackeray says memories of it haunted him all his life: "as those tender twigs are bent, the trees grow afterwards." This wretchedness lasted only a year, after which he was sent to another school, but his mother, who had married again, did not return from India until four years later. Then his passionate adoration of her, and constant fear of her leaving him again, darkened his adolescence. Some critics see him as emotionally dependent on her all through his life, but his comments on her jealous possessiveness in a later letter seem to contradict this:

> There's hardly a subject on which we don't differ ... When I was a boy ... I thought her an angel and worshipped her. I see but a woman now, O so tender, so loving, so cruel.

When he was twenty-five, he married a "child-wife" very much like David Copperfield's Dora, a beautiful young girl who was gentle and affectionate, but totally unsuited by upbringing and temperament to be the wife of a brilliant young literary man on the make. After four years of marriage, she became incurably insane, leaving him with two baby daughters. Thackeray seems to have had a feeling of guilt about having left her too much alone, which perhaps accounts for his tender and overcharitable treatment of the character of Amelia in *Vanity Fair*. Since divorce on the grounds of insanity was impossible at that time, Thackeray could not remarry, and his close relations with women seem to have been limited to his dominating mother and the beautiful and intelligent wife of his friend the Reverend William Brookfield. Thackeray assured her jealous husband that he felt only a "spiritual sensuality" toward her, but undoubtedly she contributed greatly to his emotional frustrations.

Before the publication of *Vanity Fair* (it came out in monthly parts in 1847–48), Thackeray had made his living for ten years by writing short stories, sketches, parodies, reviews and one unsuccessful novel, *The Memoirs of Barry Lyndon*. He had shown great fertility of invention and a great talent for burlesque, but while planning *Vanity Fair* he seems to have had something in the nature of a change of heart toward his creative responsibilities. He writes in a letter:

> Truth, and justice and kindness are the great ends of
> our profession . . . A few years ago I should have sneered
> at the idea of setting up as a teacher at all . . . but I
> have got to believe in the business.

Thackeray, in fact, like Fielding, proclaims the novelist's
moral function. But the *tone* he sets in his note "Before the
Curtain" is all his own. We are to visit Vanity Fair if we
care to, and watch the puppets as they are manipulated
by "the Manager of the Performance." The mood of the
Manager, although he provides "scenes of all sorts," is
"more melancholy than mirthful." He hopes to send the
spectators home "in a sober, contemplative, not uncharitable frame of mind." But it is important to remember
that Thackeray's subject is what he defines as "Vanity
Fair," and that the line of criticism which attacks the
book for not creating strong, positive figures standing
for virtuous and constructive living is simply falsifying
Thackeray's vision and his avowed purpose. He was criticized along these lines at the time of the original publication and gave his own answer.

> My object is to indicate in cheerful terms that we are
> for the most part an abominably foolish and selfish
> people . . . all eager after vanities. Everybody is you
> see in that book,—for instance if I had made Amelia
> a higher order of woman there would have been no
> vanity in Dobbin's falling in love with her, whereas
> the impression at present is that he is a fool for his
> pains, that he has married a silly little thing, and in
> fact has found out his error . . . I want to leave every-
> body dissatisfied and unhappy at the end of the story.

As a matter of fact, compared with his great contemporary social satirist Balzac, Thackeray's terms are quite
"cheerful." Balzac was a complete skeptic who knew that
in the world he was writing of, the innocent and the honest are simply used and thrown aside by the greedy and
the heartless. Thackeray's cynicism is much less thorough-

going. We may feel dissatisfied and unhappy at the end, but on the whole Thackeray's "bad" characters come to bad ends—no one could call Becky's end a successful conclusion to her own ambitions—and the kind and the good achieve security and happy contentment. Moreover, ironically, it is the humble, the innocent and the stupid (Lady Jane and Rawdon), whom Becky has despised, who finally confound her strategems.

But as he tells us, his subject is the vanity of human wishes, and it is around that center that he has organized the whole book. He does not base his structure, like Fielding or Jane Austen, on strong ironical contrasts between a Tom Jones or a Mr. Knightley, who possess clear-cut, affirmative moral principles, and varying degrees of hypocrisy and self-deception among the other chief characters. All the characters are self-deceived, pursuing phantom ambitions or clinging to phantom loyalties. No one reaches full self-fulfillment, and frustration in some measure is the common human fate. That is Thackeray's vision of human experience and the temperamental coloring of the whole book. Yet, as artist, he combines it with a creative zest and richness which controls his huge range of "puppets" into a living unity of design.

Vanity Fair purports to be a social picture of the same period as *Emma,* which was published six months after the Battle of Waterloo. In the place of "domestic life in country villages," Thackeray presents a social structure which includes the wealthy landed aristocracy in Lord Steyne, and the impoverished in the Bareacres; the "county" family of the Crawleys, with a younger son in the church; the self-made middle-class climbers, merchants and stockbrokers, like the Osbornes and Sedleys; Jos Sedley, the wealthy colonial official; Army officers, from generals to lieutenants, and their wives, together with the tradesmen, servants and hangers-on who live off these people, and are frequently ruined by them.

All the chief characters have money and privilege or are scrambling to get it, or are bemoaning the lack or the loss of it. It is the center of their lives. It is a predatory society from top to bottom, presenting a glittering surface, while below is a loveless void. We move from London to Queen's Crawley, to Brussels, to Pumpernickel (Weimar), and wherever we go money values and social snobbery reign supreme. Miss Crawley has "a balance at her bankers which would have made her beloved anywhere," and the affections of all her relations are centered in it, not in her. Old Osborne has no pity for his old friend Sedley when he fails in business, though Sedley has given him his own start in life, and he is determined to marry his son to the illiterate mulatto from the West Indies, Miss Swartz, solely because of the size of her dowry. Rawdon Crawley and Becky take all the savings of Ruggles the butler and Miss Briggs, the "companion," without a thought of their future. Even when old Sedley has lost his fortune, and he and his wife and Amelia and little George are living on an allowance from Jos, he speculates with that and reduces them to complete penury. Old Osborne boasts to his son George: "I don't grudge money when I know you're in good society, because I know that good society can never go wrong"; while Rawdon Crawley, who has social position without the money, comments on two of his friends who are fleecing George: "They get what money they like out of him. He'd go to the deuce to be seen with a lord. He pays their dinners at Greenwich and they invite the company." Of the Duchess of Richmond's ball on the eve of the battle of Waterloo, we hear: "The struggles, intrigues and prayers to get tickets were such as only English ladies will employ, in order to gain admission to the society of the great of their own nation." At the same time the great are shown us behaving with shocking ill-breeding to anyone of lower rank; none of the "county" will accept the second Lady Crawley, because she is the daughter of an ironmonger, and Rawdon Crawley ignores Dobbin, looking upon him as an "under-bred City man."

Thackeray calls it "a novel without a hero," and the

gallery of men is indeed as unromantic and as unheroic
as it could well be: the dirty, miserly, coarse old Sir
Pitt Crawley, his fox-hunting parson brother, his eldest
son, who "failed somehow in spite of a mediocrity which
ought to have insured any man a success"; the loutish
young "blood," Rawdon, the greedy City bourgeoisie, the
spoiled and treacherous George Osborne, the almost pathetic Jos Sedley, whose overeating and drinking and
dressing are so obviously compensations for his shyness
and loneliness. As Thackeray said, they are all "odious"
except Dobbin, and since, in the pattern of the book, he
too must be pursuing "vanity," poor Dobbin is doomed
to dullness. His very name is made to suggest someone
uncouth and slow in the wits; he has large hands and feet;
he is awkward and tongue-tied and speaks with a slight
lisp. He deceives himself cruelly about the value of
Amelia, yet finally speaks out about her stupid and heartless egotism. He is the only character who is allowed to
combine loyal and generous instincts with a cultivated
mind. Thackeray describes him in Chapter 62 as the only
"gentleman" Amelia had ever met, which is saying that
he is the only one in the book. But he is very dim compared with Mr. Knightley.

If the novel has no hero, it has two heroines. In Chapter
2 we are told that Amelia is to hold that position, but by
Chapter 30 Thackeray has shifted the title to Becky, and
no one can question her right to it. Nevertheless he tells
us in "Before the Curtain" that "the Amelia Doll . . . has
. . . been carved and dressed with the greatest care by the
artist," which suggests that he did not intend her to be
the complete little ninny she appears at the beginning.
Though the Victorian reading public apparently approved
of her, there were contemporary critics who called her "a
little dolt" and who saw her as "thoroughly selfish as well
as silly," and "rather mawkish than interesting." To one
such objection, made when the novel was being serialized,
Thackeray answered: "You are quite right . . . Don't you
see how odious all the people are in the book (with the

exception of Dobbin".) But he adds that Amelia is to learn humility and be saved. Thackeray, however, does seem deliberately to mislead his readers in the first half of the book. He never mentions Amelia without some endearing address—"that pure and gentle bosom," "that timid little heart," "that poor panting little soul"—and her witless passiveness and thick-headedness are contrasted favorably with Becky's skillful trickery. In her widowhood, we can admire her uncomplaining loyalty to her ruined old father, but Thackeray suggests no *criticism* of her senseless devotion to the memory of her good-for-nothing husband, or her blind stupidity in thinking it is her duty to give up her child to be spoiled by his doting Osborne grandfather, rather than giving him the ideal stepfather in Dobbin. Not until the book is two thirds finished does Dobbin read over her letters to him and realize "how cold, how kind, how hopeless, how selfish they were!" Dobbin awakens then to the vanity of his devotion to her, but it is too late to change the habit.

Yet Amelia is the only character in the book who really matures and who achieves a measure of self-knowledge. She is humbled when she finds out that it is Dobbin who has been supporting her and her child and her parents for years, and that it is through him that old Osborne has consented to a reconciliation and will give her back her boy. At last she recognizes "that beautiful and generous affection," but she is quite willing to give him nothing in return and to continue to let him give her all. Her awakening to her own selfish folly does not come until in Pumpernickel she refuses to listen to his advice not to bring Becky into her household, and the Major at last rounds upon her and tells her the truth.

> No, you are not worthy of the love which I have devoted to you. I knew all along that the prize I had set my life on was not worth the winning; that I was a fool, with fond fancies, too, bartering away my all of truth and ardour against your little feeble remnant of love. . . . Good-bye. I have spent enough of my life at this play.

Amelia is left to the unwelcome attentions of Becky's men friends. It is true that it is Becky who supplies the final blow to her illusions by showing her the note George Osborne had put in her bouquet at the Duchess of Richmond's ball, and thus proving his faithlessness, but surely we may read it that without that final proof, Amelia had already confessed her own unfairness and foolishness and had capitulated to her faithful lover. Becky pats her head and tells her to summon Dobbin:

> "And now let us get pen and ink, and write to him to come this minute," she said.
> "I—I wrote to him this morning," Emmy said, blushing exceedingly.

The characters of Amelia and Becky and their respective fates make the chief pattern in the structure of the book. The contrast between an active and a passive nature, between villainess and victim, between brains and muddle-headedness, between heartlessness and devotion, are simple and obvious. So is the seesaw movement by which Becky rises and Amelia sinks, only to be reversed later as Amelia comes into her own and Becky goes into eclipse. But activity is naturally much more entertaining than passivity, and the story is inclined to sag whenever Becky is off the stage. She is the only dynamic figure in it, lighting up all the others in turn as she uses them for her own predatory purposes.

Becky's situation reminds us of that of Moll Flanders. Like Moll, she has to face the question of what an ambitious girl without money can do in the world. As Moll rejects domestic service, so Becky rejects being a governess; she will rebel and live by her wits. Like Moll she declares she needs only money to live a virtuous life: "I think I could be a good woman if I had five thousand a year." But whereas Moll convinces us that security and a kind husband are really all she needs, we would never believe that of Becky. Whatever she had she would want more, and life would not be life to her without intrigue

and adventure. Can we really accept that she would have
retired to respectability at forty?

Becky is not afflicted with a conscience. Her early upbringing has convinced her that she owes nothing to society, that she has a perfect right to everything she can get
from it by her own abilities. Her coldly calculating nature
admits no love and no loyalty: she cannot suffer through
her affections for she has no affections. We see her weep
once only, when old Sir Pitt falls on his knees and offers
her marriage, and her grief is over an infuriating miscal-
culation.

> Rebecca started back a picture of consternation. In
> the course of this history we have never seen her lose
> her presence of mind; but she did now, and wept some
> of the most genuine tears that ever fell from her eyes.
> "Oh, Sir Pitt!" she said. "Oh, sir—I—I'm *married al-
> ready*."

In spite of her dedication to self-interest, for the most part
Becky shows none of the unpleasant traits of the other
climbers. Her part in public is to please everyone, to be as
Mrs. Bute Crawley described her: "the most clever, droll,
odd, good natured, simple, kindly creature in England." Old
Sedley sees through her at once and that she is out to
catch Jos, but that is before she has had much practice in
her role. Later her flattery is much more adroit and she is
unerring in knowing where to apply it. Listen to her playing on the young Sir Pitt's ambitions to become a peer,
with a seat in the House of Lords.

> You remain a baronet! No, Sir Pitt Crawley, I know you
> better. I know your talents and ambitions. You fancy
> you hide them both: but you can conceal neither from
> me. I showed Lord Steyne your pamphlet on Malt.

Her dauntless fight for a secure position in society (which
she attains finally by being presented at Court, in lace
stolen from the Pitt Crawleys and diamonds given her by
Lord Steyne) and her dexterity at evading bailiffs and

living on nothing a year, while giving the impression of birth and wealth—"it was only from her French being so good, that you could know she was not a born woman of fashion"—bring energy and zest into the story whenever she is on the stage. Only twice does Thackeray seem to strike false notes in the presentation. Would she have been *unkind* to her child? Her unfailing good nature is so much emphasized in her relation with others, and the Crawley children loved her when she was their governess, and little Rawdon worships his mother: "she was an unearthly creature in his eyes, superior to his father—to all the world." We may well believe she boxed his ears in a fit of temper when she caught him, as she thinks, spying as she sings to Lord Steyne, but surely she would have been much more likely to make him forget the episode by making it up to him afterward? Thackeray feels he has to make her lose the sympathy of the reader and chooses this way to do it, but it is not convincing.

Nor is his analysis of her frame of mind as she reflects on the value of security:

> It may perhaps have struck her that to have been honest and humble, to have done her duty, and to have marched straightforward on her way, would have brought her as near happiness as that path by which she was striving to attain it.

This rings very hollow. Given Becky's temperament and talents, how could she possibly have been happy as a poor little governess? Moreover, no one in the book prospers by these means. Amelia is honest and humble—and miserable—until she and little George inherit the Osborne money. Poor Miss Briggs is honest and humble, and is merely exploited by the greed and vanity of others.

A favorite adverse criticism of *Vanity Fair* nowadays is to say that the novel is weakened by the Victorian taboo on sex, and that the characters are thereby devitalized. But this could be so only if it leaves us with the feeling that the author himself feels frustrated by the limitations im-

posed upon him by his age, as Dickens did in part, and
later, Hardy. Thackeray declared himself shackled in
Pendennis, but in *Vanity Fair* it is part of the whole conception and of the tone in which it is created that neither
the good nor the evil of real sexual passion has any place
in it. Love is the loyal devotion of Dobbin or the gentle,
tender affection of Amelia and Lady Jane. As to what he
calls "vice," Thackeray is here quite willing to accept the
convention of the age as to what is permitted "on stage."
Nothing is lost to the book by his reticence as to whether
Becky is "guilty" or not. Any physical relationship she had
would be purely a business affair anyhow. Greed and ambition are the only driving forces in her, and in the great
scene where she and Lord Steyne are interrupted by the
unexpected return of her husband, though it is most effective theatrically, we have no sense that she is involved
in any real personal drama. All of Rawdon is in his
pathetic comment later on finding her hoard of money.
"You might have spared me a hundred pounds, Becky, out
of all this—I have always shared with you", but Becky's
rejoinder, "I am innocent," is meaningless. When Sir
Pitt pleads with Rawdon to forgive her, Rawdon himself
sums it up:

> "She has kept money concealed from me these ten
> years," he said. "She swore, last night only, she had
> none from Steyne. She knew it was all up, directly I
> found it. If she's not guilty, Pitt, she's as bad as guilty;
> and I'll never see her again—never."

The chief objection modern critics have had to the art
of Thackeray, however, is his manner of telling his story.
Ever since Flaubert developed the doctrine of complete
objectivity as the aim of the novelist, and was followed by
Henry James with his pained comments on the "lyric leak"
and "the terrible fluidity of self-revelation," the ideal of the
serious novelist has been to withdraw open comment in
his own person, and to let the events and characters speak
for themselves, or be analyzed with apparent imperson-

ality. But this was not Thackeray's way. Fielding was his
model, but he went far beyond Fielding in his intrusion
upon his story in his own person. His metaphor for the
whole demands it. His characters are "puppets" and he is
their "showman." The whole performance is to be "brilliantly illuminated with the Author's own candles," and
finally: "As we bring our characters forward, I will ask
leave, as a man and a brother, not only to introduce them,
but occasionally to step down from the platform and talk
about them."

Thackeray, like Sterne, treats writing as an extension
of talking, and if one of the unifying elements in the novel
is that it is all a picture of Vanity Fair, another is the all-
pervasive *tone* which the perpetual presence of the author
throws over it all. We know him to have been a young man
of thirty-five when he wrote the book, but the impression
is that of an elderly vision, compassionate but melancholy, reviewing the whole territory and reporting on it in
a sardonic but on the whole kindly and humorous fashion.
The bitterness and irony are muted and he is without
hatred for anyone. We contemplate the whole action from
a distance as it unfolds and we listen to the author's easy
discursive soliloquy as he appears to evoke the whole memory of it. "I have no idea where it all comes from" he said,
but his hope is "to convey the sentiment of reality."

He does indeed convey the illusion of actuality, richly
and abundantly. The "puppets" are not fixed in their attitudes. They do not develop much, nor do we explore their
emotions deeply, but they are most keenly observed. We
are shown different aspects of them at different times.
They surprise us by unexpected traits, as when Amelia
flies into a passion when she catches her mother giving
her baby Daffy's Elixir, or when Lady Jane Crawley rounds
upon Sir Pitt and refuses to have Becky in her house, or
when Rawdon, that "poor battered fellow" becomes a devoted father.

We do not quarrel with the author at all while he tells
his story: the leisurely panoramic method absorbs us into

its flow. Nor, I think, need we quarrel overmuch with Thackeray's constant interruptions to generalize from the particulars of what he is telling us. This is a method now out of fashion, but provided that it is well done and the comments are cogent, we can enjoy their penetration and their force. We rebel only when they are commonplace and obvious, when they are beside the point, as in the passage on Becky's thoughts, already quoted, or when we are addressed in too hortatory a tone.

> Picture to yourself, O fair young reader, a worldly, selfish, graceless, thankless, religionless old woman, writhing in pain and fear, and without her wig. Picture her to yourself, and ere you be old, learn to love and pray!

Yet the "picturesque" quality of Thackeray's writing, his evocation of happenings in their physical settings, seldom failed. The sustained narrative flow is broken continually by individual scenes, comic or serious, full of drama and movement: old Sir Pitt's proposal to Becky; the contrasts of partings between husbands and wives before the battle of Waterloo; Jos Sedley's flight from Brussels; the midnight "hurry and bustle" at Queen's Crawley when old Sir Pitt has a stroke, and Mr. and Mrs. Bute Crawley find Miss Horrocks, the butler's daughter, decked in her "guilty ribbons" and "with a wild air, trying at the presses and escritoires with a bunch of keys"; the whole series of pictures at the end of the party at Gaunt House, culminating in the confrontation of Becky and Lord Steyne by Rawdon Crawley.

Besides these longer descriptions or dramatic interludes, the emotional mood is everywhere sharpened and focused by physicial detail. Thackeray does not linger over death-beds, like Dickens, but his pathetic touches are the more effective for being glimpses only: Amelia, futile and useless, watching George packing, leaning against the wall, holding his crimson sash to her breast like a stain of blood; George's unused bedroom in Russell Square, with its whips and caps, a Bible and a pair of spurs on the mantelpiece, and "a dried inkstand covered with the dust of ten years"; Lady Steyne, back in happy memories of her convent childhood, weeping silently as she listens to Becky singing. Glimpses of horror too: the mad George Gaunt, shut away, "dragging about a child's toy, or nursing the keeper's baby doll" and crying if his wine and water was not strong enough; little Rawdon gazing at "the wondrous bronze hand on the dressing table, glistening all over with a hundred rings," as he longs for attention from his mother. Wonderful satiric comedy too, as in the picture of Becky setting out to charm the younger Sir Pitt, making him snug on the sofa by the fire and letting him talk

> ... as she listened with the tenderest and kindest interest, sitting by him and hemming a shirt for her dear little boy. Whenever Mrs. Rawdon wished to be particularly humble and virtuous, this little shirt used to come out of her work box.

Or, when she has descended to Bohemia, her preparations to welcome Jos Sedley to her room:

> "In one minute you shall come in." In that instant she put a rouge-pot, a brandy bottle, and a plate of broken meat into the bed. . . .

She then tells Jos how her brute of a husband has deserted her and how she has lost her darling child:

> ". . . they tore it from me—tore it from me" and she put her hand to her heart with a passionate gesture of despair, burying her face for a moment on the bed.
>   The brandy bottle clinked up against the plate which held the cold sausage. Both were moved, no doubt, by the exhibition of so much grief.

One Victorian critic urged Thackeray to "take his stand no longer on the platform of experience, but on the mount of vision"; but this is to ask him to be someone else. It is in the world of society and its vanities that he is at home, and which he can create with such vigorous astringent comment and such lively observation, and such easy urbanity in the management of his plot and his language. He did not have the width of understanding, or see as deeply into human psychology as George Eliot—he said of himself that he had no head above his eyes—nor does he attain to Jane Austen's perfect artistry and assured creation of human values. He takes the stand of a disillusioned yet sympathetic man of the world and lights up the essentials of human nature as seen from that view, with a "not uncharitable frame of mind." Is it so trivial? His own comment on his story is perhaps as good a summing up as any: "I am quite aware of the dismal roguery which goes all through . . . and God forbid that the world should be like it altogether: though I feel it is more like it than we like to own."

THE TRAGIC VISION

GEORGE ELIOT
1819–1880

The Mill on the Floss

Henry James said of George Eliot's novels: "there rises from them a kind of fragrance of moral elevation; a love of justice, truth and light; a large generous way of looking at things." George Eliot was an intellectual. She knew many languages and read widely in philosophy, theology, history and the science of her day. Her mind was forceful and comprehensive, and we are always in the company of this mind as we read; it is always enlarging the matter in hand by its intelligence and its sweep. She was also a great humorist, but Henry James rightly emphasizes above all her emotional and moral qualities. They outweigh everything else.

Yet in spite of this, in the eyes of the society of her time, until she had established her literary reputation by the sheer weight of her genius, she was a social outcast. After the death of her father, when she was thirty, she moved from Coventry to London and became assistant editor of *The Westminster Review*. She met many of the leading literary and intellectual leaders of the time, and among them George Henry Lewes, journalist and critic. From the age of thirty-five, until Lewes' death, two years before her own, she lived in an adulterous relationship with him. His wife was alive, and under the law of the

day he could not get a divorce from her, since he had con-
doned her adultery when she left him. George Eliot, or
Mary Ann Evans as she then was, broke up no home, and
was the most devoted of foster mothers to Lewes' two boys;
but as a result of the prejudice of the time, she suffered
complete social ostracism for years. Nevertheless the relationship brought her fulfillment and, also, the discovery
of her genius, for it was Lewes who persuaded her to try
her hand at fiction; but it made her aware of all the
cruelty of rigid conventional judgment.

In the last book of *The Mill on the Floss,* she deals with
the subject at length in relation to Maggie Tulliver's disgrace in the eyes of St. Ogg's, and sums up her own view
of herd intolerance and "general rules" applied "without
the trouble of exerting patience, discrimination, impar-
tiality," adding:

> . . . the mysterious complexity of our life is not to be
> embraced by maxims, and . . . to lace ourselves up in
> formulas of that sort is to repress all the divine prompt-
> ings and inspirations that spring from growing insight
> and sympathy.

Of her own case she wrote to one of her faithful
friends: "That is a rare and blessed lot—to know ourselves guiltless before a condemning crowd." But one cannot believe that in truth she found it so, and against one
person in particular she felt great bitterness—her brother
Isaac, who refused to see her again or to communicate
with her except through a lawyer. It is difficult not to believe that a deep compulsion for self-justification in the
face of his condemnation led to the plan of the conclusion of *The Mill.* Though Maggie Tulliver is, of course,
really innocent of any sexual offense, Tom refuses to believe it: "You shall not come under my roof. It is enough
that I have to bear the thought of your disgrace: the sight
of you is hateful to me." George Eliot's revenge was to make
Maggie's final triumph the acceptance by Tom of her superior nobility of spirit. As they are being swept to death

together, the grandeur of her sacrifice penetrates his narrow mind:

> . . . it was . . . a new revelation to his spirit, of the depths in life that had lain beyond his vision, which he had fancied so keen and clear.

He is "pale with a certain awe and humiliation," and dies suitably in that spirit.

If, however, the conclusion of the book is a subjective fantasy solution which strikes a false note (and many people do not agree that it does so), the creative achievement of the whole stands firm. George Eliot made no secret of the fact that the figure of Maggie was autobiographical. Not literally so, of course, though she herself was brought up in the country and later in a country town. But the character of Maggie is her own, and through most of the book she is presented with a remarkable double vision which is both subjective and objective at the same time. We live through all the immediate intensity of feelings of the child and adolescent, but it is all seen from a mature, adult perspective, from an over-all view of tolerant sympathetic irony.

This vision, moreover, is not occupied only with the creation of a personal drama: her characters never stand alone. She is busy with the evocation of the complete social environment which conditions the personal situation. Both Fielding and Thackeray had practiced the panoramic narrative method, loaded with realistic detail, but no one before George Eliot had established the close, organic relationship between the nature of the individual and the nature of the society in which the individual has developed and in which it has to function. She is the first sociological novelist. Long before the subject was studied as it is today, she observed that someone should investigate:

> . . . the natural history of our social classes, especially of the small shopkeepers, artisans and peasantry—and

the degree in which they are influenced by local conditions, their maxims and habits, the point of view from
which they regard their religious teachers, [and] the
interaction of the various classes on each other.

Every one of these topics is woven into the texture of *The
Mill*. George Eliot said of her own writing: "It is the habit
of my imagination to strive after as full a vision of the
medium in which a character moves, as of the character
itself." Or again: "There is no private life which has not
been determined by a wider public life." She is herself as
much at ease in the home of Bob Jakin, the peddler, as in
the drawing room of the Deanes; in the very different
vicarages of Mr. Stelling or Dr. Kenn as in the offices of
Guest & Co., merchants and shipowners; in the parlor of
Mr. Glegg, retired ship's chandler, as in that of the gentleman farmer Mr. Pullett, or the poor tenant farmer Mr.
Moss.

She knows the whole interrelated social structure of
the neighborhood and its ways of living. We see these people intimately in their homes: Mrs. Tulliver weeping in
her storeroom, among the household treasures which must
be sold—her linen, her "chany," her silver teapot; Mrs.
Glegg, with her "fuzzy front" of false curls, which is not
put on for breakfast; Mrs. Pullett solemnly unlocking first
a door, then a shutter, then a wardrobe, to show her sister
the glories of a new bonnet.

George Eliot knows, too, all the social currents and
stresses operating between the various hierarchies: the
Miss Guests shuddering at the thought of any connection
by marriage with such people as the Gleggs and the Pulletts; the pitying scorn of the Gleggs and the Pulletts for
the incompetent, struggling Mosses; the exasperation of
Mr. Deane, who has worked himself up to a partnership
in the firm in which he started as warehouse hand, for
Tom Tulliver's useless "gentleman's education"; the snobbery of the rascally lawyer Wakem, "who always knew the
stepping stones that would carry him through very muddy

bits of practice," but who thinks it would degrade his son to marry Maggie. She knows all their various turns of speech, their maxims and their mores. More particularly she both dissects and dramatizes the characteristics of the pastoral Tullivers and the urban Dodsons, contrasting the serene background of the mill and the ancient history of the town of St. Ogg's with the quality of their present inhabitants. The opening paragraph of the book evokes a picture of the harmony between nature and the works of man: the river flowing among the rich pastures and cornfields and carrying the ships laden with the produce of the land to the city and thence across the seas. Against "this rich plain where the great river flows for ever onward" and what George Eliot calls "the poetry of peasant life," she sets Mr. Tulliver, the present owner of the mill. He has much kindly warmth, but he is self-complacent, narrow, improvident, ignorant and bitterly vindictive.

St. Ogg's itself is "one of those old, old towns which impress one as a continuation and outgrowth of nature," with a history dated from the Roman occupation of Britain. St. Ogg, its patron saint, was a simple ferryman who heeded the pleas of a woman with a child to cross the river at night in bad weather, saying: "I will ferry thee across, it is enough that thy heart needs it." His passenger miraculously turned into the Virgin Mary. We are told, however, that the minds of the present inhabitants "had no eyes for the spirits that walked the streets." Against the romantic history and Christian visions of earlier ages George Eliot puts the creed that governs the substantial lower middle class as represented by the Dodson clan. While admitting its solid unimaginative virtues of rigid honesty, thoroughness of work and loyalty to its customs and its kin, she analyzes every cranny of its smallness of mind, its obsession with money and respectability, its insensitivity to any spontaneous feeling, its prejudice and its hypocrisy. More important from the point of view of the novelist's art, George Eliot gives us scene after scene where all these people reveal themselves in concrete dramatic terms: the childhood scenes of family life, the aunts and uncles gathered to discuss Tom's education, and best of all the tragicomedy when Mr. Tulliver has lost his case about the water rights and is declared bankrupt. The contents of the mill must be sold, and the family gather to put into practice the core of their creed—the right thing must be done toward kindred: "Never to deny them bread, but only require them to eat it with bitter herbs." They will buy the bare necessities to furnish the mill, but Mr. Tulliver has disgraced the family and "must be made to feel that he could never humble himself enough."

When George Eliot has thoroughly established the social background, by description and by narrative action, she exclaims:

> It is a sordid life, you say, this of the Tullivers and Dodsons—irradiated by no sublime principles, no romantic visions, no active self-renouncing. . . . I share with you this sense of oppressive narrowness; but it is necessary that we should feel it, if we care to understand how it acted on the lives of Tom and Maggie.

The central theme of the book is the interaction of the lives of the brother and sister, both raised in this environment, but reacting to it in different ways. Just as George Eliot is the first sociological novelist, so she is the first truly psychological novelist. She is the first to practice the deliberate exploration into the springs of human motives and human mistakes, and into the inexorable continuity of cause and effect in human behavior. The center of tragic irony is the contrast between what the human will of the individual sets out to do, and thinks it can do, and what it actually does; the contrast and conflict between aspiration and achievement. Maggie, as tragic heroine, struggles throughout in a triple conflict: the struggle within her own divided self, between impulse and reason, and later between passion and duty; the clash between her own temperament and that of Tom; and the collision with her environment and with external events, which are outside her own control. All merge to bring about the tragic outcome.

The pattern is established in childhood. Maggie is not in the least ill-treated at home. She has an adoring father and a kind though quite uncomprehending mother. She suffers because she is dreamy and forgetful, thoughtless and impulsive, because she is oversensitive and mentally precocious, and because her brother, whom she adores, is none of these things. He is reliable, unimaginative, with all the oversimplified moral doctrines of the Dodsons: "He was particularly clear and positive on one point—namely that he would punish everybody who deserved it." In the first episode Maggie, who has been living for the day of Tom's return from school, has to confess that his rabbits have died because she forgot to feed them. Tom punishes her by refusing to take her fishing and Maggie rushes sobbing to the attic, where she keeps her fetish, an old wooden doll which she punishes for her own misfortunes, driving nails into its head and then comforting and cosseting it when her mood has changed. On this occasion, since childish quarrels end in reconciliation, she and Tom are soon friends again. But their characters are already established: Maggie passionate, loving, but always doing the wrong thing; Tom commonplace, self-righteous, trustworthy, never tempted to any excess, quite uncomplicated by any emotions at all. Maggie never stops to think of the results of her actions before she acts. Driven to frenzy by her aunts' comments on her shaggy black hair, she rushes upstairs and cuts it off; taunted about her brown skin, and wildly jealous of her neat little blond cousin, she pushes Lucy into the mud; the outcry about that decides her to run off to the gypsies. And she is desperately lonely, because no one around her has the least interest in her love of reading, or can share in her longings to enlarge her life and develop the faculties she knows she possesses.

Help comes there when she meets Philip Wakem, the crippled boy who goes to school with Tom, but the seeds of tragic irony are innate in that friendship, for fate arranges it that his father should be the lawyer to whom Mr. Tulliver attributes his humiliation and against whom he swears, and makes his family swear, unending vengeance.

After the bankruptcy, when the children leave school, Tom goes to work for his uncle Deane, and all his planning is for the future and the paying off of his father's debts. He gives no thought to Maggie, left with her embittered parents, and "with a soul untrained for inevitable struggles," to a life filled only with dull duties, vain daydreams and bursts of adolescent fury or despair. Pathetically she finds temporary serenity in the reading of *The Imitation of Christ,* by the fourteenth-century mystic St. Thomas a Kempis, which Bob Jakin has brought her in a package of second-hand books. She disciplines herself in the gospel of renunciation and the suppression of self-love.

That unnatural peace is broken by a chance meeting in the woods with Philip, whom she has not seen for several years. Maggie longs for the old companionship, but knows that any meetings between them must be secret, and feels that "anything so near doubleness would act as a spiritual blight." Philip argues urgently against her negative asceticism and plays on her pity for his own crippled body and lonely life. She is plunged into the hardest of all conflicts, not that between good and evil, but that between one good and another good. Philip wears down her scruples, arguing for the necessity of self-development, not self-mortification.

"I shall have strength given me," said Maggie, tremulously.

"No, you will not, Maggie: no one has strength given to do what is unnatural. It is mere cowardice to seek safety in negations.... You will be thrown into the world some day, and then every rational satisfaction of your nature that you deny now, will assault you like a savage appetite."

It is inevitable that Philip should succeed in persuading

her to continue the harmless meetings, and inevitable that he should fall in love with her. Maggie does not fall in love with him, she is quite unawakened sexually, and it is only the warm affection and the pity she has for him that make her promise to marry him if it should ever be possible.

Inevitably their secret is discovered. Ironically again the blow comes from the most unlikely quarter. It is the amiable and well-meaning Aunt Pullett who remarks at the Sunday dinner table that she has noticed Philip coming from the Red Deeps. Instantly Tom's suspicions are aroused; he surprises Maggie setting out for the rendezvous, and his response is thoroughly characteristic. The alternatives are simple: either Maggie swears never to meet Philip again,

> or I tell my father everything; and this month, when by my exertions he might be made happy once more, you will cause him the blow of knowing that you are a disobedient, deceitful daughter, who throws away her own respectability by clandestine meetings with the son of a man that has helped to ruin her father.

Tom insults Philip and taunts him with his deformity. Maggie says she must put her father first, but when Philip has left, she rounds on Tom as she has never done before:

> You have been reproaching other people all your life ... If *you* were in fault ... I should be sorry for the pain it brought you ... But you have always enjoyed punishing me ... You have no pity ... You are nothing but a Pharisee. You thank God for nothing but your own virtues.

Tom, however, forges ahead in the Dodson world, which, having a similar lack of imaginative understanding, appreciates his practical virtues and does not recognize his emotional limitations.

Few critics have any quarrel with *The Mill* up to this point. Action, environment and character have been interfused to produce a sense of rich texture and of the inevi-

table course of development. But ever since the first publication of the novel in 1860, the last two books in it have
been attacked: partly on the score of the melodramatic
ending, but more on the count that Stephen Guest is not
the sort of man Maggie could ever have fallen in love with,
and that it degrades her to do so. Meeting this criticism,
George Eliot owned that she planned her material badly;
she enjoyed writing the earlier part so much that she had
not left room to develop the tragic catastrophe as she
wished. But she denied violently that her psychology was
at fault in making Maggie fall in love with Stephen: "If
I am wrong there ... if I really did not know what my
heroine would do under the circumstances in which I deliberately placed her—I ought not to have written the book
at all." She goes on to say that Maggie is a character
"essentially noble, but liable to great error," and that she
must represent her truthfully.

George Eliot is quite sound here on the point she is making—the possibility of Maggie being overwhelmed by an
attraction to a man who was as good as engaged to her
much beloved cousin Lucy, and of this attraction over-
riding her loyalty not only to Lucy but to Philip. When the
novelist made Philip tell Maggie that the repression of her
natural instincts would mean that they would later assault
her "like a savage appetite," she prepared us to expect
that Maggie's next conflict would involve sex as well as
moral sensibility. But George Eliot does *not* meet the criticism of the character of Stephen Guest himself. Is it possible that Maggie could be attracted to the figure of
Stephen as represented at the opening of the sixth book;
this young man "whose diamond ring, attar of roses, and
air of nonchalant leisure, at twelve o'clock in the day,
are the graceful and odoriferous result of the largest oil-
mill and the most extensive wharf in St. Ogg's"? The
reader winces at the picture of this bejeweled and per-
fumed young spark, and everything that follows is unfortunately tainted with that introductory image. This is a
pity, for I think a close reading of the text makes it clear

that George Eliot's intention, which she did not have room to develop fully, was that Stephen's new experience of deep feeling in his relations with Maggie should open his eyes to his former self-complacency and triviality, and that this development in him would make *her* response emotionally acceptable.

As it is, though perhaps rather hurried, Maggie's attraction to Stephen is made plausible psychologically. Since her father's death, she has been teaching in a school, with no outlet for adult relationships. After the first evening with the emotional stimulus of the music and the obvious attentions of this handsome young man, George Eliot describes Maggie as being excited in a way that was mysterious to herself:

> It was not that she thought distinctly of Mr. Stephen Guest, or dwelt on the indications that he looked at her with admiration; it was rather that she felt the half-remote presence of a world of love and beauty and delight, made up of vague, mingled images from all the poetry and romance she had ever read, or had ever woven into her dreamy reveries.

The meeting, too, comes before she again sees Philip. The development of the mounting sexual tension between Maggie and Stephen is convincing, with the inevitable issue that she becomes caught in a situation from which no happy escape is possible. The conflict of loyalties is insoluble.

The final symbolism by which she drifts into an irrevocable situation through the drifting of the boat on the river is skillfully managed. There is irony again in the fact that the river expedition had been planned with Philip, and Maggie looks forward to it, "for perhaps it would bring her some strength and calmness to be alone with Philip again." But Philip is sick, and Stephen takes his place, and the lovers are carried by the tide and "the dreamy gliding of the boat" until when Maggie realizes their position it is too late for any decision of hers to save pain to others. Her final resolution that she can't go forward to marriage with Stephen, so that he too must be sacrificed as a sop to her conscience, and her whole family also involved in the scandal associated with her flight, makes it difficult for the reader to sympathize with her fully. It is here that we question George Eliot's artistic objectivity. Maggie's awakening too late to the results of her own actions is characteristic, so is her instinct of self-sacrifice and renunciation; but whereas in earlier episodes George Eliot has always presented Maggie from a perspective that can criticize her as well as sympathize with her, that now seems lost. Now it appears that we are to take Maggie's estimate of her own course of action as the only possible one consistent with fine ethical standards. When we pass on to her martyrdom by the tongues of the St. Ogg's gossips, to Tom's repudiation of her, and to her final supreme sacrifice, we feel that the overflow of subjective sentiment is altogether too strong for her creator and that she too is lost in the flood!

Henry James, who admired George Eliot deeply, has only one major adverse criticism: "her conception of the novelist's task is never in the least as the game of art." Some modern critics have tried to prove that she practices the game more than she is given credit for. They point to the constant references to the river which are "planted" all through the book, and say that they "give one the feeling that [Maggie] is swept along by a current of circumstances she can neither resist nor control," and to other recurrent images of animals and music. These allusions are all in the text certainly, but I do not think they weave any organic symbolic pattern. George Eliot's gifts lie elsewhere, above all in the straightforward presentation of character in dialogue and description.

Her minor figures are as surely sketched as her major ones. Though the Dodsons are a clan, each aunt and each uncle has a precise individuality. But the most important minor character in the design of the book is Bob Jakin, the peddler, who provides a contrast with all the rest of the cast. In the social scale Bob is at the bottom, but in maturity of outlook and qualities of head and heart he is the superior of everyone else—even of Maggie, since he has so much of the shrewd common sense which poor Maggie never acquires. In comparison with the Dodsons, it is Bob's generosity which is emphasized. Against their refusal to do more than the absolute minimum to help their sister and her family, though they can well afford more, Bob offers Tom his entire capital of £10, with which he had planned to equip his peddler's pack. He is the only person who senses Maggie's loneliness and hunger for reading, and so brings her the package of second-hand books. But the main comparison and contrast is with Tom himself. Bob's business code is not strictly ethical: he uses his "big thumb" to falsify the yardage he sells to his skinflint customers. His explanation to Maggie has a certain justice: "I never cheat anybody as doesn't want to cheat me, Miss." Instead of having a rigid business rectitude and a cold heart, like Tom, Bob takes great delight in his capacity to "get round the women with me tongue" —witness the wonderful comedy of his duel with Aunt Glegg—but he has the warmest heart in the world for all those in trouble. He is like Ogg, the son of Beorl, who ferries the poor woman across the river, because "it is enough that thy heart needs it." When Tom refuses to have Maggie under his roof, Bob takes her in without question. And as a token of his perfect faith in her, he puts his baby in her arms, saying: "it 'ud be better for your takin' a bit o' notice on it."

Bob is the only complete human being in the book. He is as much at home in the country as in the town, in the water as on land. He has no illusions about the quality of the society around him, but he can accommodate himself to it without loss of his own integrity. He is the only truly fulfilled and creative person we meet, and George Eliot has emphasized this subtly by leaving him at the end at home with mother, wife and child. He is the incarnation of "the spirits that walk the streets" from the old traditions of the past.

If we find the ending of the book a lapse into moral melodrama, that does not invalidate the sureness and truth of George Eliot's large human understanding. Her digressions and analyses, though the modern reader may find them too lengthy, all grow out of the revelation of character and background, and enrich her vision. They are the comments of a fine mind, a deeply tolerant probing of the facts of human behavior, and an expansive grasp of both outer and inner reality. The abundance of her humanity and luminous wisdom is something that no other English novelist possesses in like degree.

THOMAS HARDY
1840–1928

Far from the Madding Crowd

Hardy classed *Far from the Madding Crowd* among his "Novels of Character and Environment." These included all his best-known "Wessex" novels. It is the earliest of them, the one in which he first used the name, and it was followed by *The Return of the Native, The Mayor of Casterbridge, The Woodlanders* and *Tess of the D'Urbervilles.* Published fourteen years after *The Mill on the Floss,* it deals with the same sort of England; more still with the England of *Adam Bede,* for like that book it is a purely pastoral novel. In fact when it was first published anonymously in serial form in 1874, many people thought that George Eliot had written it. It recreates the English countryside of the early nineteenth century in which Hardy grew up. Weatherbury is an English village before the coming of railways, or the mechanization of farming operations, or of compulsory education; a village where life has gone on unchanged for hundreds of years, carrying on its old traditions, not only in farming, but in social relations, in dress, and local habits and superstitions.

Hardy shares the immense creative energy of the great Victorian novelists, but his imaginative world is entirely his own. The ironic social cynicism of Thackeray, the zestful faith in human nature of Dickens, or the mature critical intelligence and psychological insight of George Eliot are all alien to him. His vision is almost wholly tragic. The Victorian critics and public, who did not care much for tragedy, attacked him continually for his pessimism. Hardy replied that he held no pessimistic philosophy, that a novel was not an argument but "simply an endeavour to give shape and coherence to a series of seemings or personal impressions." He speaks, however, of the "ingenious machinery contrived by the gods for rendering human possibilities of amelioration to a minimum"; and we may justly complain that Hardy often invents a good deal of this ingenious machinery himself. Luck in Hardy is always bad luck.

He lost his faith in Christian theology early in life. As a young man he intended to be a clergyman, like many of his relatives. He found, however, that he could not accept the doctrines of the church and substituted his own ethical and traditional values. He became an architect and practiced his profession in Dorchester, London and Weymouth. His architectural interests often appear in his novels, as in his loving description of the old shearing-barn in Chapter 22 of *Far from the Madding Crowd*. The success of that book decided Hardy to devote himself to writing, and he lived in the country outside Dorchester for the rest of his life. As a person he was gentle and quiet, devoted with simple integrity to his calling. With his dark vision went a deep human sympathy and understanding; fiction, he said, was founded on "a power of observation informed by a living heart."

His "observation," however, is of a very different kind from George Eliot's. It concerns itself much more with large outlines than with minute particulars. George Eliot builds up the psychological characteristics of her major figures from the details of their daily lives and surrounds them with a detailed environment. We pass from household to household; we hear all their personal gossip in the various "domestic interiors"; we know their houses, their rooms, where they kept their linen and china and their best bonnets and false "fronts" and medicine bottles. From the outset we are in the midst of small human dramas which hold our attention before the large outlines of the theme emerge. That is not Hardy's way. *Far from the Madding Crowd* opens very slowly; indeed it is heavy going at first. But gradually it envelops us in its atmosphere and design. The psychology is very simple. The characters are individuals, of course, but at the same time they are types, often becoming large symbols. We seldom see them quietly at home. They are busy living out the large lines of development that Hardy has invented to give "shape and coherence" to his "impressions."

Bathsheba Everdene, his heroine, is a capable but willful and egotistical young women who owns her own farm. Her faithful lover is Gabriel Oak, who has lost his own flock of sheep by a stroke of fate and is engaged by her as her bailiff. She involves herself first by her own folly with Farmer Boldwood, a middle-aged neighbor whom she cares nothing about, but later falls in love with the swaggering Sergeant Troy, the illegitimate son of one of the "gentry." He has seduced and promised marriage to Fanny Robin, one of Bathsheba's servant girls, but he forsakes her and marries Bathsheba. The marriage proves disastrous. By accident Bathsheba discovers Troy's treatment of Fanny, who has died in childbirth. He leaves Weatherbury and is believed drowned. Bathsheba makes a half promise to marry Boldwood if her husband does not return in seven years. A little over a year later, Boldwood is giving a Christmas party when Troy breaks in to claim his wife. Boldwood shoots him and tries to shoot himself. He is declared insane and condemned to life imprisonment. This leaves the way open for a quiet union between Bathsheba and Oak.

Far from the Madding Crowd is the only one of the Wessex novels which is allowed a "happy ending." For Hardy, a story with only three deaths in it, one life sentence and a final marriage between the two chief characters can almost claim to be comedy. Yet the tragic elements much outweigh the final reconciliation. Like all tragedy it leaves us face to face with the mystery of human evil and suffering. As Hardy sees it, the personal fate of the individual is largely at the mercy of impersonal forces over which he has little control, or at the mercy of minor mistakes which prove to have incalculable major consequences. The innocent and guilty alike are struck down by these forces and errors, differing only in the way they react to the blows of fate and chance. People blame Hardy often for the lack of adequate *cause* for many of his tragic happenings, but it is exactly in this lack of adequate cause that much of the irony inheres. Fanny Robin mistakes the church at which she is to meet Troy for their wedding. He is so angry that he postpones the date. Meanwhile he meets Bathsheba Everdene and deserts Fanny, which leads to the death of Fanny and her child and the ultimate ruin of Bathsheba's marriage. Or Bathsheba sends a silly valentine to Farmer Boldwood, in a moment of thoughtless bad taste, and the chain of events set up by that leads to the madness of Boldwood and the murder of Troy.

Hardy's vision is centered on the ironic contrast between man's aspirations and his performance; between his will and his compulsive emotions; between the illusions of his pride and the realities of his self-ignorance. "The grimness of the general human situation" is always his subject. Yet his attitude toward the individuals caught in these baffling circumstances is deeply humane and compassionate. What he emphasizes as the most remarkable quality in man is his courage and his dignity. He sees Egdon Heath in *The Return of the Native* as "a place perfectly accordant with man's nature—neither ghastly, hateful nor ugly; neither commonplace, unmeaning nor tame; but, like man, slighted and enduring." His heroes and heroines, though so often defeated, are never abject; they go down fighting. Around them stands the apparently indifferent universe, working out, maybe, some inscrutable purpose of its own, but entirely uncaring whether the individual lives or dies. But even so man braves it out. We see it in the symbolic picture of Fanny Robin, the simple, ignorant farm servant, seduced and deserted by her lover, as, alone and penniless, she drags herself, mile by mile, and finally yard by yard, along the road to the workhouse. Nothing supports her but sheer determination to reach a shelter where her child can be born. "I can do it," she gasps, as she crawls from post to post of the iron fence, which, however, ends half a mile from her destination. Finally she clings to a large dog, and with him as prop reaches the gate of the poorhouse and is carried in. The conclusion is very Hardyesque:

> "There is a dog outside," murmured the overcome traveller. "Where is he gone? He helped me."
> "I stoned him away," said the man.

The final irony is that death comes to Fanny and her child exactly as it would if she had *not* made her pitiful and valiant struggle. There seems no meaning in the courage and no escape rewards it. But to Hardy it points to something inextinguishable in the spirit of man which makes him not only wretched but noble. In spite of his manifest weakness, he is not to be condemned nor scorned.

Hardy always admitted a comparison between his own work and that of the Greek dramatists, and to a certain extent it is true. *Far from the Madding Crowd* has five main characters and a chorus—the "rustics"—against a background of the irony of fate. But the comparison ends there. Hardy's cumbersome plottings and melodramatic contrivances arise from a strange mixture of both classic and romantic strains with the naturalism of his own day. We can accept incredible happenings in the plots of the Greeks and the Elizabethans because they are cast in conventions far removed from actuality. As long as they are true to their own imaginative worlds we do not rebel. But if the characters are a part of what we think of as "real life" it is not so easy to make this imaginative adjustment. Hardy described his own world as "partly real, partly dream-country" and the clash between the two is sometimes disastrous.

He himself was well aware of his dilemma: "... the writer's problem is to strike the balance between the uncommon and the ordinary. In working out this problem human nature must never be abnormal. ... The uncommonness must be in the *events,* not in the characters." He did believe, however, that the events must be uncommon: ". . . a story must be exceptional enough to justify its telling." If this were true Jane Austen or Henry James or Virginia Woolf would not be worth reading. Hardy's genius, however, was not of the kind that can create intense interest without strong *action.* He needed large epic outlines and simplifications to present what seemed to him the basic elements in human destiny.

The central element to him is sexual love. "Life being a physiological fact, its honest portrayal must be largely concerned with the relation of the sexes." The actual plot of *Far from the Madding Crowd* is concerned solely with the relation of two women and three men, though we shall see that the *theme* is a much larger one. In Hardy's work, as in that of the Greek dramatists, sexual attraction appears as a catastrophic passion. It happens suddenly, violently, irrationally. He makes very little attempt to explore it or analyze it. In fact he emphasizes only one large psychological truism about it: "We colour and mould according to the wants within *us* whatever our eyes bring in." Love is a subjective passion that will project itself upon any object and endow it with any qualities it desires to find there. Thus when Liddy warns Bathsheba that Troy has a bad name for wildness and fickleness in his relations with women, Bathsheba's answer is: "He's a sort of steady man in a wild way, you know." Passion eclipses reason, leaving the strong man as helpless as the silly, trusting woman. Solid, middle-aged Farmer Boldwood is as much its slave as Fanny Robin and Bathsheba, with all her pride, will throw everything overboard to capture the worthless Troy.

The men are all romantic types: Gabriel Oak (though he becomes much more) is the faithful chivalric suitor, Boldwood the victim of a grand passion, Troy the born philanderer, false and fickle. Hardy was clearly though hardly successfully trying to do more with Boldwood; he evidently intended him as a symbol of the dark unconscious forces which can overwhelm apparent sanity and stability and lead to madness. On his first entrance Boldwood promises to become more of an individual than he does in performance. We are told that the receipt of Bathsheba's valentine has destroyed the perfect balance of "enormous antagonistic forces . . . in fine adjustment," and even his face shows that "he was now living outside his defences for the first time, and with a fearful sense of exposure." But this "exposure" degenerates too often into ranting melodrama. When Boldwood uses very few words we believe most in his feelings. These are vividly communicated to the reader in the scene where Gabriel Oak meets him after Oak has been working frantically to thatch the ricks which Troy's carelessness has neglected. Boldwood confesses listlessly in passing that his own are unprotected.

"I overlooked the ricks this year."
"Overlooked them!" repeated Gabriel slowly to himself. . . . A few months earlier Boldwood's forgetting his husbandry would have been as preposterous an idea as a sailor forgetting he was in a ship.

What of Bathsheba herself? Do we believe in her, as a symbol of Woman, and as a living individual? Again, Hardy is no psychologist. His women are all primitive creatures, whose hearts invariably dupe their heads. The gentle ones, like Fanny, are types of clinging femininity, made to be deserted by faithless lovers. The stronger ones crave excitement; they are vain and self-willed, despising sensible and sensitive men, responding at once to flattery and possessing an immense power of self-deception.

Our first sight of Bathsheba is a charming picture: a beautiful girl in a crimson jacket, sitting in a gaily painted farm wagon, surrounded by her household goods and window plants. She is looking at herself in a mirror and smiling at what she sees there. Since this is a Hardy novel, we guess at once that her doom is rooted in her vanity; Gabriel Oak, who is watching unseen, sees it as symbolic of basic feminine nature: "Woman's prescriptive infirmity had stalked into the sunlight." He falls in love with her nevertheless, but when she retorts lightly to his proposal of marriage: "I want somebody to tame me, and you would never be able to," we know that she will have plenty to tame her before long. In spite of having sound intelligence and a good heart, she refuses to marry either of the stanch and loyal farmers, but falls an easy victim to the swaggering and heartless Troy. Her awakening is justly bitter, but she becomes a much more sympathetic character in her humiliation and disillusion. The great central scene in which she opens Fanny's coffin and discovers the dead child with Fanny's body, and which ends with Troy's return and her realization of his utter indifference to herself, is very effective both dramatically and pictorially, in spite of its outmoded and stilted dialogue.

The rest of her story, though, is anticlimax. She does not grow in self-knowledge. Her willingness to accept a loveless marriage with Boldwood as punishment for her original sending of the valentine is as immature as the original action, and her snobbish sense of social superiority to Oak lasts far too long. The weakness of the conclusion is that, like that of *The Mill on the Floss*, it is an imposed one. Nothing in Bathsheba's own development brings it to pass. By a series of improbable crises the difficulties to an obviously suitable marriage are removed and the way left open for a sound if sober future.

Plot and characterization in the novel, then, are unsatisfactory. The action is too complicated, the characters too simple. The emotions often seem forced, the events often unconvincing. But these are only elements in a much larger design, and this design is the theme of the book and creates its real quality.

To call this design Hardy's "setting" or "background" is to falsify it. That suggests something detachable from the human drama, whereas the two are inseparable and together fuse into a whole. "Wessex" is not a geographical entity; it is a special element, an enveloping ether, in

which the world of the book has its being. Much has been
written on Hardy's observation and his wonderful sensitivity to sound and sight. It is wonderful. He knows every
fine shade of vibration made by wind through grasses:
"One rubbing the blades heavily, another raking them
piercingly, another brushing them like a soft broom." He
notices how waterdrops on plants have "the effect of minute lenses of high magnifying power," how the fern
sprouts are like bishops' croziers, or the withered grass en-
cased in icicles takes on "the twisted and curved shapes of
old Venetian glass." He has the true countryman's knowledge of how toads and slugs and sheep all follow different
instincts at the coming of rain, and how the ash and the
beech hold fog longer than other trees.

Of central importance, however, are what he himself
speaks of as "the deeper realities underlying the scenic,"
the realities in which nature and man play out interrelated dramas. In one sphere of being, that of sexual passion, we watch the movements of men and women as
undirected, violent, leading to ruinous disintegration. In
the other, that ruled by the courses of the stars and the
cycles of the seasons, the great ordered rhythms of the
universe pursue their everlasting continuity. Yet in spite
of these apparently independent and hostile movements,
man is an inseparable part of nature, and all that is
most enduring in him recognizes that fact, consciously
and unconsciously. To Hardy, slavery to sexual impulse,
or to trivial egotism, is to betray man's bond with the
eternal wisdom of the earth and all that is deepest in his
own nature; it is to try to stand alone, to divert his course
from the deeper creative rhythms which alone can bring
peace and fulfillment. Troy's bastard birth is a symbol of
the loss of a vital continuity; Boldwood's madness a symbol of the disruption that results from the divorce of the
human spirit from its ties with natural law. Bathsheba's
involvement with both these men springs from what is
trivial and egocentric in her nature, and it is punished
by the temporary loss of all harmony between her external

life and its roots in the farm inherited from her fore-bears.

Over against these emblems of disorder and disruption of natural law is Gabriel Oak, symbol of man's true place in his universe, of the control of passion by self-discipline, and of all that which to Hardy gives man dignity and worth. In the first chapter Oak seems a typical, though obviously very intelligent, countryman, but in the second chapter much more is established. Hardy describes the sweep of earth and sky, the wind, the trees, the stars, and the sensation to the observer of "riding along" as a part of the majestic cosmic motion. From this wide magnificence the notes of Gabriel's flute brings us back to the particular, and we move from the swing of the stars to the shepherd's hut and his flock, and to him at work on "his great purpose." He brings in a newborn lamb, placing "the little speck of life" on a wisp of hay before the small stove. From there we move again to the stars, as Oak experiences a moment when all earthly fellowship slips away in contemplation of the immense loneliness and beauty of the night scene. From that we go with him to the scene of another birth, that of a calf, at which Bathsheba and her aunt have been assisting. So that by the end of the chapter Hardy's vision has been affirmed. Man and woman, earth and sky, and the creatures of earth, are all brought into unity. We see man and woman, by their activities and the arts of their civilization, aiding nature in creative continuity.

This sense of creative collaboration between man and nature is the theme of the book, with its central symbols of the farm and Gabriel Oak as the ideal farmer. He is present in all the scenes dealing with the ordinary daily life, or with the extraordinary emergencies or tragedies of country doings. We see him at the lambing, the sheep dipping, the sheep shearing, the haying, the harvest; all the productive natural processes of farm life. And we see him too where nature proves her power to defeat man and to render useless all his service in her cause. The incident of the loss of Gabriel's flock of two hundred sheep and their unborn lambs illustrates this. A young untrained sheep dog, with no vice in him at all, stampedes the ewes in the night, and Gabriel awakes to the tinkle of their sheep bells as they hurl themselves down the hill and into a chalk pit. Not only are the sheep killed, but Gabriel's hopeful future as an independent farmer goes with them. He goes through "an ordeal of wretchedness," but emerges with "that indifference to fate, which, though it often makes a villain of a man, is the basis of his sublimity when it does not."

In the next incident he is triumphant in saving the fire from spreading beyond the blazing straw rick, and twice again his knowledge, skill and enterprise prevent disasters springing from the savageries of nature: when he lances the poor bloated sheep who have got into the clover field and "blasted" themselves, and again when he spends the night thatching the ricks to protect them from the oncoming storm. In opposition to these scenes where the science and dexterity of man's hands are used to conserve and protect his natural heritage, Hardy puts the scene of the dazzling exhibitionism of Troy's swordplay, a dexterity which serves no purpose but to gratify his own vanity.

As Oak's actions control the destructive forces in nature herself, so he controls his own rebellious emotions. He accepts that his love for Bathsheba must be put aside: "I must get used to such as that; other men have and so shall I." Bathsheba herself, in the agony of her own personal jealousy, recognizes the source of his inner strength: he "looked upon the horizon of circumstances without any special regard to his own standpoint in the midst. That was how she would wish to be."

The duration and dignity of the pastoral tradition is suggested by the frequent references to Greek legend and even more by the pervasive Biblical atmosphere in the names of the characters and in the cadences of the prose. Bathsheba loses her temper with Gabriel when he has rebuked her.

"Don't let me see your face any more."

"Very well, Miss Everdene—so it shall be."

And he took his shears and went away from her in placid dignity, as Moses left the presence of Pharaoh.

In the English tradition, Hardy sees the old shearing-barn as more truly a symbol of "functional continuity" than either church or castle.

The fact that four centuries had neither proved it to be founded on a mistake, inspired any hatred of its purpose, nor given rise to any reaction that had battered it down, invested this simple grey effort of old minds with a repose, if not a grandeur.... For once, medievalism and modernism had a common standpoint.

All the good fellowship and warmth of the sheep-shearing feast grows out of its traditional roots, as does the atmosphere created by the "rustics" in the old malt house. These supply as it were a "chorus," whose artistic purpose is as varied as the Greek chorus, with some additions of Hardy's own. Though each figure is lightly individualized, together they represent the common humanity which is changeless. They keep the old customs of their forefathers and their talk is full of reminiscence of the past. While strictly limited in outlook and faculties, their comments show the particular events of the plot through the eyes and experience of the general human level. Hardy speaks of their "sad but unperturbed cadence" and that is their "tone" toward the tragic happenings. When Gabriel upbraids Joseph Poorgrass for leaving the wagon with Fanny's coffin out in the rain while he goes into the tavern for a drink with his friends, Jan Coggan and Mark Clark point out to him the stark truth of the matter.

Nobody can hurt a dead woman.... All that could be done for her is done—she's beyond us.... If she'd been alive, I would have been the first to help her.... But she's dead, and no speed of ours will bring her to

life. . . . Drink, shepherd, and be friends, for tomorrow
we may be like her.

They are tolerant and good-tempered to all, and like
Shakespeare's clowns, provide "comic relief" in anecdote
and argument. The only person who disturbs the simple
harmony of their work and pleasures is the outsider,
Troy. His idea of giving them a good time is to stupefy
them with brandy, so that when the damage to the ricks is
threatened, they are all too drunk to help Gabriel to avert
it.

Though mostly extraneous to the main plot, Hardy uses
them to further the central episode and to emphasize the
tragic irony of the course of events. The fact that Joseph
goes to the Buck's Head tavern and drinks beer with his
friends, delays the arrival of Fanny's coffin, so that it is
too late for burial that afternoon. As a result, the coffin is
put in Bathsheba's house for the night, and she discovers
that Fanny died in childbirth and that Troy was faithless.
This, of course, gives an ironic overtone to Coggan's
speech about the delay doing no harm to the dead, and
how he would always help the living, since ultimately it is
the living who are injured.

The book is very uneven in interest. Hardy has no artistic conscience about contrivances and coincidences. The
whole scene at the fair, where Troy from outside a tent
manages to extract a note, telling of his return, from
Bathsheba's hand, as she sits inside, is preposterous. So is
the heavy irony of the rain from the gargoyle spout wash-
ing out the flowers which Troy has planted on Fanny's
grave. At the same time the *picture* of Troy in the darkness working by the light of a lantern hung from a yew
tree, his heart filled with his own dark remorse, is very
vivid. Hardy excels in descriptions of light and darkness:
the glimpse of Troy, at the half-opened door, with a candle,
thrusting the newspaper with the notice of his marriage to
Bathsheba at Boldwood, who reads it in the flickering
light; the waves of fog in the trees as Joseph drives the

wagon with Fanny's body through the lonely woods; or the Rembrandtesque scene in the old malt house.

> The room inside was lighted only by the ruddy glow from the kiln mouth, which shone over the floor with the streaming horizontality of the setting sun, and threw upwards the shadows of all facial irregularities in those assembled round.

The same unevenness of accomplishment marks Hardy's use of language. No one can write worse. He can be heavy and pretentious, using involved sentence structures and clumsy words, so that he sounds as lumbering and jolting and creaky as one of his own farm wagons. But against that is the ease and saltiness of the rustic dialect and much simple and moving speech, like that in which Bathsheba gives orders for the fetching of Fanny's body from the workhouse. Joseph says there is no time to get a hearse, and she replies:

> "A pretty waggon is better than an ugly hearse, after all. Joseph, have the new spring waggon with the blue body and red wheels, and wash it very clean. . . . Carry with you some evergreens and flowers to put upon her coffin—indeed, gather a great many, and completely bury her in them. Get some boughs of laurustinus, and variegated box, and yew, and boy's-love; ay, and some bunches of chrysanthemum. And let old Pleasant draw her, because she knew him so well."

Virginia Woolf has perhaps given the best summing up of the Wessex novels in her essay on Hardy in *The Second Common Reader*.

> As we consider the great structure it seems irrelevant to fasten on little points. . . . Inevitably they are full of imperfections. . . . But undoubtedly, when we have submitted ourselves fully to them . . . we have been freed from the cramp and pettiness imposed by life. Our imaginations have been stretched and heightened; our

humor has been made to laugh out; we have drunk deep of the beauty of earth. . . . It is no mere transcript of life at a certain time and place that Hardy has given us. It is a vision of the world and of man's lot, as they revealed themselves to a powerful imagination, a profound and poetic genius, a gentle and humane soul.

JOSEPH CONRAD
1857–1924

Lord Jim

Conrad brought a new vision into English fiction, and if, as many people think, the sense of human isolation and the search for individual identity is the most characteristic feature of the serious twentieth-century novel, the fact that *Lord Jim* was published in 1900 makes it a symbol of the new trend. All the novels we have discussed, though they were created by very different personalities, are concerned with man and woman in society. The central characters are deeply imbedded in traditional social and moral systems, and these codes govern their lives, which are lived among like-thinking people. The tragic heroes and heroines face emotional isolation; it is thrust upon them. They transcend it by the renunciation of self within the society of which they form a living part. The problem of Jim is quite different. He has broken the code and is an exile physically from his own people. Marlow, the skeptical, sympathetic man of the world, who tells so many of Conrad's stories, reports it with all his own doubts and hopes, suspending judgment throughout. The single figure of Jim, however, is the ethical and emotional center of everything; all the other characters and events exist simply to reveal some facet of his complex situation.

Conrad's own life reveals many reasons why the theme of human isolation should be almost obsessive in his writing. His father, a Polish poet and dramatist as well as a landowner, was a victim of the rebellion against Russia in 1863, when Conrad was five years old. His mother went with his father into exile in Russia and died two years later. His father returned, broken in health, in 1868 and died within a year. When Conrad was seventeen, against the wishes of all his relations, he went to sea. His wish had always been to get to England—translations of the adventure stories of Frederick Marryat had kindled his dreams of seafaring—but when finally he arrived there at the age of twenty-two, he could not speak a word of the language and it was years before he achieved British nationality. For seventeen years, however, he sailed in English merchant ships. A journey up the Congo River —the trip described in *Heart of Darkness*—ruined his health and in 1894 he had to give up his career. For the next twenty years he lived in great poverty, struggling to make his name as a writer, but with very little success: *Lord Jim* sold less than two thousand copies on first publication. It was not until he wrote *Chance,* in 1914, that he won any popular recognition.

His reputation then was that of a writer of sea stories, full of exotic local color and composed in richly ornate prose style. Conrad himself never ceased to chafe under this, and his letters show his impatience with the failure of the critics, and even of his close friends, to see what his books were really about. He says everybody seems to think "that I sit here and brood over sea-stuff," and when a friend is going to write something about him, he pleads: "Do try and keep the damn sea out of it. My interests are terrestrial after all." He goes on to point out that only about a tenth of his fiction is about the sea, and that even when it is, his material is the psychological problems of human beings who happen to be in ships. He felt he lacked an understanding audience, and again, in spite of his English wife and his home in the English countryside, he seems to have remained an alien. He wrote English prose brilliantly, but spoke with so strong an accent as to be difficult to understand. (He had to refuse an offer to lecture in America for that reason.)

So it is not surprising that his vision of man shapes itself so often into the drama of some exile, some man without a country, some outcast, some lonely sea captain, someone in the grip of solitary struggle, someone trapped in an unalterable past, which must be surmounted if the soul is to survive. Conrad would not agree with Hardy that the honest portrayal of life "must be largely concerned with the relation of the sexes." He might rather quote Dr. Johnson: "Love is only one of many passions, and it has no great influence upon the sum of life." He wrote many love stories, but they are not his best. In *Lord Jim,* two thirds of the book is over before love enters, and even then it is a very minor interest. Our interest is centered in one human personality and his fate. As in Hardy, mere chance seems to play a part of active evil in that fate. Marlow, thinking of the submerged derelict which probably caused the disaster to the *Patna,* comments:

> The incident was rare enough to resemble a special arrangement of a malevolent providence, which, unless it had for its object the killing of a donkeyman and the bringing of worse than death upon Jim, appeared an utterly aimless piece of devilry.

The same might be said of the arrival of the villainous Gentleman Brown when Jim seems to have "mastered his fate" in Patusan. Not, however, the malignant irony of external events, but the moral and emotional quality of man's response to them, is Conrad's theme.

Baldly, Jim's fate is the result of an act of physical cowardice. In the earlier chapters, before Marlow comes on the scene, we are told what has led up to this psychic catastrophe. Jim has always been a daydreamer. His choice of the merchant marine as a career (like Conrad's own) is the result of "a course of light holiday reading" in adventure stories. Even during his training, when a small emergency arises, he flinches from a very minor risk. It passes unnoticed and Jim himself learns nothing from it and continues to feed his romantic ego with heroic fantasies. Very young he becomes mate of a ship,

but "without ever having been tested by those events of
the sea that show in the light of day the inner worth of
a man, the edge of his temper and the fibre of his stuff."
Not only does he not know himself, but he is no judge of
others. When he has to leave his own English ship because
of a slight accident, and finds himself stranded in an
Oriental port, he is attracted to those who have chosen the
easy way. "In all they said—in their actions, in their
looks, in their persons—could be detected the soft spot,
the place of decay." But Jim does not detect it. While con-
temptuous of them as seamen, he is fascinated by "their
appearance of doing so well on such a small allowance
of danger and toil." He takes the job of mate on the *Patna*,
carrying eight hundred pilgrims on the way to Mecca.
The ship hits a submerged hulk in the night and the
officers are convinced it will sink very quickly. They de-
cide to leave the sleeping passengers to their fate and save
themselves. At the last moment Jim too jumps into the
boat. But the *Patna* does not sink. She is rescued by a
French gunboat and towed into port. By the time the officers have been picked up by a passing ship and taken
back to land the facts are known and Jim's career as an
honorable seaman is finished. He is forever disgraced,
cast out, "under a cloud."

By a piece of good fortune that Hardy would never have
permitted, Marlow attends the trial, and we see the rest
of the story through his eyes. Marlow too is a sea captain.
His training and tradition make him want to believe in
"the sovereign power enthroned in a fixed standard of
conduct"; but at the same time he is sensitive, intelligent
and questioning, and he recognizes Jim as "one of us."
This phrase echoes through the book and takes on different meanings according to its context. At its lowest it
means a member of the white race among the colored
races of the East, but it also denotes the men of honor
and sensibility in contrast to the baseness of the *Patna*'s
other officers and of Cornelius and Gentleman Brown.
In its widest meaning it includes the whole human race;

all guilty, all with secret knowledge of tarnished ideals and acts of moral if not physical cowardice. Marlow recognizes Jim as "one of us" in all these contexts, in spite of the irreparable act which has set him apart. He differs from the rest of us only in that he has been "found out."

> The commonest sort of fortitude prevents us from becoming criminals in a legal sense; it is from weakness unknown ... from weakness that may lie hidden, watched or unwatched, prayed against or manfully scorned, repressed or maybe ignored more than half a lifetime, not one of us is safe.

The imaginative apprehension of this pervasive lurking danger is what binds Marlow to Jim. It makes him "one of us" in spite of his failure in the test, and it throws a doubt on the validity of all absolute codes of conduct. Jim has come to Marlow "like a man panting under a burden in a mist. ... I cannot say that I had ever seen him distinctly ... but it seemed to me that the less I understood the more I was bound to him in the name of that doubt which is the inseparable part of our knowledge. I did not know so much more about myself."

The whole narrative is colored by similar remarks. Marlow is "fated never to see him clearly"; the gleams he gets are "glimpses through rents in the mist."

> It is when we try to grapple with another man's intimate need that we perceive how incomprehensible, wavering and misty are the beings that share with us the sight of the stars and the warmth of the sun.

As Marlow leaves Jim for the last time, in Patusan, and sails away himself until he loses sight of him as a tiny white speck on the beach, still "he seemed to stand at the heart of a vast enigma."

Marlow himself speaks of Jim as a symbol. "I don't know why he should always have appeared to me symbolic. Perhaps that is the real cause of my interest in his fate." Jim is universal: he has no family name, and wher-

ever Marlow travels—all over the Orient, or in Australia,
or England—the problem pursues him.

I could not bring myself to admit the finality. The
thing was always with me, I was always eager to take
opinion on it, as though it had not been practically
settled: individual opinion—international opinion ...

Marlow sees Jim first in the courtroom. He alone among
the ship's officers has not bolted to escape trial. Brierly,
one of the assessors at the investigation, has been willing
to put up money to get him away; not only to save him
"from eating all that dirt," but for the reputation of the
white community. Jim stubbornly refuses to go. "I may
have jumped, but I don't run away." All he can do now
to dissociate himself from "them" is willingly to stand
and take his punishment in public. We see him in the
dock, tall, fair, blue-eyed, clean-limbed, answering the
questions:

... while his utterance was deliberate, his mind posi-
tively flew round and round the serried circle of facts
that had surged up all about him to cut him off from the
rest of his kind: it was like a creature that, finding itself imprisoned within an enclosure of high stakes,
dashes round and round, distracted in the night, trying
to find a weak spot, a crevice, a place to scale, some
opening through which it may squeeze itself and escape.

The court gives its verdict: "certificates cancelled."
Society has announced its practical penalty for the offense. For Jim, however, the spiritual issue remains: how
to make peace with himself in his dire humiliation? For
the first time the problem of his selfhood confronts him
in all its dismaying confusion. All Marlow can do to
help at this point is to listen: "I don't want to excuse myself, but I would like to explain." Jim's "explanation" is
a pathetic mixture of determination to accept responsibility for his action and at the same time to preserve some
shreds of self-respect and self-justification. His confidence

in himself before the accident had been so complete that his disgrace is proportionately shattering, and he is unable to see his act clearly. He is busy "rationalizing" the whole thing, trying to find some opening through which a ray of self-esteem can squeeze itself. Marlow challenges nothing; he doesn't even know if Jim believes himself; for "no man ever understands quite his own artful dodges to escape from the grim shadow of self-knowledge."

So we hear that Jim wasn't "ready"; "one must have time to turn round." He had been "taken unawares"— though he has already testified that it was "twenty-seven minutes by the clock" between the accident and his jump into the boat. He assures Marlow what a competent officer he had always been: "I always believed in being pre- pared for the worst." He insists that it was not *self*- betrayal; he had no chance with the others behaving as they did: "It was their doing as plainly as if they had reached up with a boathook and pulled me over."

Marlow watches him reliving the whole thing, even losing himself for a moment in a romantic vision of him- self if he *had* stuck to his post: "with his nostrils for an instant dilated, sniffing the intoxicating breath of that wasted opportunity." Marlow does not know whether to be glad or sorry that Jim can't accept any finality about his fate: "Some day one's bound to come upon some sort of chance to get it all back again." He goes off, with a letter from Marlow, still talking about starting again with a clean slate. Left alone, Marlow comments:

A clean slate, did he say? As if the initial word of each our destiny were not graven in imperishable char- acters upon the face of a rock.

So it proves with Jim, and it is not Marlow but his friend Stein, the old German merchant, who sees a pos- sible escape for him. To Marlow's story of Jim's later failures to find any security and stability, he says, "I understand very well. He is romantic." He goes on to analyze the difficulties of such a nature.

> A man that is born falls into a dream like a man who falls into the sea. If he tries to climb out into the air ... he drowns ... No! I tell you! The way is to the destructive element submit yourself, and with the exertions of your hands and feet in the water make the deep, deep sea keep you up. So if you ask me—how to be? ... In the destructive element immerse.

What is Stein saying in this rather cryptic passage? He sees that since Jim is a born romantic, his true existence is in a dream world. That has betrayed him, or he has betrayed it; it has proved to be the destructive element. Yet in spite of this, it is his true life element. Therefore, in order to *be,* he must turn the dream, the illusion, into fact. He must live it in *action.* Jim's life is useless to him because he can't fulfill his real nature, can't live his dream. He has tried to climb out into the air, but he can't sustain himself there. The hope is that the destructive element can be made creative. Stein suggests, therefore, that Jim go to Patusan, a white man alone among squabbling native factions, face its dangers and gamble on making his dream come true.

He succeeds. Two years later Marlow visits him there, hears of his many fighting adventures, of his final peacemaking, and his building of a model community. His original act of cowardice had been the betrayal of a trust toward the human community of the pilgrims. Now it is the human community which is the core of his new life. Marlow asks him if he would like to leave, and Jim bursts out:

> Look at those houses; there's not one where I'm not trusted. . . . Leave! No, on my word, I must feel—every day, every time I open my eyes—that I am trusted—that nobody has a right—don't you know? Leave! What for? To get what?

In the trust of the people he feels safe; " 'I shall be faithful,' he said quietly. 'I shall be faithful.' " To Marlow he seems to have "survived the assault of the dark powers" and to have won peace.

The dark powers, however, have not finished with Jim, and the pattern of tragic irony works itself out to its full circle with "a sort of profound and terrifying logic," as Marlow later comments. The psychological critics make much of the inner meaning of the advent of Gentleman Brown, declaring: "He is no chance intruder: he is as inherent in the situation within Jim as Banquo's ghost," because "the evil is within himself." But surely this goes outside the text, and Conrad makes no suggestion of such a reading? The irony of fate plunges him into an insoluble conflict of loyalties. It would have been a simple matter to have exterminated Brown and his boatload of roughs after they have killed one of Jim's people. It is not any guilty conscience in Jim which prevents it. It is the remembrance of how his own guilt was resolved as the result of being given a second chance. Brown is of course quite astute enough to know what blackmailing approach will be most fruitful:

> He asked Jim whether *he* had nothing fishy in his life to remember, that he was so damned hard on a man trying to get out of a deadly hole.

We think at once of Jim's despairing description of his own act: "It was as if I had jumped . . . into an everlasting deep hole." Brown goes on to emphasize his sense of loyalty to his men: "By God, I am not the sort to jump out of trouble and leave them in the damn lurch!"

So Jim trusts Brown, who cynically betrays the trust, and Jim gives his own life in atonement. Is his death defeat or victory; failure or triumph; courage or abdication of his responsibilities; supreme sacrifice or theatrical flourish? Is he tragic hero or romantic fool? Again critics differ widely in their interpretation. David Daiches says: "He betrays his people . . . and then makes amends to *himself* by going to his certain and useless death in a gesture of purely romantic histrionics." This is to regard his end as senseless suicide. Others read the pattern as that of sin, punishment and expiation. But do not both these views oversimplify? Conrad himself has no easy answers to tragic dilemmas. He made a misleading but often-quoted declaration that to him, the temporal world rests on a few very simple ideas: "It rests, notably . . . on the idea of Fidelity." But the immediate response to that is: Fidelity to what?, which is perhaps answered by a passage in one of his letters:

> Everyone must walk in the light of his own heart's gospel. No man's light is good to any of his fellows. That's my creed from beginning to end. . . . Another man's truth is only a dismal lie to me.

Hence the paradoxes and ambiguities of Jim's fate. Marlow ends his narrative with "Who knows?" Yet in spite of all the ruin that fate has brought, Marlow sees the pattern of "profound and terrifying logic," and the fact that "of all mankind Jim had no dealings but with himself." In the past he had missed his great opportunity to translate dream into actuality, and Marlow wonders about his death "whether this was perhaps that supreme opportunity . . . for which I had always suspected him to be waiting." He reminds us that those who saw it said that Jim looked around "with a proud and unflinching glance," and in that picture Marlow sees him, "ready to surrender himself faithfully to the claim of his own world of shades."

Just as Conrad's vision of life, his grave, lonely and ironic perception of the human condition, reveals a new atmosphere in fiction, so do his experiments in technique. Revolutionary writers are always forced into new technical experiments, because what they have to say will not fit into the old molds: a new way of seeing life demands a new way of writing about it. "Life does not narrate," says Conrad, "it makes impressions on our brains." Hence he had to find a new way of telling his story. If we except Sterne, all novelists before Conrad narrate in direct chronological sequence. The author may pretend he is writing an autobiography, or he may be outside his material and present it with differing degrees of objectivity; but wherever he takes his stand, the plot development, the growth of the characters and the over-all theme emerge in a linear pattern of cause-and-effect progress.

Conrad changed all that. *Lord Jim* is one of Marlow's memories, and though Conrad never read any Freud, nor of course any Proust, he was well aware that association and not chronology is the basic principle of the memory process. The opening chapters of straight narrative are technically clumsy, in spite of some wonderful writing, because there is really no way by which Conrad, who is supposed to know the story only through Marlow, could be familiar with the inner and outer aspects of Jim's earlier life. But from the entrance of Marlow in Chapter 4, the sequence becomes that of the associations and digressions in Marlow's mind. They play all over time and place, picking up new illuminating perspectives at every turn.

All chronological sequence is abandoned. In the middle of Jim's story of the *Patna* episode, first we go back to Marlow's account of the ways in which the other officers escaped the inquiry, and then forward to the mysterious suicide of Brierly shortly after he sat in judgment on Jim. From that we jump forward several years to the occasion on which Marlow heard the first-hand account of the rescue of the *Patna*, from the French naval lieutenant in Sydney, Australia. When we get back to Jim, it is only to be interrupted by the memory of Chester and his guano island. From that we return to Jim at the nadir of his fortunes, "on the brink of a vast obscurity," the evening after the verdict of the court has been given. Marlow's recollection of the letter he wrote at that moment carries him several years ahead to various episodes, ending in the visit to Stein, and on from that to the conclusion of his spoken narrative, his last meeting with Jim at the height of his triumph in Patusan. In the final part, described in Marlow's letter and journal, a portion of Jim's fate is disclosed by a visit to Stein's house, and the rest eight months later, through the dying lips of Brown; while the whole is being read, in very different circumstances, by the nameless "privileged man" (Conrad himself) who is Marlow's confidant.

The fact that Jim's story comes to us involved with so many times and places is only one aspect of a larger element in it: that it comes involved with so many other people and points of view. Jim is the central character, his "case"—the question of the response of the individual to the events he must meet—is the central theme. It is all reported through Marlow. Marlow's experience and his compassionate, speculative intelligence provide throughout the central standard of judgment which controls all the material and gives it its special flavor. But through Marlow's "impressions" we see the facts filtered through the minds of a great number of other eyes and personalities. Jim's character is not complex; on the contrary it is simple, but Conrad knows that the fulfillment of any individual destiny is conditioned not only by the qualities and needs in itself, and its conscious or unconscious compulsions, but by the qualities and needs possessed by all the people who surround it. The whole range of reaction to Jim comes into focus, from the moral dregs of humanity, like the officers of the *Patna,* Chester, Cornelius and Brown, up through the materialistic neutrality of the businessmen who employ him as water clerk, to the unimaginative French lieutenant and finally to the penetrating idealism of Stein.

To the entirely base, Jim's situation is simply something to be exploited for their own ends. Chester, after the verdict, declares to Marlow, "he is no earthly good for anything," so he may as well be sacrificed to the guano gamble. Brown cares nothing about what has brought Jim to Patusan, but he is greedy to get his hands on the money he is sure Jim is making there, and is quite sure his devotion to his colored people is sheer humbug. To the traders the moral question of Jim's past is irrelevant: he has proved an able and honest employee and that is all that concerns them. The wheezy old French lieutenant simply can't imagine what life could be once personal honor is lost. His description of his own dangerous part in the rescue of the *Patna* discourages Marlow, though as a test the circumstances were totally unlike, and the lieutenant had all the support of a disciplined naval crew. In contrast to his bovine conventionality, Stein, whose own life has been full of individual risk and courage, accepts the facts of Jim's failure with full understanding and sympathy.

Finally, when fate has again trapped Jim, we see his final stand viewed through the eyes of his new associates, who judge his loyalty to his own code as harshly as the world has judged his disloyalty to it. They all see him as faithless. To Jewel, he has broken his word: he had promised he would never leave her. To his personal servant he is a coward: why doesn't he at least put up a fight? To his former friend, Doramin, he is the man who has betrayed them to white men, who have murdered Doramin's son.

Through all these personalities we see Jim and his conduct from many points of view, and in essence, see the human condition in the same way. What each of these people sees is to him the reality of the matter. The facts are added to, or distorted, or ignored as they are refracted through different eyes. No wonder that Marlow declares that reality and illusion cannot be separated: "there is so little difference and the difference means so little." No wonder too that Marlow feels fated "never to see him clearly," and that we leave him "at the heart of a vast enigma."

That mistiness, with its confusing outlines, through whose rents the "moments of vision" form themselves into

clear-cut external events, is sustained as a symbol throughout. Conrad is again a forerunner of the twentieth-century
novelists in his careful creation of symbolic significance.
In certain passages he elaborates his imagery so as to
give a new dimension to descriptive writing. The external
details are vivid in themselves but they do not remain
merely scenic. Each has a symbolic value which deepens
and enriches the emotional and moral elements involved
in the picture. One of the finest pieces of such writing
is at the opening of the third chapter, the description of
the *Patna* immediately before the accident. Conrad's
method here merges three elements: the perfect serenity
of the night and the apparent safety of the ship; the inner
moral significance of that in terms of the apparent ease of
keeping a straight course as long as all is calm and peaceful; Jim's personal sense of his own security, and his habit
of escape into daydream fulfillment.

The whole thing can be left at the level of description,
but a study of the language reveals that Conrad is playing "the game of art" in every detail. The universe, the
ship, and Jim all *seem* part of a changeless placid pattern: a pattern of simple lines, curves and circles; of simple effects of light and dark on a flat surface: the rays of
the stars, the curve of the moon, the sea extending "its
perfect level to the perfect circle of a dark horizon"; and
this "circular stillness of water and sky with the black
speck of the moving hull remaining everlastingly in its
centre." Conrad then suggests that this apparent static
peace is not really all-inclusive. The black smoke from the
funnel, the discordant grinding of the wheel chains, the
fragmentary light from the binnacle are all disharmonies;
and the intermittent glimpses of the black fingers of the
steersman, "alternately letting go and catching hold of the
revolving spokes" remind us of the wheel of fortune. But
Jim is unmindful of anything but the apparent "invincible" aspect of peace. He glances "idly" at the ship's
chart "portraying the depths of the sea," but to him it is

only "a shiny surface," as level and smooth as the waters, and the course can be easily calculated by compass, rulers, dividers and a pencil, drawing a straight black line on the white paper to the ship's destination. Jim loses himself in romantic dreams of imaginary achievements, which, with deadly irony, he regards as "the best parts of life, its secret truth, its hidden reality."

Again in the crucial scene in Stein's house, the sequence of the discussion of Jim's situation in its psychological terms is dramatically intensified by the symbolic use of the light and the darkness in which it takes place. The circle of lamplight is Jim's "case," which they seek to illumine. Marlow remains in that, but Stein moves between it and the shadows in which his butterfly cases are stored. This darkness seems to represent both the presence of all the dim unconscious forces which Stein recognizes in human personality, and also his own memories, from which he draws wisdom and insight. It gives him assurance, but when he returns to the light, "the austere exaltation of a certitude seen in the dusk vanished from his face." He, like Marlow, cannot be sure that his solution is the right one, and the rest of the scene is played out among the "fleeting gleams" of the candles as Stein leads Marlow through empty dark rooms on their way to bed. The waves of doubt and certainty surrounding the two men, about Jim, about themselves, about life itself, are all given depth by the flickering alternations of the scenic details.

Yet another different use of the imagery of light and dark is at the opening of Chapter 36, where Conrad himself, the "privileged man" who was the only one to hear the last word of Jim's story, comes into his room and finds Marlow's last letter and journal. He is the writer, the artist, who is going to use this material. He goes to his window, high above the dark city, and looks out, as though from the lantern of a lighthouse. Below is all the multiplicity and confusion of raw experience: the roofs and ridges like endless waves; the unceasing mutter of voices and sounds; the church spires, "like beacons on a maze of shoals without a channel"; the obscuring dusk and driving rain; the striking of the clock, "with a shrill vibrating cry at the core." He draws the curtain, shutting out all that turmoil of time-ridden experience. He becomes, as it were, disembodied; his footfalls make no sound on the carpet, his own firsthand physical and emotional life is over. He is alone with his memories in the "sheltered pool" of the artificial lamplight—the light of imaginative vision. He directs the rays of the lamp upon Marlow's message, this one particular instance before him, runs over it swiftly, and then "like one approaching with slow feet and alert eyes the glimpse of an undiscovered country," sets out to examine this new imaginative territory.

It is easy to find fault with certain aspects of Conrad's writing. F. R. Leavis says that he is sometimes too intent "on making a virtue out of not knowing what he means," and that he insists too often that "the vague and unrealizable are profoundly and immensely significant." Yet this impossibility of comprehension is exactly what Conrad is trying to convey. He does perhaps overwork words like *inscrutable, unspeakable, inconceivable,* and in places his prose is overdecorated and overcadenced in his enjoyment of "purple patches." Yet when these things are said, he remains a great and original artist, whose work lives up magnificently to what he himself put forward as his aim. In his Preface to *The Nigger of the Narcissus* Conrad describes his conception of what the novelist's art should be. It should evoke both the sense of isolation of the human soul and its sense of solidarity with its fellows; it should appeal primarily to the spontaneous, intuitive emotions rather than to the intellectual side of man's nature; and its moral truths should be implicit in the actions, the characters, the scenes, without the direct intrusion of interpretation by the author.

My answer to those who demand specifically to be
edified, consoled . . . or frightened or charmed, must
run thus:—My task is, by the power of the written
word, to make you hear, to make you feel—it is before
all to make you *see*. That—and no more. . . . If I succeed, you shall find there, according to your deserts:
encouragement, consolation, fear, charm—all you demand, and perhaps also that glimpse of truth for which
you have forgotten to ask.

INDIVIDUAL WORLDS

EMILY BRONTË
1818–1848

Wuthering Heights

The value of a novel rests ultimately on the quality of the personality behind it, or more exactly, on the skill with which that personality can use form and language to communicate his vision and knowledge. Ways of looking at life are as varied as novelists themselves, but we can easily distinguish certain large types of literary personality which recur in every age. First, there are the possessors of that large comprehensive human understanding which gives us a panoramic view of a whole society, who create the worlds of *Tom Jones* and *Vanity Fair* and *The Mill on the Floss;* then the psychologists, who explore inward, into Clarissa or Lord Jim; then those, like Sterne or James or Virginia Woolf, who are passionately interested in what James calls "the refinements and ecstasies of method." But certain writers have a genius which is so personal and peculiar to themselves that they create worlds in their books which seem to exist as separate entities. Each has a unique atmosphere which encloses it and into which we become absorbed. The social environment as we know it, or recognize it, sinks out of sight, and the characters live and breathe in a literary climate whose laws are its own. This world need only be consistent with itself to impel us to imaginative belief.

The strangest and most powerful of these individual worlds is that of *Wuthering Heights*. Emily Brontë herself remains a shadowy, enigmatic figure, who lived a life of almost complete seclusion in a Yorkshire parsonage, wrote a few poems of mystical ecstasy or impassioned romantic loneliness, and died at the age of twenty-nine, a year after the publication of her novel. Of what went to the making of the story we know next to nothing. We know that she and her sisters, as children, invented imaginary kingdoms of romance, and kept chronicles of these realms of fantasy even when they were adults; we know that they read "mad Methodist magazines," full of dreams and frenzied fanaticism; we know that they had a brother who drank himself to death. But that is about all. The critics of the first edition, while recognizing the vigor of the book, found it "revolting" and "unquestionably and irredeemably monstrous." Her sister Charlotte, who loved Emily deeply, but quite failed to understand her, wrote an introduction to the second edition, in which she tried to interpret Emily's temperament and the quality of her genius. "Stronger than a man, simpler than a child, her nature stood alone. . . . Her will was not very flexible; her spirit altogether unbending"; and she notes "a certain harshness in her powerful and peculiar character." Charlotte recognizes the "strange and sombre power" of the book, but feels that she must apologize for its immaturity and immorality. She points out that the creative mind "strangely wills and works for itself," producing creatures like Heathcliff, Earnshaw or Catherine, but that Emily, "having formed these beings did not know what she had done," and that only time and experience could have taught her better.

Modern criticism has, of course, swept away Charlotte's attitude of apology and moral disapproval, and has rated Emily's genius far above that of her sister. But her book remains mysterious, just as she herself does, in spite of all the attempts to elucidate both. Her own reserve stands impenetrable; her own voice interprets nothing. The story comes to us through two narrators—a commonplace young city spark and a country housekeeper. They report faithfully what they have seen and heard, and interpret it by their own standards, though these are clearly often inadequate; any further implications of vision and meaning beyond their insights the reader must create for himself.

Hence the widely differing expositions of the thematic pattern of the book behind its melodramatic plot. It is impossible to be unaware of the immense energy and pressure of emotional forces at work in the writing, but how do these shape themselves into "meaning"? Virginia Woolf found no answer:

> She looked out upon a world cleft into gigantic disorder and felt within her the power to write it in a book. That gigantic ambition is to be felt throughout the novel—a struggle, half thwarted but of superb conviction, to say something through the mouths of her characters which is not merely "I love" or "I hate" but "we, the whole human race" and "you, the eternal powers" ... the sentence remains unfinished.

Arnold Kettle, at the other extreme, quoting Virginia Woolf, declares: "I do not think it remains unfinished," and sees Heathcliff as the spirit of human revolt against injustice, and the book as "an expression in the imaginative terms of art of the stresses and tensions and conflicts, personal and spiritual, of nineteenth-century capitalist society." Mark Schorer asserts that, as he understands it, Emily Brontë set out to write a work of edification. "She begins by wishing to instruct the dandy Lockwood in the nature of a grand passion." The final significance, however, is the insistence on "the impermanence of self and the permanence of something larger." David Cecil calls it a "metaphysical" novel, where the great characters exist "in virtue of their attitude to the universe and to the huge landscape of the cosmic scheme." He sees the pattern as "the expression of certain living spiritual principles—on the one hand the principle of storm—of the harsh, the ruthless, the wild, the dynamic; on the other the principle of calm—of the gentle, the merciful, the passive and the tame." He sees those two principles combining to form a cosmic harmony, and "it is the destruction and re-establishment of the harmony which is the theme of the story."

That the uplands and lowlands of the moors are ever-present in Emily Brontë's imaginative vision is evident. The very title implies it, with Lockwood's heavy explanation in the first chapter that "wuthering" is a "provincial adjective, descriptive of the atmospheric tumult to which its station is exposed in stormy weather." We are told at the outset of the gaunt and stunted trees "all stretching their limbs one way" as a result of the force of the north wind. That picture becomes metaphor when Heathcliff has got the child Hareton Earnshaw into his power and gloats: "Now, my bonny lad, you are *mine!* And we'll see if one tree won't grow as crooked as another with the same wind to twist it." Wuthering Heights, in fact, is a symbol of the "atmospheric tumult" which is the dominant force in the world of the book; a wild, destructive force twisting the lives of everyone exposed to it. It does not triumph ultimately in the temporal world. Heathcliff's plans for ruining Hareton prove illusory and the future for him and the young Cathy is to be at Thrushcross Grange in the quiet valley. We may question though whether this conclusion establishes the harmony described by David Cecil, or whether it does not point rather to separate planes of existence which remain disparate and irreconcilable in the world of men.

For it is not really true to say that the chief characters exist in virtue of their attitude to the universe and the huge cosmic landscape. It would hardly be possible to create a novel in those terms. True, we are never far from the natural world. Although Emily, unlike Charlotte in *Jane Eyre,* gives no long descriptive accounts of the moors, yet they are fused into the life and language of the characters on every page; their winds, skies and streams,

their rock-ribbed surface and rolling stretches of heather
and bluebells, their sunlight and moonlight, their stillness
and storms, their many birds, their "suffocating snow,"
and summer days with "the whole world awake and wild
with joy." Yet though one dimension of the book is cosmic
in sweep, which gives it what Virginia Woolf calls its
"huge stature" among novels, at the same time, like all
other novels, it deals directly with human relationships,
which differ intrinsically from natural forces in that they
are inevitably bound up with emotional and moral problems and conflicts and choices. The novel moves indeed
on three levels, all interfused; the realistic, the emotional
and moral, and the world of pure spirit. We shift from one
to another within a few lines. We can start with Nelly
in the farm kitchen, singing the baby Hareton to sleep
with a folk song, go on to Catherine confiding to her
her intention to marry Edgar Linton because he is young
and rich and handsome, and then listen to her crying out
her indissoluble bond to Heathcliff:

> If all else perished, and *he* remained, *I* should still
> continue to be; and all else remained, and he were
> annihilated, the universe would turn to a mighty
> stranger: I should not seem a part of it.... Nelly, I
> *am* Heathcliff!

With a formal audacity which predates that of Conrad
by fifty years, Emily Brontë starts her story only a few
months before its ending, though it is to span three generations of the families concerned. In its first three chapters, however, all its elements are revealed to us and we
are at once enveloped in the savage, stormy and mysterious atmosphere of the whole.

Lockwood, a young nonentity from London, has rented
Thrushcross Grange as a retreat in which to recover from
a mild disappointment in love, and imagines himself both
cynic and misanthrope. He goes to call on his landlord
at Wuthering Heights. The forbidding house and surroundings match the grim, black-browed figure of Heath-

cliff himself, and the rest of the household are a young girl, his daughter-in-law, whose beauty is marred by ungracious rudeness and an expression "between scorn and desperation," an uncouth boorish youth, a fanatically self-righteous old farm hand, a woman servant and a bevy of snarling dogs. A "dismal spiritual atmosphere" of hatred and tension hangs over them all. A snowstorm blows up and Lockwood is refused hospitality for the night. Snatching up a lantern to light his way, he tries to set out alone, but is set upon and mauled by two of the dogs. The men laugh at his plight, but the maid rescues him and puts him to sleep in a small room with an old-fashioned enclosed bed built against the window. On the sill are some mildewed books and the names *Catherine Earnshaw, Catherine Heathcliff, Catherine Linton* scratched all over the paint. On blank pages among the books are scraps of a diary in a childish hand dated some twenty-five years before. They tell of the cruelty of "Hindley and his wife" to Heathcliff, of the tyranny of old Joseph, who preaches to them of hell-fire for hours together, of a plan between herself and Heathcliff to escape and "have a scamper on the moors." Falling asleep as he pores over a book of Calvinistic sermons, Lockwood dreams first of listening to one of the sermons concerning the seventy times seven sins which must be pardoned, with an unspecified "seventy-first" which is unforgivable. The meeting breaks up in a shower of blows, as the congregation attack both Lockwood and one another, and "every man's hand was against his neighbour." Waking, the blows are translated into the tapping of a branch on the windowpane. Dozing off again, Lockwood has another dream, which is much more disturbing. In it, he recognizes the tapping branch at the window, and breaking a pane of glass to get at it, he finds himself holding "a little, ice-cold hand," while a voice sobs, "Let me in—let me in," and a child's face seems to look through the window. In terror, Lockwood dreams that he pulls the wrist to and fro on the broken pane "till the blood ran down and soaked the bedclothes."

He wakes, yelling, from this nightmare, and Heathcliff, rushing in, is both furious and agonized by his story. As Lockwood leaves the room, he sees his host wrenching open the lattice, bursting into tears and crying, "Come in! come in!... Cathy, do come.... Oh! my heart's darling; hear me *this* time," while the snow whirls wildly through the window and blows out the candle.

On returning next morning to the Grange, Lockwood falls ill, and during his convalescence Nelly Dean, the housekeeper, tells him the full story leading up to his experience at the Heights. But already the reader is aware of dark, malignant forces into which the self-complacent young Lockwood has been as it were hurled from the tame, commonplace existence he has left. The very fact that this civilized social being can have a dream in which he turns savage enough to rub a child's wrist on broken glass suggests the alien world of horror lurking in Wuthering Heights. The house is not only set in bare, bleak and harsh surroundings and has the atmosphere of a prison, it is full of physical violence and moral ugliness. With the exception of Zillah, its inhabitants, human and animal, are either savage or sullen, living without grace or gaiety, or even common courtesy, "where every man's hand is against his neighbour." The cold, deserted closet, with its moldering books and childish diary, tell of equal cruelty, hatred and imprisonment a generation earlier; while the final chilling nightmare, the sobbing little ghost and Heathcliffs' outburst create the presence of some thwarted passion in the past and a present anguished human need.

Nelly Dean has been in the service of the Earnshaws and the Lintons since her own youth, so she is in a position to report the story in its realistic, intimate development. It starts with the arrival of Heathcliff at Wuthering Heights, "a dirty, ragged, black-haired child," whom Mr. Earnshaw had found homeless in the streets of Liverpool and had brought back to the farm from an impulse of pity. At once his presence sows dissension among the

Earnshaw children. Heathcliff and Cathy become fast
friends, but his father's favoritism of Heathcliff—of
which Heathcliff takes full advantage—makes Hindley
furiously jealous. His father's early death gives Hindley
power to pursue his revengeful malice, and he reduces
Heathcliff to the position of farm drudge. Chance in-
troduces Cathy to the children at Thrushcross Grange,
Edgar and Isabella Linton, and Edgar's good looks and
good manners undermine Cathy's loyalty to Heathcliff.
He overhears her telling Nelly that it would degrade her
now to marry him, and without listening further he runs
away and is not heard of for several years. He returns,
educated and obviously well-to-do, six months after
Cathy's marriage to Edgar. Cathy insists that she can keep
Heathcliff as friend, but after stormy scenes among the
three of them, she falls ill. Meanwhile, to revenge himself
on Hindley, now reduced to poverty by drink and gam-
·bling, Heathcliff gets him completely into his power
financially, so that Wuthering Heights will become his
on Hindley's death. To revenge himself on Edgar, Heathcliff, in spite of his passion for Cathy, takes advantage
of Isabella's infatuation for him to elope with her and
get her money. Two months later they return, Heathcliff
forces his way into the Grange to see Cathy, and after a
scene of frenzied passion, leaves her insensible. That
night she dies in giving birth to a daughter. Heathcliff
then dedicates his life to the ruination, both material
and spiritual, of the two houses. He lives at Wuthering
Heights, bringing Hindley to complete degradation and
pauperization, while he brings up Hareton, Hindley's moth-
erless child, as a brutal young savage. At the same time
the young Cathy grows quietly and happily to girlhood at
the Grange, knowing nothing of the family history. Heathcliffs' next fiendish plan is to marry his feeble, ailing
son, Linton, who lived with his mother, Isabella, until
her death, to Cathy, and so secure *her* property and en-
sure *her* misery. This too he accomplishes. Linton dies

shortly afterward, leaving the situation into which Lockwood has stumbled. Nine months later he returns unexpectedly, finds Nelly at the Heights, and hears from her of Heathcliff's strange death and sees the happy issue of the whole tragic tale.

Lockwood's point of view in the early chapters is that of would-be sophisticate from the outer world. He serves the purpose of contrast. His callow experience of life and love and shallow cynicism are set against the intensity of Heathcliff's savagery and suffering. But Nelly Dean's point of view is very different. She has been a participant in the whole course of events, the confidante of all the chief characters, and she speaks as both narrator and chorus. Emily Brontë is careful to tell us what sort of person Nelly is. Lockwood comments on her insights and thinks her wisdom comes from living in the country rather than among the superficial standards of cities. Nelly laughs and says people are alike everywhere, but she adds:

> I certainly esteem myself a steady, reasonable kind of body . . . not exactly from living among the hills and seeing one set of faces, and one series of actions, from year's end to year's end; but I have undergone sharp discipline, which has taught me wisdom; and then, I have read more than you would fancy, Mr. Lockwood. You could not open a book in this library that I have not looked into, and got something out of also.

It is true that Nelly's integrity fails at many of the practical crises of the story, and that she is in a sense responsible for its tragic development. She does not tell Cathy that Heathcliff has overheard her saying that it would degrade her to marry him, and that he then left without listening to the rest of her confession; it is she who carries Heathcliff's letters to Cathy when he returns to Wuthering Heights, and who lets him in secretly, during Edgar's absence, for the final meeting before her death. Later she fails to report to Edgar that young Cathy has been corresponding with Linton; she suppresses the truth about Linton's true state of health, and actually lies about her own responsibility in Cathy's abduction. But we may put all that down to necessary plot machinery rather than to any intention to suggest a criticism of Nelly's character. Rather she is created to embody the standards of good feeling and good sense which remain steady in the midst of the raw, uncontrolled actions and passions with which she is surrounded. We know that in spite of her reading and experience she does not understand these, and we often rebel at her oversimplified moralizing, but her stability and self-assurance create a framework of familiar emotional patterns without which we could hardly accept the story she tells.

For certainly we cannot agree with her opinion that "here we are the same as anywhere else, when you get to know us." At Wuthering Heights horrible realistic cruelties match the emotional tortures inflicted on one another by both children and adults. When they are children, Hindley knocks Heathcliff down with a heavy iron weight and kicks him under a pony's hoofs. Of Heathcliff himself we learn later from Cathy of how he set a trap over a lapwing's nest so that the parent birds could not get to it, and how they found it in winter full of little skeletons; he boasts of his wish to fling old Joseph off the highest gable of the Heights and paint the house front with Hindley's blood; he dashes a tureen of scalding applesauce full in Edgar Linton's face. When Hindley himself is a father, Nelly has to hide Hareton in a closet to keep him safe from drunken savagery. Later Isabella sees Hareton as a child "hanging a litter of puppies from a chairback." We see Heathcliff slitting up the flesh of Hindley's arm, kicking and trampling on his fallen enemy and dashing his head repeatedly against the flagstones; later he snatches up a dinner knife and flings it at his wife's head. He treats his dying son with complete brutality and when he has tricked young Cathy into the house, hits her over the head and threatens to kick her if she disobeys him. Looking at the two of them he confides to Nelly: "Had I been born when laws are less strict, and tastes less dainty, I should treat myself to a slow vivisection of those two as an evening's amusement."

In the writing, men are often likened to animals— wolves, mad dogs, reptiles—but the brutalities in *Wuthering Heights* are not only physical, like those of beasts; all the common standards of kindness and justice are outraged. Nelly owns that young Hindley's treatment of Heathcliff "was enough to make a fiend of a saint"; Cathy forces Isabella to listen while she tells Heathcliff gibingly of the poor girl's infatuation for him; she insults her loving, gentle husband in Heathcliff's presence, calling his control cowardice, and then tries to win his sympathy by staging a fit of hysterics, "dashing her head against the arm of the sofa and grinding her teeth, so that you might fancy she would crash them to splinters." Edgar himself abandons his sister to her fate and refuses her any help.

But all these mental cruelties sink into insignificance beside those of Heathcliff. Up to the time of his disappearance he has the reader's pity, for though Hindley's childish jealousy is understandable, his revenge is disproportionate, and Cathy's disloyalty, though also understandable, is nevertheless shocking. But after his return, Heathcliff's determination to ruin Hindley, body and soul, and his black hatred of the Lintons becomes devilish. It is not, after all, they who have wronged him, but Cathy who has betrayed his love. His behavior to Isabella is revolting in its sadism; he shows himself, as she truly says, "a lying fiend, a monster, not a human being." He is pure hate personified as he mutters: "I have no pity! I have no pity! The more the worms writhe, the more I yearn to crush out their entrails." After Cathy's death, when the second generation of Earnshaws, Lintons and Heathcliffs grow into adolescence, it is still revenge that dominates him. His only interest in his son, that "whey-faced whining wretch," is that he can be used as an instrument for his father to get control of the Linton estates, as he has already got control of the Earnshaws.

> I want the triumph of seeing my descendants fairly lord of their estates, my child hiring their children to till their father's land for wages. That is the sole consideration which can make me endure the whelp.

He cannot really break young Cathy's spirit, even with his final torture of destroying all her books, but he does confess at the end that to her he'd made himself "worse than the devil." For the rest, when Nelly urges him to repent, he can still say: "I've done no injustice and I repent of nothing." All that happens to change the situation is that his compulsive drive for vengeance on his dead enemies exhausts itself: "I have lost the faculty of enjoying their destruction, and I am too idle to destroy for nothing." As for the property he had planned so madly to get, he can say: "I wish I could annihilate it from the face of the earth." In place of the demonic thirst for revenge, the memory of the dead Cathy usurps his entire consciousness, and the "one universal idea" of a final union with her spirit.

This abdication by Heathcliff of his destructive fury leaves the way open for the swift growth of the love—already latent—between Hareton and the young Cathy, and for a final resolution in the emotional and moral pattern of traditional humanism. As long as hate breeds hate, Heathcliff triumphs. Those who return hate for hate he can crush: Hindley, who screams in his frenzy, "Oh, if God would but give me strength to strangle him in my last agony, I'd go to hell with joy"; or Isabella, who will not be satisfied unless she can return "a wrench of agony" for each that Heathcliff inflicts on her. Edgar Linton is too passive to put up any effective resistance and Heathcliff's own son, conceived in hate, wastes away to early death. Heathcliff can boast of his destruction of Hareton:

I've got him faster than his scoundrel of a father se-
cured me, and lower, for he takes a pride in his brutish-
ness. . . . I've taught him to scorn everything extra-
animal as silly and weak. . . . He had first-rate qualities
and they are lost, rendered worse than unavailing. . . .
And the best of it is that Hareton is damnably fond
of me! You'll own that I've out-matched Hindley there!

But that is just where Heathcliff himself is outmatched.
He cannot corrupt Hareton and render his qualities unavailing, simply because Hareton returns love for hate.
Moreover, by forcing young Cathy into his power, Heathcliff frustrates his own plans. At first, after Linton's
death, she shows her mother's snobbish pride and thinks
it would degrade her to consort with the oafish Hareton.
But she has her father's sweetness of nature too, which
finally asserts itself. She learns humility from her sufferings. Hareton, says Nelly, has "an honest, warm and
intelligent nature"; he has only to learn the external graces
of life from Cathy. All these qualities will heal the wounds
of the past, and lead to a calm, fruitful domestic future
at the Grange.

Yet this harmony on the simple moral and emotional
level excludes all the "huge stature" of the novel, and its
ultimate intensity and mystery. At the end Wuthering
Heights remains abandoned, bereft of either creative or
destructive powers—"For the use of such ghosts as choose
to inhabit it," suggests Lockwood, but Nelly rebukes him:
"No, Mr. Lockwood . . . I believe the dead are at peace."
Lockwood believes so too, as he looks at the graves on the
moor under the "benign sky," but the country folk think
differently, and even Nelly doesn't like to go out on the
moor at night or be alone in that house.

Indeed the figures of Cathy and Heathcliff haunt the
book as they are said to haunt the moors. They radiate a
blazing vitality which dims everybody else. The problem
of the bond between them and its significance remains
the central mystery, just as its creation into language is

the central triumph. As children they seem to represent
the spirit of freedom rebelling against tyrannical authority (Hindley) and religious bigotry (Joseph). Cathy has
a dream that when she was in heaven she wept because
it didn't seem her home, and the angels were so angry
that they flung her out onto the heath near Wuthering
Heights, where she woke sobbing for joy. She and Heathcliff are creatures of the wild moorland existence beside
which conventional social standards are meaningless.
Cathy owns that she has no more right to marry Linton
than she has to be in heaven, but declares too that marriage could not separate her from Heathcliff. The rhythm
of the prose rises in intensity as she tries to define that
world of being that unites them:

> . . . he's more myself than I am. Whatever our souls are
> made of, his and mine are the same: and Linton's is as
> different as a moonbeam from lightning, or frost from
> fire. . . . He's always, always in my mind . . . So don't
> talk of our separation again: it is impracticable.

To Nelly, such talk suggests that she is ignorant of what
marriage is or is "a wicked, unprincipled girl."

Yet when Heathcliff has left and she marries Linton,
for six months "the gunpowder lay as harmless as sand,"
and Nelly is sure that she and Edgar "were really in possession of deep and growing happiness." On Heathcliff's
reappearance she rushes to her husband, flings her arms
around his neck and bursts out: "Oh, Edgar, darling!
Heathcliff's come back!" In spite of Edgar's dismay, they
sit looking at one another "too much absorbed in their
mutual joy to suffer embarrassment." Yet this is no romantic, erotic infatuation. Cathy describes Heathcliff to
Isabella as "an unreclaimed creature . . . an arid wilderness of furze and whinstone . . . a fierce, pitiless, wolfish
man." Heathcliff himself makes no excuses for Cathy's
treachery to her own nature and to him:

I want you to be aware that I *know* that you have treated me infernally—infernally! . . . And if you flatter yourself I don't perceive it, you are a fool.

To Nelly, Cathy appears as a spoiled, selfish, little termagant in her response to the situation: "I had little faith in her principles, and still less sympathy for her feelings." Yet again from the quality of the language, the reader senses that behind all this is the awakening of that wild force, now imprisoned, that united her and Heathcliff in their childhood. As Cathy tears her pillow with her teeth and scatters the feathers, she is a child again, reliving their days on the moors; as she struggles to open the window so she can feel the wind on her face, she knows herself "exiled and outcast" in her present life, and cries despairingly:

Why am I so changed? Why does my blood rush into a hell of tumult at a few words? I'm sure I should be myself were I once among the heather on those hills.

Heathcliff's comments to Nelly on her sickness have the same echoes of his knowledge of her exile from a dimension of living unknown to Edgar—of her "frightful isolation" at the Grange and its killing insufficiency: ". . . as well plant an oak in a flower-pot and expect it to thrive."

It is her betrayal of her true self that they both recognize in their final frenzied meeting. However much Cathy may pretend that it is Heathcliff who is breaking her heart and killing her, she is forced to accept the justice of his agonized mixture of anger and despair.

You loved me—then what *right* had you to leave me . . . for the poor fancy you felt for Linton? Because misery and degradation, and death, and nothing that God or Satan could inflict would have parted us, *you,* of your own will, did it.

In his paroxysm of wild passion at the news of her death he prays that she may not rest as long as he lives:

> Be with me always—take any form—drive me mad!
> Only *do* not leave me in this abyss, where I cannot
> find you! . . . I *cannot* live without my life! I *cannot*
> live without my soul.

Heathcliff is doomed in his turn to the torture of exile
and imprisonment in an alien world until his own release.
We hear nothing more, however, of his true life and soul,
but only of his hideous plots and ferocities against others,
until eighteen years later. Then, after Edgar Linton's
death, he describes to Nelly how he had persuaded the
sexton who was digging the grave to remove the earth
from Cathy's coffin and open it. Nelly exclaims against
the wickedness of disturbing the dead, but Heathcliff
speaks in quiet passionate rhythms of his own response.

> Disturbed her? No! she has disturbed me, night and
> day, through eighteen years—incessantly—remorse-
> lessly—till yesternight; and yesternight I was tranquil.
> I dreamt I was sleeping the last sleep by that sleeper,
> with my heart stopped and my cheek frozen against
> hers.

He goes on to tell, with moving simplicity, of the racking
torture of Cathy's elusive figure, never seen, but never
absent, during all this time.

> When I sat in the house with Hareton, it seemed that
> on going out, I should meet her; when I walked on the
> moors I should meet her coming in. When I went from
> home, I hastened to return: she *must* be somewhere at
> the Heights, I was certain! And when I slept in her
> chamber—I was beaten out of that. I couldn't lie there;
> for the moment I closed my eyes, she was either outside
> the window, or sliding back the panels, or entering the
> room, or even resting her darling head on the same
> pillow as she did when a child. And I must open my lids
> to see. And so I opened and closed them a hundred
> times a night—to be always disappointed.

No moral harmony calms the conclusion of Heathcliff's story. In its social aspect he himself can describe it wryly as "an absurd termination of my violent exertions." He has spent his whole energies on wrecking the lives and fortunes of the Earnshaws and the Lintons, only to find that the love between Hareton and young Cathy is to prove stronger than all his hate. He will not accept that his enemies have defeated him. To him, his rage has simply spent itself; he is indifferent to everything in the present, living only in the past and the future. He sees Hareton as the personification of his own youth, "of my wild endeavour to hold my right, my degradation, my pride, my happiness and my anguish." For the rest, his whole being and faculties are obsessed with the longing for the final union in death with his beloved. Nelly's pious talk of repentance and preparation for a Christian heaven reminds him only to insist on being buried with no coffin wall between himself and the dead Cathy. His heaven is as she has said hers will be, "that glorious world" of escape from the prison of an aching heart. He looks "wild and glad" as he nears it, and finally his dead eyes have a "lifelike gaze of exultation," though the rest of the "savage, sarcastic face" seems to sneer at the moral judgments of the world it has left behind.

What is this untamable passion, thwarted in the lives of Cathy and Heathcliff and consummated only in death? It is not harmonized with anything else in the book. It is different in *kind* from both the loves and the hatred in the rest of the story, which can and do work themselves out to a creative equilibrium in the family union of the Earnshaws and the Lintons at the Grange. Heathcliff has no part in that. His blood dies with him: he has no issue. Yet in spite of his brutal cruelties and vindictiveness we are left believing in some potential in him which has been betrayed by Cathy's rejection of it, and perverted from any temporal fulfillment. We are given no hint of what creative adult fulfillment it could have had in those tempestuous natures. We see only the "gigantic disorder" of this shattered and fettered life force, yet its presence creates the timeless qualities in the book, in spite of its carefully planned time scheme and its strong local flavor. The fragments of that thwarted passion, struggling to frame their unfinished sentence, "We, the whole human race and you, the eternal powers . . ." hold the undying force and fascination of *Wuthering Heights*.

CHARLES DICKENS
1812–1870

Great Expectations

The contemporary readers of Dickens, and indeed all readers until about twenty years ago, accepted him uncritically as a spontaneous genius of prodigious vitality who created an original world of fiction in which all ages and classes found delight. It was a world of melodrama and sentiment, of humanitarian zeal, of exhilarating humor, of cozy domesticity, of inns and coaches and good cheer. Dickens conformed scrupulously to the proprieties and conventions of his public; nothing in his novels could bring a blush to the cheek of Mr. Podsnap's young person and his novels all end happily; but that he himself rebelled inwardly from the limitations imposed by his society can be proved from his own comments. In an editorial written in 1864 (two years after the publication of *Great Expectations*), for his weekly journal *All the Year Round,* he challenges the prevailing code:

> Why is all art to be restricted to the uniform level of domesticity? Whenever humanity wrestles with the gods of passion or pain, there, of necessity, is that departure from our diurnal platitudes which the cant of existing criticism denounces. . . . The mystery of evil is as interesting to us now as it was in the time of Shakespeare, and it is downright affectation and effeminacy to say that we are never to glance into that abyss.

Since Edmund Wilson published his essay on "The Two Scrooges" in *The Wound and the Bow* in 1941, modern criticism has become more and more aware of how much of Dickens' imagination inhabited that abyss, and how steadily his novels darkened and deepened in atmosphere toward the end of his life. It is difficult to say how conscious Dickens himself was of what contemporary critics have found in the later novels. We read now with a knowledge of Freud and Jung, of the displacements and distortions of unconscious processes; our insights have been sensitized by interpretations of Kafka, Joyce, Faulkner or D. H. Lawrence. We respond emotionally, therefore, to much in the vision of Dickens which his older readers regarded as melodrama or caricature, and find inner symbolic significance when Dickens himself may have *consciously* felt none.

But that the "mystery of evil" and "the gods of passion and pain" are very much alive in the strange world of *Great Expectations* is plain. Dickens was to complete one more novel, *Our Mutual Friend,* but *Great Expectations* is, as George Bernard Shaw called it, his "most compactly perfect book," and the one in which the themes he felt most deeply are most fully realized.

Dickens was a man of little formal education, like his own David Copperfield, or Pip in *Great Expectations.* He had no training in philosophy, science, ancient or modern history, or art. He was not a man of ideas, he was simply a born literary artist: that is to say he took an endless delight in observing the world around him and identified himself spontaneously with all the joys and sorrows of common humanity. His own vitality was inextinguishable. It would seem that the writing of some twenty novels of the length and variety of his would be enough for one man, but his fiction was only one part of his activity. He loved the theatre, and wrote plays, acted in them and directed them constantly. In addition, he owned and edited a weekly magazine, lived an immensely busy social life, did a great deal of public speaking for good causes, lived in the midst of a family of ten children, and could nevertheless write: "I am at a great loss for means of blowing my superfluous steam off . . . and that is always my misfortune." Nor was he simply a natural storyteller who dashed off his novels without preparation and planning. He speaks himself of those "conceited idiots who suppose that volumes can be tossed off like pancakes, and that any writing can be done without the utmost application, the greatest patience and the steadiest energy of which the writer is capable." His strong theatrical bent, however, gifted him with the power to identify himself with his audience, like an actor—and indeed he finally became one, in his immensely successful dramatic readings from his own novels. The books are full of scenes where action and character combine in vivid visual outline. He creates an external world full of exuberant extravagance and absurdity, of the grotesque and the fantastic; crowded with concrete figures and faces, malignant or benevolent or ridiculous, all bearing the stamp of his own imaginative coinage.

The question whether this is matched by an inner world of any emotional intensity is not so easy to answer. Dickens was a man of action, not of contemplation, and he is often accused of a poverty in the revelation of human insights. This is true, I think, of his creation of personal relationships. They are apt to be crude and oversimplified. The pressures under which character changes, the tensions and conflicts between mature adults, the subtleties of loving or loveless interchange are lacking in his novels. His emotional strength lies elsewhere; in the presentation of certain general themes which persist all through his work. In the earlier novels these appear as highly charged subject matter which remains at an external level and is not explored, but in the later novels the serious content penetrates much more deeply and is fused into the atmosphere and texture of the created whole, haunting each book with its own particularly pervasive presence of evil and pain, and giving even much of the comedy an ironic and savage twist.

What are these themes? Prisons and criminals, cruel and unjust institutions, helpless and unhappy children, greed for money and power—these are constantly recur-

ring motifs in Dickens' plots. They all appear in *Great
Expectations,* and are woven into an interlocking pattern
of great subtlety and intensity among the four central
figures.

Before the adult relationships develop, an eerie atmosphere of depression, alienation and isolation has established itself. Two backgrounds, equally dismal, surround
young Pip. The opening scenes paint, first, the tangled,
weed-grown graves of the churchyard, and beyond that
the dark, flat wilderness of the marshes, the empty sky,
the "low leaden line" of the river and the "savage lair"
of the sea in the distance. Then, at Satis House, in semi-
darkness, lives Miss Havisham, who halted her life on the
morning of her wedding day, twenty years earlier, when
her faithless lover deserted her. She is dressed still in her
faded bridal gown of yellowed white satin; the wedding
feast remains on the table, the cake draped in cobwebs,
while speckle-legged spiders with blotched bodies, grop-
ing black beetles and scavenging mice feed on the decay.
Outside, the rank, flowerless garden, "so cold, so lonely,
so dreary," lies deserted.

Both these backgrounds suggest emptiness and desola-
tion, and mingled with them is another suggestion which
permeates the whole book: human guilt and imprisonment. On the marshes is an old gibbet, hung with chains;
moored in the river are the hulks which hold the criminals. In the opening scene, Pip meets the terrifying and
terrified convict (Magwitch), who is to play so vital a
part in his expectations. The leg iron, got rid of for the
time by the file Pip steals from Joe's forge, proves the
instrument of an attempted murder, and Pip's feelings
later, when he is hoping for Magwitch's escape, might
apply to the whole atmosphere: "the dismal wind was
muttering round the house . . . the tide was flapping at
the shore, and I had the feeling that we were caged and
threatened." As a child, while Pip is still helpless and innocent of any wrongdoing, he is treated as if he were
guilty. His sister's attitude to him has always been that

toward "a young offender"; Pumblechook pushes him before the magistrate, when he is to be bound apprentice to Joe, "exactly as if I had that moment picked a pocket or fired a rick." Pip is to find that his "great expectations" are to prove nothing but a cage; as he says, "the taint of prison and crime" seem to pursue him. After his first meeting with Estella at Satis House, when he thinks he has escaped to a new life, he is at once reminded of the past by the unknown man in the bar, who stirs him rum and water with a file and gives him a shilling, wrapped in two pound notes. Pip thinks with horror of "the guiltily coarse and common thing it was, to be on secret terms of conspiracy with convicts." His first view of London is of the grim outline of Newgate prison, the group of criminal clients waiting to see the lawyer Mr. Jaggers, and in his office, the two fearful casts of murderers' faces leering down from the walls. As he goes later to meet Estella he tries to beat the dust of Newgate off his coat, but feels impregnated with its atmosphere. His final complete involvement is the discovery that he owes his "expectations" not to the rich and respectable Miss Havisham but to the convict Magwitch, in whose miserable fortunes both he and Estella are inescapably enmeshed.

Crime and imprisonment inevitably implicate the law. The law is the mechanism which society has developed and enforces to protect its own interests and embody justice. Allegedly it protects strong and weak alike, the "gentleman" and the commoner, the adult and the child. Dickens' books, however, are full of the bitterest satire on legal pretentions in particular, and in general on the vicious cruelties perpetrated by the powerful upon the helpless, especially upon children. When the convict appears first in the opening scene, he is "a man who had been soaked in water, and smothered in mud, and cut by flints, and stung by nettles, and torn by briars." Symbolically, this is what society has done to him to bring him to his present pass, and when we hear his story later, we see how from earliest childhood he was doomed to become a criminal by poverty, degradation and the indifference and inhumanity of authority. When Mr. Jaggers is explaining to Pip how he came to take the baby (Estella) from Magwitch's wife and give her to Miss Havisham for adoption, he outlines his attitude toward his own action:

> Put the case that he lived in an atmosphere of evil, and that all he saw of children was, their being generated in great numbers for certain destruction. Put the case that he often saw children solemnly tried at a criminal bar, where they were held up to be seen; put the case that he habitually knew of their being imprisoned, whipped, transported, neglected, cast out, qualified in all ways for the hangmen, and growing up to be hanged. . . . Put the case that here was one pretty little child out of the heap who could be saved . . .

Dickens' final comment on the ruthlessness of the law is the picture in the court as Magwitch is condemned to death. He is one of thirty-two men and women who have received death sentences during the session. They are herded together, surrounded by legal officials in their regalia, and by a great gallery of people, "a large theatrical audience," who have come to watch the show. The judge gives a pompous, moralistic speech to the condemned, singling out the already dying Magwitch as a "scourge to society." Dickens comments:

> The sun was striking in at the great windows of the court . . . and it made a broad shaft of light between the two-and-thirty and the Judge, linking both together, and perhaps reminding some among the audience, how both were passing on, with absolute equality, to the greater Judgment that knoweth all things and cannot err.

This is an attack on a public institution which abuses its authority, but Dickens is equally outraged by the inhumanity of man to man. The directly personal cruelties of power are best symbolized in Pip's sister, Mrs. Gargery, tall and bony, with a red skin which makes Pip wonder if she washed herself with a nutmeg grater instead of soap. But her most characteristic attribute is a coarse apron "having a square impregnable bib in front, that was stuck full of pins and needles." She never takes this off and it speaks vividly of her negation of all womanly love. The breasts on which the head of husband or children should rest are instead covered with this harsh and wounding armor.

Some of the most poignant scenes in the book are the opening ones, which describe the atmosphere in which Pip grows up. He is introduced as "a small bundle of shivers" alone in the graveyard, which is followed by the terrifying intrusion of the world of active violence and fear as the convict seizes him. Then we see the household at the forge, where he is made to feel guilty and ashamed of his very existence; the Christmas party at which he is baited and bullied by his elders; his treatment at the hands of the hypocritical Pumblechook; his introduction to Estella, who reveals to him that he is coarse and common. Dickens knows that in children "there is nothing so finely perceived and so finely felt, as injustice," and looking back on his childhood, Pip too knows that truth: "Within myself, I had sustained, from my babyhood, a perpetual conflict with injustice."

The bulk of the book, however, deals with adult suffering, and with the *states of mind* of imprisonment, isolation and lovelessness, of which the concrete illustrations of the marshes, the decayed house and garden, the prisons, the cruelties toward the weak and helpless, are the outward symbols. During his last years, after the separation from his wife, Dickens' own relations with the actress Ellen Ternan, who (most unwillingly, it seems) became his mistress, were unhappy and frustrating, and no doubt the presentation of Pip's compulsive infatuation for Estella had a basis in Dickens' own experience. But thwarted sexual love is only one of the negative elements in the emotional texture. The lives of the main characters are all deformed by the lack of love, or by the distortion of love into revenge and emotional greed. Just as Pip's first impression of "the identity of things" is interrupted by the convict, who tilts his little body upside down until he is sick and giddy, so all his relationships and moral values continue to be turned upside down repeatedly as he pursues his quest for his identity through the story. His "great expectations" of money and of love are all reversed into ironic paradox, as are the expectations of those with whom his fortunes are entangled.

Pip's "snob's progress" begins on the first day he goes to Satis House as a child and meets Estella. He accepts at once that her standards are correct and that he and his connections are coarse and common. The forge, which before had seemed "the glowing road to manhood and independence," seems only to dirty him with its dust and grime, and he is ashamed of Joe's ignorance and simplicity. When Mr. Jaggers informs him that he has great expectations and is to be removed from the forge and "brought up as a gentleman" in London, he never doubts for a moment that it is Miss Havisham who is his benefactor and that the seemingly aristocratic Estella is part of the design of his fortunes, that he has been "set apart for her and assigned to her." As he goes out alone on his last evening at home, "proposing to finish off the marshes at once," he remembers with shame his meeting with the convict, but comforts himself with the thought that it was all a long time ago and that the man was now dead to him and "might veritably be dead into the bargain." He daydreams of coming back later to entertain the villagers to "a dinner of roast beef and plum pudding, a pint of ale and a gallon of condescension."

Dickens' picture of the life of a "gentleman" in Pip's position is indeed a bitter satire on the possession of money without any sense of responsibility for its use. Dickens would be the last person to underrate the importance of money. He raised himself from being the neglected child of impoverished parents to being the possessor of a large fortune, and he loved the good things that his position brought him. He does not pretend that a return to Biddy and Joe and the forge would be any solution of Pip's problem. Through possession of the money Pip learns the manners of good society and a knowledge of the world, and picks up enough education through Mr. Pocket and his own diverse reading to be able finally to make a good living in a sphere of "modest usefulness." The money is, in fact, of great value to him. But his life in the years of his good fortune is purely parasitic, and it is perhaps not surprising that the story of these years is the dullest part of the book. We watch Pip in an existence of empty futility; spending his allowance, and more, on furnishings, clothes, cards, sport and empty show; and leading his good friend Herbert Pocket into expenditures he cannot afford, and therefore into debt. Even Pip's one "good action" of setting up Herbert in a business position is not carried through without Miss Havisham's help; and when his "expectations" fail, Joe has to step in and pay his creditors. In personality Pip becomes absorbed into the background of his associates, who have no real human fellowship, no intellectual or artistic interests, and no *purpose* whatever. He lives in a world of make-believe and self-deception, "restless, aspiring, discontented," tortured by the guilt of his repudiation of Joe, and most of all, by the compulsive centering of all his hopes on the winning of Estella. He insists on seeing his feelings as "high and great emotions," and blinded by his infatuation, cannot recognize how totally unworthy of such devotion Estella is.

Into this world of false values and delusive hopes breaks the harsh truth. The reader has been partially prepared for it by the constant interweaving in Pip's life of episodes involving convicts and criminals, the atmosphere of Mr. Jaggers' office and the glimpses of Newgate prison, with the opposite strands in his development—Joe and the forge, Miss Havisham and Satis House, and his "gentle-

man" existence in London. But Pip has consistently tried
to ignore everything except his own romantic preconceptions. The shock is therefore overwhelming when, with
the arrival of Magwitch, his illusions are shattered and
his world in ruins. With terrible irony, Magwitch seizes
Pip affectionately by both hands *five times* in their first
interview, as if to emphasize their close association and
linked destiny. He pours out his pathetic joy in working
and saving in Australia for Pip's welfare, and his pathetic
pride in the evidences that he, "the hunted dunghill dog,"
has been able to "make a gentleman." He has thus tri-
umphed over the colonists who despised him as "an ignorant common fellow."

> I says to myself "If I ain't a gentleman . . . I'm the
> owner of such. All on you owns stocks and land; which
> on you owns a brought-up London gentleman?"

Finally he recounts how he determined to return and
make himself known to Pip, and to claim his emotional
reward: "Look' ee here, Pip. I'm your second father. You're
my son—more to me nor any son." He takes it for granted
that Pip will respond in like measure. To add to the horror
and repugnance this produces in Pip, which "could not
have been exceeded if he had been some terrible beast,"
comes the knowledge that Magwitch's life will be forfeit
if his return is discovered.

> Nothing was needed but this; the wretched man, after
> loading me with his wretched gold and silver chains
> for years, had risked his life to come to me, and I held
> it there in my keeping.

Just as Magwitch's planning for Pip has mingled dis-
interested love with the desire to *use* another for a vicarious revenge upon society for his own victimization by it,
so has Miss Havisham used Estella. With much less excuse than Magwitch, and with much more bitterness and
injury to others, she has combined a ravenous possessiveness in herself with a training in cold callousness that

has petrified Estella's heart and has made it impossible for her to respond emotionally to others. She has brought her up in the candlelit darkness and decay of Satis House —symbol of her own ruin—and has destroyed her capacity to live in the daylight of natural affections. Miss Havisham in the past chose an ideal of love which crushed her own identity. "I'll tell you what real love is," she says to Pip: "It is blind devotion, unquestioning self-humiliation, utter submission . . . giving up your whole heart and soul to the smiter—as I did." When her lover betrayed her, she chose to shut out the light of day and to make that moment of shock and grief a cause for revenge upon all men. Estella is to be trained to be inhuman: "I stole her heart away and put ice in its place." Deliberately Miss Havisham encourages Pip in his infatuation that it may cause him pain. At the same time, however, she expects warmth and tenderness from Estella toward herself. When the girl proves that her heart is indeed ice throughout she cannot believe it:

"But to be proud and hard to *me!*" Miss Havisham quite shrieked, as she stretched out her arms. "Estella, Estella, to be proud and hard to *me!*"

Magwitch has no cause to reproach Pip with such ingratitude as *his* great expectations are toppled into ruin. Pip hides his "frenzy of fear and dislike" from the poor convict, and as Magwitch's story is unfolded it is clear how much more he is victim than victimizer. Pip finds his own true identity as unselfish loyalty and love gradually fill his heart. Finally he sees in Magwitch a much better man than he had been to Joe, and can promise him, as he faces his trial and death: "Please God, I will be as true to you as you have been to me." The handclasp between Magwitch and Pip on the convict's deathbed is the loving reality of faithful union which had seemed such a horrible mockery to Pip on his first arrival.

We feel that Magwitch has little need of redemption, and that Pip's prayer for him—"O Lord, be merciful to him, a sinner"—is superfluous. As Magwitch himself has said earlier: "What I done is worked out and paid for!" Indeed it is strange that Pip continues to regard the money as "tainted," since it has all been earned honestly by Magwitch's own labors in Australia. Though his great expectations for Pip have been intertwined with a wish for a vicarious revenge on the society that has destroyed him, he has never betrayed or distorted love, or injured others by defective love. These are the sins of which Pip and Miss Havisham and Estella are all guilty. All have been victims of the same sins at the hands of others, but their own reactions have been equally negative and un-flowering. They are allowed redemption through the loss of their self-deceptions, the acceptance of responsibility for their own sufferings and their forgiveness of one an-other. Miss Havisham recognizes the "master mania" which has shut out the sunlight not only from her own life but from that of Estella and Pip, and she can pray to Pip for his compassion. He can reply: "There have been sore mistakes . . . I want forgiveness and direction far too much to be bitter with you."

Finally, Estella and Pip can come together. Most critics deplore the happy ending, which Dickens did not origi-nally plan. But it is, surely, in tune with the resolutions of the other relationships. There is certainly no reason why, in eleven years, Estella should not have achieved self-knowledge and unselfish love, as the other characters have done. As she says herself: "I have been bent and broken but—I hope—into a better shape." Moreover, it is a satis-fying conclusion that, as Magwitch's daughter, she should find happiness with Pip. I myself find no difficulty in acquiescing and sharing in that "broad expanse of tranquil light" in which we leave them.

The conflicting themes, then, conclude in resolution: We leave all the main characters, dead or living, in peace and charity. Yet one minor figure remains totally evil: "Old Orlick." Orlick used to be accepted as an example of Dickens' melodramatic villains, used simply for the mechanism of the plot and having no organic significance. Recent criticism, however, makes a good deal of him as a kind of Dostoevskian "double" to Pip—the embodiment of the evil in Pip's own nature. We have seen the same kind of criticism making Gentleman Brown a "double" of Lord Jim. It is true that Orlick constantly intrudes on Pip's progress: he too works at the forge; he assaults Mrs. Joe, and Pip recognizes the weapon as the leg iron the convict has rid himself of with the stolen file; Pip's affection for Biddy is matched by Orlick's lust for her; he shadows Magwitch on his visit to Pip's rooms, and later betrays his presence in the country to Compeyson; he gets a position at Satis House. Finally he tricks Pip to the hut on the marshes and intends to kill him there and burn his body in the limekiln. In that scene he declares that Pip was responsible for his sister's death: ". . . it warn't Old Orlick as did it; it was you. You was favoured and he was bullied and beat. . . . You done it; now you pays for it." But while we can well believe that Pip as a child often wished Mrs. Joe dead, it is difficult to accept that we are meant to take it that this represents some real guilt in Pip's mind, and that we must judge him as containing the qualitites of Orlick within himself. *Great Expectations* is full of subtleties, and we are ready to believe that the subconscious processes of the creative artist produce effects he may not have consciously planned, but this particular kind of psychological subtlety seems quite foreign to Dickens.

Structurally Orlick appears to symbolize a purely destructive and unredeemable element in the whole "mystery of evil." No one knows his origin; and to Pip he "conveys an idea of something savagely damaging." When Pip is "very small and timid," Orlick terrifies him with a tale that the Devil lived in a black corner of the forge and that "it was necessary to make up the fire, once in seven years, with a live boy, and that I might consider myself fuel." Later he is jealous that Pip becomes an apprentice while he remains a hired hand; jealous also because he believes that Pip has come between himself and Biddy;

he bears a heavy grudge because Pip has had him dis-
charged from his job as porter of Satis House. It is an
element in the irony of circumstance that it is this action
of Pip which drives Orlick to London and into the pay of
Compeyson and thus causes Magwitch's capture. However, the truth about Orlick is, as Pip says: "I could have
done you no harm, if you had done yourself none." The
motivation of jealousy is surely enough to make it plausible that Orlick could declare, "You was always in Old
Orlick's way since ever you was a child," which accounts
sufficiently for his malignancy without any subtle psychological probings.

The comic villain of the piece is Mr. Pumblechook.
Pretentiousness and hypocrisy are particularly hateful to
Dickens, and they are the essence of Pumblechook. He bul-
lies and baits Pip unmercifully as a child, but takes all
credit for his good fortune (since he had originally introduced him to Miss Havisham), while toadying revoltingly
to him as soon as he hears of his new riches. The scene
where he repeatedly takes Pip by both hands, murmuring,
"May I—may I—?" is a parody of that later scene where
the real author of the good fortune, Magwitch, passionately seizes Pip's hands so frequently in their first interview. It is poetic justice that Orlick and his friends should
raid Mr. Pumblechook's store, steal his money, give him a
beating and stuff his mouth full of seeds from his stock
as a gag. But the victory is only temporary. Pumblechook,
like Mrs. Elton in *Emma,* is really invincible, and goes out
of the story the same "windy donkey," protesting his own
generosity and Pip's ingratitude.

The forces opposed to the total evil of Orlick, the crim-
inality of Compeyson, the injustices of society in general,
and the betrayals of love exemplified in Miss Havisham,
Estella and Pip himself, are the good will of Magwitch,
the simple loyalty of Joe and Biddy and the sophisticated
values of Mr. Jaggers and Wemmick. These last are the
only characters in the book who on their first appearance
have already solved their complex human problems in a

satisfactory way. In his office, or on legal business elsewhere, Mr. Jaggers is ferocious, inflexible and without a hint or chink of sentiment. "I'll have no feelings here," he roars savagely at a client who is about to "snivel." He has absolutely no illusions about the criminals who haunt his office, and washes his hands with scented soap, gargles his throat and takes out a penknife to "scrape the case out of his nails" before going home. He has "a manner expressive of knowing something secret about every one of us that would effectually do for each individual if he chose to disclose it." He is uncompromisingly blunt as he tells Pip of his "expectations": "If my advice had been taken, I should not have been here;" he is much too cynical and worldly-wise to see any good in Magwitch's romantic scheme. But his honesty is incorruptible and his legal judgment infallible, and his clients can trust him completely. In private, he has put "poor dreams" of love and domesticity behind him, but he has saved Magwitch's wife from a conviction for murder and "tamed" her into useful service as his housekeeper. In the office, his clerk Wemmick models his behavior on that of Jaggers, but the most heartwarming scenes in the book are those of Wemmick at home in his "private and personal capacity" at his miniature Castle in Walworth, with its battlements and drawbridge, cannon and flag, his numerous other mechanical gadgets, his fowls and rabbits and vegetables, his Aged Parent, and Miss Skiffins to tea on Sundays to provide romance.

These scenes are the only appearance in the book of the "eccentric" comedy figures created so lavishly and with such zest by the earlier Dickens. The Pocket family fail as comic creations, and in Mrs. Joe and Pumblechook the bitterness of the satire eclipses the comedy.

The novel is full of unforgettable dramatic scenes where the atmosphere and the action fuse into pictorial outline. It opens with a whole quick series of them in the first five chapters: the entrance of the convict in the graveyard; the robbery of the pantry; the Christmas party; the hunt for the fugitives from the hulks on the marshes. But in addition to the scenes of direct narrative excitement, again and again the action becomes symbolic and communicates much more than the mere external picture. Miss Havisham, pointing her finger at little Pip and saying "Play!" suggests both the whole theme of the attempt to manipulate persons as if they were puppets, and also the futile "play" at being a "gentleman" with nothing to do, which is to be Pip's fate a little later. It is ironic too that the only game the children do play is called beggar my neighbor. Pip's sudden vision of Estella's beautiful hands knitting, turning to the scarred wrists of Mr. Jaggers' housekeeper—her real mother—or the scene when Pip patronizingly repays the two pound notes to Magwitch, who proceeds to burn them in the candle, remind us of the inextricable interweaving of reality and illusion in the situation of all the chief characters. Each step in revelation brings the "great expectations" of each to their source in the dregs or dross of society, as the fates of the younger generation prove to be linked inextricably with past crimes. Again, Pip's hallucinations of seeing Miss Havisham, in her faded bridal array, hanging in the deserted brewery is a symbol of how she has strangled her own life; and the glimpse of her kissing her hand to Estella, "with a ravenous intensity that was of its kind quite dreadful," expresses the whole horror of her distorted love.

Scenes of pure comedy lighten the serious and symbolic content: Pip's fantasy account of his first visit to Satis House; Trabb's boy mimicking Pip in his fine new clothes; Mr. Wopsle's performance as Hamlet. Everywhere, too, Dickens' extraordinary felicity in description and metaphor flashes out: Mrs. Joe cutting bread and butter, or preparing Pip for his first visit to Miss Havisham:

> ... she pounced on me, like an eagle on a lamb, and my face was squeezed into wooden bowls in sinks, and my head was put under taps of water butts, and I was soaped, and kneaded, and towelled, and thumped, and

harrowed, and rasped ... (I may here remark that I suppose myself to be better acquainted than any living authority, with the ridgy effect of a wedding ring, passed unsympathetically over the human countenance.)

Or Mr. Trabb at his breakfast:

[He] had sliced his hot rolls into three feather beds, and was slipping butter in between the blankets and covering it up.

Or Wemmick throwing pieces of dry biscuit into his wide slot of a mouth "as if he were posting them."

Any book by Dickens, however, is full of drama and of verbal wit. What distinguishes *Great Expectations* from the others is its emotional intensity and insight, the fact that, as George Bernard Shaw said, it is "consistently truthful as none of the other books are." In spite of its richness and variety, it is pervaded by a unity of moral purpose which finally subdues all the material to one conclusion. It portrays vividly a society riddled with injustice, greed and cruelty. Each of the chief characters seeks an identity of the self within this society; each is in isolation, yet entangled with others in a common guilt. Each is forced to face the mystery of evil, passion and pain. Reconciliation and forgiveness come from the discovery of the basic element in human relationship and understanding: that true identity and escape from isolation is reached in humility and compassion. It is symbolized in Pip's feelings toward Magwitch after his capture, as he chooses to go with the convict on the galley which is taking him to prison, and feels that henceforth his place is by Magwitch's side.

For now my repugnance to him had all melted away, and in the hunted, wounded, shackled creature who held my hand in his, I only saw a man who had meant to be my benefactor, and who had felt affectionately, gratefully, and generously towards me with great constancy through a series of years.

D. H. LAWRENCE
1885-1930

Women in Love

D. H. Lawrence wrote a Foreword to the first American
edition of *Women in Love* (1920), stating what the book
was about. He denies the charge of pornography: "the
sensual passions and mysteries are equally sacred with
the spiritual mysteries and passions," and declares that
the novel "pretends only to be a record of the writer's own
desires, aspirations, struggles." It is his "passionate struggle into conscious being." This is basically true, since all
Lawrence's novels are almost obsessively personal, and
evoke his own desperate confusions, as well as his fierce
affirmations. He said his motto was "Art for My Sake," that
"one sheds one's sicknesses in books; repeats and presents
again one's emotions, to be master of them." At the same
time, though Rupert Birkin is obviously himself, the novel
is much more than "self-expression." In order to place
himself, Birkin must objectify his total environment,
which he does with startling originality and insight.

Everything about Lawrence is startling. Aldous Huxley
said of him: "To be with Lawrence was a kind of adventure, a voyage of discovery into newness and otherness. For being himself of a different order, he inhabited
a different universe from that of the common man." It is
the same in his writing. We are taken at once into "otherness"; he demands that we refocus our vision and see a
new order of living, which is a disturbing experience. The
first introduction to Lawrence inevitably produces some
kind of shock, even revulsion, and this may, of course,
persist.

Indeed no modern writer has provoked such diametrically opposing opinions about his work. F. R. Leavis sees him as "the great creative genius of our age, and one of the greatest figures in English literature." Virginia Woolf writes in her diary: "D. H. Lawrence comes off occasionally . . . has great moments; but he is a most incompetent writer." E. M. Forster, so utterly different in temperament, so civilized and fastidious, yet agrees with Leavis that Lawrence is the greatest imaginative writer of our time. Herbert Read accepts his greatness, but sees him as great prophet and moralist: "The novels are relentlessly crude in plot, characterization, form, style, atmosphere. . . . As an artist he is not merely flawed, he is grotesque." David Daiches, on the other hand, sees him as "an esthete who keeps mistaking himself for a moral teacher." Comparing him with Eliot, Leavis thinks the two will be seen to dominate their age, but "Lawrence appears to me decidedly the greater genius." We have no record of what Lawrence thought of Eliot, but Eliot's opinion of Lawrence in *After Strange Gods* is unequivocal. He sees him as the perfect example of the diabolic principle in modern tendencies, an instrument of the demonic powers. He owns that Lawrence stands for life as against the living death of modern materialism, but it is for quite the wrong sort of life. He quotes Scripture against him: "Woe unto the foolish prophets, that follow their own spirit and have seen nothing."

Lawrence certainly followed his own spirit. He was aggressively individual, and was ready to scrap all traditions and all existing institutions, religious, political, social: "I find my deepest desire to be a wish for pure unadulterated relationship with the universe . . . for truth of being." He combined this, however, with a very strong desire to dominate others, to be a prophet of his own deeply felt instincts and ideas, and a leader toward "the goodness, the holiness, the desire for creative and productive happiness" which he was convinced they would bring. He failed, however, to create any corporate life for his beliefs and remained all his life an exile in his "otherness."

After he had freed himself from his strangling family environment (described in *Sons and Lovers*) and married his wife (the Ursula of *Women in Love*), he spent his life wandering from place to place in search of a happy social environment. He went from England to Italy, then left Europe in disgust, finding everything "played out, done for, finished." But Australia proved no better and America even worse. Sooner or later he quarreled with all his friends, who, in his opinion, failed to reach his standards, just as in *Women in Love* Birkin cannot establish any satisfactory relation with anyone except Ursula, and that is achieved only after tormenting growing pains on both sides. Everyone else is either spiritually sick or dead. As Birkin says: "Not many people are anything at all. They jingle and giggle. It would be much better if they were just wiped out. Essentially they don't exist . . . they aren't there." It is no wonder that Lawrence wrote despairingly, shortly before his death—he died of tuberculosis when he was forty-five—"What ails me is the absolute frustration of my societal instincts. . . . I think societal instinct is much deeper than sex instinct and societal repression much more devastating."

Lawrence had no gift for the art of social living, but fortunately he could transmute his intense personal vision into literary art. There he could project his picture of the perverted civilization he hated and despised, and there he could embody those values in which he so passionately believed. "The business of art," he said, "is to reveal the relation between man and his circumambient universe *at the living moment* . . . the Now." He regarded the novel as the art form which can accomplish this better than any other; it is "the one bright book of life," because it can reveal true and vivid relationships in all their flow and change; "the whole of the strange assembly of apparently incongruous parts, slipping past one another." It is the flow and change and incongruity he wants to capture. He sees religion and philosophy "busy nailing things down, to get a stable equilibrium of right and wrong," but the beauty of the novel is that it can "develop an instinct for life . . . instead of a theory of good and bad."

Lawrence was well aware that his ideas about both life and art were heretical. He wrote to a critic-friend: "I am doing something not attempted before. You must drop the preconceptions you bring from other novels: they will get in the way." He fully expected the attacks made on him: "Obviously to read a really new novel will always hurt to some extent. There will be resistance." When Arnold Bennett complained in a review of *Women in Love* that the book was badly constructed, Lawrence's reply was: "All rules of construction hold good only for novels that are copies of other novels," and that his book was not based on "the old stable Ego of character" where the figures were conceived in a moral scheme and made consistent.

Lawrence has of course plenty to say about his own unorthodox beliefs, but his pattern is conceived not as social or moral drama but as psychic drama. Yet, as Leavis points out, Lawrence combines this with a realistic surface which evokes a complete sense of most varied social environments: the mining village, similar to one in which he himself was born; the life of the wealthy mineowner and his family; the "county" socialite background of the Roddices; the lower-middle-class status of the Brangwens; the Bohemian London set and the tourists in the Austrian Alps. All these settings are made strange and unfamiliar because Lawrence never sees anything external apart from the psychic life which he feels pulsing in and around it: the "host of licentious souls" in a London café; the "glamorous thickness of labour and maleness" among the miners, these "powerful underworld men," whose voices are voluptuous "like strange machines, heavy, oiled"; the evening house party at Breadalby with "the women lurid with colour," and underneath the social chitchat "an accumulation of powerful force in the room, powerful and destructive."

The social environments are not important in the plot, which indeed is negligible, but they play their part as negative forces in the thematic pattern. The book opens with the two Brangwen girls discussing marriage. They are both disillusioned about it as a solution to their problems, and indeed about any fulfillment or fruition in their lives. Gudrun says bitterly: *"Nothing materializes!* Everything withers in the bud," and she declares: "I get no feeling whatever from the thought of bearing children." Ursula is not so strident as her sister, and we are told that she feels a force within herself, striving to lay hold on life, but frustrated: "She seemed to try and put her hands out, like an infant in the womb, and she could not, not yet."

In these two images, the withering bud and the child in the womb, which recur several times in the book, Lawrence suggests the two forces of destruction and creation, whose conflict is sustained throughout. Essentially it is the conflict between contemporary civilization and the attitudes it produces in human beings and what Lawrence calls "the blood," which is the dark unconscious life force which is the root of all life, uniting man to man, and man to the universe of which he is a part. It is "the you that your common self denies utterly," says Birkin to Ursula. This force is in itself neutral. It can be ignored, and life lived from the purely conscious level, as is done by all the minor characters; or it can be perverted into the death drive, as happens to Gerald and Gudrun, Hermione and Loerke; or it can be directed into the renewed and enriched living which is finally achieved by Birkin and Ursula.

The two girls set out for the Crich wedding, passing through the "shapeless, barren ugliness" of the mining village, "an uncreated, hostile world." While they watch the arrival of the wedding party at the church, Gudrun is immediately attracted to Gerald Crich, the brother of the

bride. Ursula is interested in Rupert Birkin, a school-
teacher, but with a mixture of attraction and repulsion.
Another of the guests is Hermione Roddice, richly dressed,
impressive "yet macabre," intellectual, interested in social
reform and in the arts. We are told that though she tries
to make herself invulnerable to the world's judgment,
"there was always a secret chink in her armour. . . . It was
a lack of robust self . . . a terrible void, a lack, a deficiency
of being within her." She needs her lover, Birkin, to give
her support, but she knows he is trying to end their relationship. At the wedding reception we feel the strange un-
dercurrents in the Crich family, and Birkin establishes
himself as a champion of individualism in an exchange
with the conventional Gerald. The attitude of the two men
to one another is "a strange, perilous intimacy which was
either hate or love, or both." We are told that "they had
not the faintest belief in deep relationship between men
and men, and their disbelief prevented any development
of their powerful but suppressed friendliness." On the personal level this seems to suggest a suppressed homosex-
uality, which is enforced later by the scene of the wrestling
match, and the suggestion of a blood-brothership pact,
and of which Lawrence seems unaware. But at the thematic level the relations of the two men are second in
importance only to the relation between Birkin and Ursula.
For Gerald is the symbol of the social element which
Birkin hates and yet desperately needs to complete himself. He longs to save Gerald, who is perverting the spontaneous life within him, supplanting it by the conscious
will, dedicated to the service of the machine: "translating
the mystic word harmony into the practical word organi-
zation." It leads to his destruction—he is frozen in the
barren white snows of the Alps—but in the final words of
the book, Birkin is overwhelmed with regret that the love
between them was frustrated. Again it is put in personal
terms, but it speaks of the despairing failure of Lawrence

himself to satisfy his "societal instincts." Ursula argues that her love is enough.

> "You can't have two kinds of love. Why should you!"
> "It seems as if I can't," he said. "Yet I wanted it."
> "You can't have it, because it's false, impossible," she said.
> "I don't believe that," he answered.

At the same time it is difficult to believe from the text that Lawrence saw any hope for his society. "Humanity is a huge aggregate lie," or "Man is a mistake, he must go," Birkin says; and he pours out contempt and fury on "the dying organic forms of social mankind," their hypocrisies, their rottenness, "the ghastly, heavy crop of Dead Sea Fruit." He clashes violently with Gerald, who argues for practical social reforms and what Birkin calls "the plausible ethics of productivity," the ideal of "making things *go*," and Gerald is made to own that it gives no real center to life, which becomes "artificially held together by the social mechanism." The discussion of Gerald's "go" is immediately followed by the story of his having accidentally killed his brother, and Birkin's remark that there is no such thing as accident, "it all hung together in the deepest sense." Gerald in fact is the central human symbol of the death drive. Since to Lawrence the creative element is always associated with the dark and the warm, it is significant that Gerald's "gleaming blondness" is always emphasized: his fair hair is "a-glisten like sunshine refracted through crystals of ice."

In its public social aspect, Gerald's egocentric will expresses itself in the mechanization of both the work and the lives of the miners. He acts consistently as "the God in the machine," with the sole ideal of functional efficiency: "what he wanted was the pure fulfillment of his own will in the struggle with natural conditions." In the chapter called "The Industrial Magnate," Lawrence analyzes Gerald's ideas in direct rational terms, but elsewhere he creates his meaning much more powerfully in directly sensuous ones. There is a scene where Gerald forces his Arab mare, symbol of pure living organism, to face a clanging, grinding train, and brings her terror to exhausted submission by rein and spur.

> He bit himself down on the mare like a keen edge biting home . . . with an almost mechanical relentlessness, keen as a sword pressing in to her . . . her paws were blind and pathetic as she beat the air, the man closed round her, and brought her down, almost as if she were part of his own physique.

It is indeed part of himself, to Lawrence the essential part, that Gerald is trying to destroy.

Gudrun looks on in horror here, but in the equally powerful scene with the rabbit, in the chapter with that name, she too is involved. The rabbit again is the pure life force, described with all Lawrence's brilliance in evoking natural things. As Gudrun drags it from the hutch by its ears, it lunges wildly, "it's body flying like a spring coiled and released, as it lashed out." Gerald takes it from her.

> The long, demon-like beast lashed out again . . . looking something like a dragon, then closing up again, inconceivably powerful and explosive . . . a sudden sharp, white-edged wrath came up in him. Swift as lightning he drew back and brought his free hand down like a hawk on the neck of the rabbit. . . . It made one immense writhe, tore his wrists and his sleeves in a final convulsion, all its belly flashed white in a whirlwind of paws, and then he had slung it round and had it under his arm, fast. It cowered and skulked. His face was gleaming with a smile.

Gudrun smiles too: there is a "mutual hellish recognition" between them, and Lawrence sees the gashes on their arms as a horrible initiation rite which unites them. The gashes symbolize the spiritual wounds they will receive from the explosive subconscious forces within themselves which they thus misuse and attempt to destroy. "They were implicated with each other in abhorrent mysteries," and this would kill the possibility of any fruitful union between them.

Lawrence senses mystical depths of evil below sexuality which match the mystical heights above it. His symbol for this is one of the African statuettes Birkin has seen in Halliday's room. It comes into his memory at the time when he is in deep conflict over his relations with Ursula. He is sure that he does *not* want with her "a further sensual experience—something deeper, darker than ordinary life could give." As an illustration of what this would mean he thinks of the beetle-faced, long, elegant body and protuberant buttocks of the statuette, with all the feeling of inexplicable degradation that it arouses in his consciousness. It represents an "inverted culture," based on "knowledge of one sort, mindless progressive knowledge through the senses . . . far beyond the phallic cult" and ending in a world of corruption and dissolution. With Africans, "controlled by the burning death-abstraction of the Sahara," this would be fulfilled in "the putrescent mystery of sunrays"; but the white races, "having the Arctic north behind them . . . would fulfill a mystery of ice-destructive knowledge." Birkin immediately thinks of Gerald and wonders "was he fated to pass away in this knowledge, death by perfect cold?"

While it is not very clear what this means, it is obvious that both Gerald and Gudrun are to take this path, and destroy and corrupt themselves as a result of their passion. Gerald is first driven to a sexual union with Gudrun because of an inward disintegration he feels at the death of his father. He goes to her bed from a visit to the graveyard.

Into her he poured all his pent-up darkness and corrosive death, and he was whole again. . . . She was the great bath of life ... mother and substance and all life was she. And he, child and man, received of her and was made whole.

We might suspect from this that Lawrence was describing a fulfillment through sexual harmony, if we had not heard Birkin bursting out furiously in the preceding chapter against sex at the "emotional personal level," and against woman as "the bath of birth":

> This horrible fusion of two beings, which every woman and most men insisted on, was it not nauseous and horrible?

Neither Gerald nor Gudrun gains any further satisfaction from their union, which dwindles into a battle of wills in which she finally worsts him. Her later relationship with the vague but repellent figure of the artist Loerke is headed toward further debasement. Lawrence describes Loerke as a negation, "gnawing at the roots of life." We are told, moreover, that they both "kindled themselves" at "the subtle lusts of primitive art and worshipped the inner mysteries of sensation," which again Lawrence analyzes in almost hysterical terms of disgust.

On the other hand, Hermione Roddice, a character Lawrence seems particularly to hate, is accused of intellectualizing sex, which is just as bad. In a brutally frank conversation between them, Birkin says her only real motivation is her bullying will. "You and spontaneity! You, the most deliberate thing that ever walked or crawled!" She has none of "the great dark knowledge you can't have in your head," and her rich and colorful clothes are made to accentuate her inner poverty of spirit. The only time, in fact, she enjoys genuine voluptuous ecstasy is when she tries to brain Birkin with the lapis lazuli paperweight. He approves of that as a spontaneous act, but otherwise she is "a consuming destructive mentality."

Against all these death-directed social and sexual rela-

tions Birkin and Ursula work out their final creative affirmation. The way to it is slow and difficult. In the beginning
Birkin confesses that inwardly, "at the really growing
part," he is a knot "all tangled and messed up." Ursula
dislikes his preaching, what she calls his "priggish Sunday-
school stiffness," and she is jealous of his worn-out affair with Hermione. When she goes alone to have tea
with him he announces the terms, as it were, on which any
developing relation must be based. Love is not to be an
emotional meeting and mingling:

> It is something much more impersonal and harder. . . .
> One must commit oneself to a conjunction with the
> other—for ever. But it is not selfless—it is a main-
> taining of the self in mystic balance and integrity—
> like a star balanced with another star.

Ursula cannot accept this at all. She uses her feminine
charm and sex appeal, and is rebuked for her "meretri-
cious persiflage," but finally he yields to her embrace. This
is followed by a revulsion on Birkin's part: "it seemed to
him woman was always so horrible and clutching, she had
such a greed of possession, a greed of self-importance in
love." On her side, Ursula resents Birkin's power of self-
possession: "she saw him as a strange gem-like being
whose existence defined her own non-existence." She refuses to marry him, and as they drive in the country, they
engage in a very Lawrencian slanging match, hurling
insults at one another. The reconciliation which follows,
however, is the final one: "they left behind them this
memorable battlefield," and we are told that Birkin experiences a sense of rebirth: "life flowed through him as
from some new fountain, he was as if born out of the
cramp of a womb." As for Ursula, touching the back of
his thighs, she experiences "the full mystic knowledge of
his suave loins of darkness," and so reaches the "creative
quick."

> And now behold, from the smitten rock of the man's
> body, from the strange, marvelous flanks and thighs ...
> came the floods of ineffable darkness and ineffable
> riches.

This is "the resurrection and the life," and we are assured
that they are to "give each other this star-equilibrium
which alone is freedom."

Thus the personal man-woman conflict is resolved, but
some of the larger relations remain insoluble, as they did
to Lawrence himself. In his essay on "Mortality and the
Novel," he declares the whole meaning of life is the estab-
lishment of harmony between himself and everything in
the universe:

> Between me and another person, me and other people,
> me and a nation, me and the race of men, me and the
> animals ... trees and flowers ... skies and sun and
> stars ... This, if we knew it, is our life and eternity.

Lawrence had no difficulty with his "pure relationship"
to the natural world: that was instinctive and complete.
Birkin, after his violent scene with Hermione, rushes off
to roll naked among the spring flowers in the wood: "He
did not want a woman ... the leaves and the primroses
and the trees, they were really lovely and cool and de-
sirable, they really came into the blood and were added on
to him." He can find joy in the thought of a universe
purged entirely of "foul humanity": "Don't you find it a
beautiful clean thought, a world empty of people, just
uninterrupted grass, and a hare sitting up?" But the relation between "me and other people, me and a nation" remains frustrated. As he and Ursula look at the eighteenth-
century chair in the market place, he laments that his "beloved country" can now produce nothing but "foul me-
chanicalness; and he laments too very wistfully their
own dual isolation.

> "One has a hankering after a sort of further fellow-
> ship."
> "You've got me," she said. "Why should you *need*
> others?"

But Lawrence can suggest no public aspect of the creative
principle. The relation of Birkin and Ursula to society remains sterile. We leave them to the wandering, homeless
life of exiles which Lawrence was to find so torturing in
actuality.

As Lawrence himself said, however, it is no part of the
novelist's function to supply solutions to the problems of
the individual and society. We cannot, therefore, blame
him because he presents no unity of plot, theme and characters ending in some resolution of comedy or romance or
tragedy. His aim is to evoke the "change and flow and incongruity" of life processes, and to create "truth to the
living moment." Any adverse criticism, therefore, must
be based on his failure to do that. Even F. R. Leavis, a
great admirer of Lawrence, admits that certain passages
in the book fail, for example, the chapter "Excurse." He
offers this explanation:

> It seems to me that in these places Lawrence betrays
> by an insistent and over-emphatic explicitness, running
> at times to something one can only call jargon, that he
> is uncertain—uncertain of the value of what he offers;
> uncertain whether he really holds it—whether a valid
> communication has really been defined and conveyed
> in terms of his creative art.

If, however, it is true that Lawrence lapses into this "jargon," this repetitive verbiage, because he is "uncertain of
the value of what he offers; uncertain whether he really
holds it," Leavis is denying to Lawrence the central tenet
of his beliefs. This is the most damaging, indeed annihila-
ting, criticism which could be made of anyone who holds
his beliefs as passionately and preaches them as dog-

matically as Lawrence did. Indeed Leavis shifts his ground in the last sentence here, and while appearing to pursue the same point, really proffers a different one altogether: "whether a valid communication has really been defined and conveyed in terms of his creative art." This becomes an aesthetic question, not one of belief. Of his aesthetic failure in direct description and analysis, I think there can be no doubt, whether he is trying to convey the ultimate mystical ecstasies of Ursula or the ultimate evil represented by the African statuette and pursued by Gudrun and Loerke.

Lawrence, in fact, is a mystic, and as all mystics know, the mystical experience is absolute and inexpressible. As Lawrence himself says, it "can never be transmuted into mind content, but remains outside, the living body of darkness and silence." It cannot be translated into intelligible expository language, for it is an experience which cannot be grasped by the intelligence. Nor does Lawrence's insistent repetition of turbulent descriptive epithets add any conviction. The question is whether he succeeds in communicating his meaning in the *in*direct ways of symbol or metaphor, appealing not to the mind, but to the emotions and senses. Several times he uses the star image: "steadfast in perfect suspended equilibrium," or "this star-equilibrium which alone is freedom." As a central image, however, it suggests only *part* of the whole. The two stars have an equilibrium of tension but they never come together in physical contact. The metaphor does not suggest the dual individuality within the close physical union. Perhaps Lawrence is most successful in the scene on the cross-Channel ship, when the sensation of their "pure trajectory" together from the outer world of fact to the inner world of rebirth creates itself in words:

> There was no sky, no earth; only one unbroken darkness, into which, with a soft, sleeping motion, they seemed to fall like one closed seed of life falling through dark, fathomless space.

Here too there is a hint of the tenderness and gentleness of relationship which is usually absent.

Critics differ as much about Lawrence's success in formal quality as about his ultimate place in literary history. Mark Schorer likens the pattern to a ritual dance, and says: "... the configuration of the characters, their thematic significance, is perhaps the strictest of all English novels," while another commentator sees the characters like a nomadic tribe, carrying the story with them like a tent, to be put up at any interesting spot. Certainly the power of the book rests in the moments of intense vision, "the strange assembly of apparently incongruous parts slipping past one another," and these are linked by psychic development and not by causal sequence. But the "parts" and the relationships they create vary greatly in the success of their communication. Some are frankly absurd, like Gudrun performing her eurythmics to the cows, and in so many the violence of the vocabulary seems much in excess of the given cause. The description of Hermione, for instance, after a difference of opinion with Birkin about a Chinese painting:

> Her thin bosom shrugged convulsively. He stared back at her, devilish and unchanging. In another strange, sick convulsion she turned away, as if she were sick, could feel dissolution setting in her body. ... She swallowed, and tried to regain her mind. But she could not, she was witless, decentralized. ... She suffered the ghastliness of dissolution, broken and gone in a horrible corruption ...

Again and again we are *told* that people are having these convulsive and shattering feelings, but all intensity and clarity are lost in the emotional extravagance and the smothering, incantatory prose. The "truth to the living moment" emerges blurred and distorted.

Yet we can match these with episodes where the external scene and the psychic content are perfectly fused into a complete harmony. Gerald and the Arab mare in front of the clanking clatter of the train; or the struggle with the rabbit, where the adult, sinister forces working in Gudrun and Gerald are made more revolting by contrast with the childish innocence of Winifred, who is taking it all at the level of watching her kicking pet and how to tame him. Or the famous scene of Birkin throwing stones at the reflection of the moon in the lake. Here the frenzied irritation of his mood, the turmoil that man's passions can create in the waters of life, are most vividly communicated by the description of the violent, disfiguring movements, sounds and lighting effects caused by his frantic anger, while the image of the moon reforms each time "in triumphant reassumption," as nature shows her power "to be whole and composed and at peace."

In such passages the truths Lawrence is asserting are allowed to reach us through their sensuous embodiment without any feverish, high-pitched insistence or wasteful interpretation. And these truths are piercing and profound, for Lawrence has an unerring instinct for the things that make for creative and productive living and for those that stultify and impoverish it. He knows that for fulfillment man must live from deeper sources than the purely conscious surface of the mind, and he awakens and reveals these. At the same time he exposes the deadness and shams behind outworn formulas of love and marriage, of friendship and family feeling, of conventional social relationships and unconventional Bohemia. He said the use of the novel was that it could develop in its readers "an instinct for life," an extension of being; and that surely he does.

THE GAME OF ART

HENRY JAMES
1843–1916

The Portrait of a Lady

Literature, said Henry James, *"makes* life, makes interest, makes importance ... and I know no substitute whatever for the force and beauty of its process." He dedicated his powers to that process—"Oh, celestial, soothing, sanctifying *process"*—through which, when he had the *donnée,* the given situation, he would "fumble it gently and patiently out." For life, he says "is capable of nothing but splendid waste. Hence the opporunity for the sublime economy of art"; life is "all inclusion and confusion," while art is "all discrimination and selection."

Yet James was in no doubt that "the deepest quality of a work of art will always be the mind of the producer"; its value and intensity rest on "the kind and degree of the artist's prime sensibility, which is the soil out of which his subject springs." This sensibility he defines as

> a kind of huge spider-web of fine silken threads suspended in the chamber of consciousness, and catching every air-borne particle in its tissue. It is the very atmosphere of the mind.

His own work is the revelation of a sensibility quite unparalleled before or since in a novelist, translated into dramas of human relationships unparalleled in their minuteness and subtlety and perfection of formal beauty. *The Portrait of a Lady*, written in his late thirties, is the crown of his earlier work, some think of all his work, though others prefer the extreme density and technical elaboration of his last novels. He himself, at the end of his life, thought it the most perfectly organized and designed of his compositions after *The Ambassadors*, his last long novel. His mother reports in a letter in 1878, when he was writing it: "he says compared with anything he has yet done it will be as wine to water." He himself at the same time calls it his "big novel," adding that "it is from that I myself shall pretend to date—on that I shall take my stand." It is saddening that though it was serialized in both America and England in 1880–1881 and then published in two volumes, it made little impression, and confirmed James in his belief that the public were incapable of reading him with the attention his art demanded.

His vision and method were indeed all his own, and unfamiliar to the reading public. He admired the ironic social comedy of Jane Austen, the psychological and moral preoccupations of Hawthorne, and still more those of George Eliot. All these influenced him in some degree, but in the Preface to *The Portrait*, written twenty-five years after its first publication, he tells us that it was from Turgenev that he learned that a plot was not of first importance, but rather a group of characters so alive that the only problem becomes to invent and select such complications as such characters would be likely to produce and feel. Many suggestions have been made of originals, in fact or in fiction, for some of the leading characters in the book, but in any case it is only what James made of them himself that is of consequence, and the amount of what he calls "felt life" that he manages to infuse into them. Elements in the story are romantic, even melodramatic: the unexpected inheritance of a fortune; the innocent young heroine trapped into marriage by a sophisticated, fraudulent fortune-hunter and his ex-mistress; the devoted lovers who remain true to her through all. Yet it is never the facts, but the way the facts emerge, and all that surrounds the facts, that fascinate us. James creates many highly charged scenes of direct confrontation between his chief actors, but the scenes of inner drama have as much or more importance than the outer. What goes on within the consciousness before acting or speaking, and after it; "the very note and trick, the strange irregular rhythm of life"; the hidden vibrations between minds—those are his especial field. We share the thought processes of his heroine in their contradictions, their acceptances and discards, their self-deceptions and evasions. The straight narrative line and the substantial, clear-cut worlds of Jane Austen or Thackeray or George Eliot melt into the atmosphere of inner reactions, of ambivalent judgments, of hovering conjectures and veiled hints; of relations based on misapprehensions and suppressions, and the whole outer and inner interplay of appearance and reality.

James never moves out of his own social environment. We are always in the world of leisured, cultivated, well-to-do people, traveling in Europe or at ease in large country houses or Italian villas and palaces, furnished with family heirlooms or a profusion of rare *objets d'art*. Some of these figures are English, some American, some expatriates. James's "international" theme, the American in Europe, runs all through the book. Yet this does not make a good basis for the grouping of his cast. Elsewhere he divides his characters into the "fixed" and the "free," and this is a more fruitful classification. In the Preface he speaks of those who are but wheels to the coach and those who are of its body or who have a seat inside. Some belong only to the conventional world of social appearances. Lord Warburton's sisters, for instance, with "such an air of hereditary quiet about them," but quite without personality; or the amiable colonists from America in Paris whose lives are, "though luxurious, inane." Poor little convent-bred Pansy Osmond, the European *jeune fille*, whose only desire is to please, is equally "fixed." She can have no mind of her own and must always submit to authority. In this group too is Mrs. Touchett, arid, sophisticated, egotistical, who uses her wealth to please no one but herself. She has strangled her opportunities for emotional relationships and responsibilities, so that Isabel can see her in the future as that pathetic figure, "an old woman without memories." Or there is the raffish Countess Gemini, Osmond's sister, married to a decadent Italian aristocrat, whose only distinction is the number of her lovers; or the lightweight Ned Rosier, who nevertheless loves Pansy so truly that he will sell his treasured collection of *bibelots* to try and win her.

On the other side are those figures who have potentialities for free development in their own natures, either for good or evil. Again, some are American, some European. Their lives are all closely involved with that of the heroine, Isabel Archer. The two full-length evil characters are American expatriates, Madame Merle and Gilbert Osmond, while the rest all love Isabel and long to help her. Lord Warburton, the English aristocrat with radical views, possesses "a happy temperament fertilized by a high civilization," and is contrasted with Casper Goodwood, Isabel's American suitor, who owns a cotton mill in Massachusetts. Lord Warburton, handsome, polished, reserved, is a sophisticated man of the world, while the American is direct and positive. To Isabel Casper appears, with his square jaw and clear, burning eyes, "the stubbornest fact she knew." She has to admire his "supremely strong, clean make," though she feels in him "a want of easy consonance with the deeper rhythms of life." At the end he finally awakens in her by his embrace the physical knowledge "that she had never been loved before," but he is not allowed to prevail, and returns to America, feeling "hopeless, helpless, useless." Goodwood and the American woman journalist, Henrietta Stackpole, are both symbolic of American youth as James saw it. Henrietta is, as Ralph Touchett says, "an excellent fellow," but one "who walks in without knocking at the door." She is in many ways crude, glib and superficial. James apologized in his Preface for putting in so much of her, and wondered why he had allowed her "so officiously, so strangely, so almost inexplicably, to pervade." He imagines that he felt the danger of "thinness" in the book, which must be avoided "tooth and nail" by "the cultivation of the lively," and that, at that time, Henrietta was his notion of the lively. He declares she is only a "wheel" character, but surely she is more, and James has created her in the round. We could perhaps do without her romance with the colorless Mr. Bantling, but she herself is full of vitality. She has had to make her own way in the world and in spite of her surface crudity, she has courage and kindness, loyalty and good sense. She has a much sounder insight into human nature than Isabel herself and emerges as not nearly such a pure figure of fun as James seems to think.

Finally there is the invalid Ralph Touchett, born of American parents but thoroughly Europeanized, who is in a sense the "directing intelligence" in the book. He represents the yardstick of civilized mature emotion and understanding against which all the other characters are measured. He is the Mr. Knightley or the Marlow or Mr. Stein whose consciousness is more delicately aware than anybody else's of the whole pattern of values and relationships of the group. He has "all the illumination of wisdom and none of its pedantry." His poor health forces him into "mere spectatorship at the game of life," and it is perhaps a comment on James's own vision in this book that this wisdom should be alive only in someone marked for death and incapable of the joys of action. Nevertheless he sees more through his amused ironic contemplation and his hopeless adoration of Isabel than any of those engaged in the active drama of events.

It is not, however, through Ralph's eyes that we see the development of the drama, which, as the Preface tells us, springs from "the conception of a certain young woman affronting her destiny," and what it is open to her destiny to *be*. Wondering how to tackle this theme, and to make the heroine *matter* enough among the satellite characters, the author hit upon the method he will use:

> Place the centre of the subject in the young woman's own consciousness . . . and you get as interesting and as beautiful a difficulty as you could wish. Stick to *that*—for the centre; put the heaviest weight into *that* scale, which will be so largely the scale of her relation to herself.

He felt himself, he tells us, in complete possession of the central character, and as he queried, "Well, what will she *do*?" the other characters seemed to form themselves, to ask to be trusted to show him.

We do not of course see everything through Isabel's consciousness. In fact, another grouping of the characters would be into those whose *minds* we enter and those who are revealed only dramatically, in speech or action. We enter the consciousness of Ralph and of Madame Merle and Gilbert Osmond, but not, I think, of any of the others. James himself, however, adds a considerable amount of comment and description of character. But everything in the book contributes to Isabel's portrait, and is subservient to it, and no one intrudes who is not related to her destiny. If we are not looking at her with her own eyes, we are looking at her through the eyes of others. "What she *does*" issues in perpetual subtle shifts of perspective in herself and her associates, shifts in moral viewpoints, in social relations and in emotional awareness.

Although James's method is so much more inward and complex, and the circumstances of his heroine so different, he is doing just what Jane Austen did in *Emma*. In both books we watch a flawed and immature personality revealing her limitations of head and heart by her thoughts and actions; finding herself trapped in a painful situation entirely of her own making; discovering thereby her own egregious self-ignorance, and growing through suffering to a position of maturity. Jane Austen declared that she had chosen a heroine whom no one but herself would like, and James has to own, after a long analysis of Isabel's weaknesses—"her meagre knowledge, her inflated ideals, her confidence at once eager and dogmatic, her temper at once exacting and indulgent"—that "she would be an easy victim of scientific criticism if she were not intended to awaken on the reader's part an impulse more tender."

Isabel's situation, however, is very different from Emma's. Whereas Emma's position in her social milieu is stable and secure, Isabel's is that of an emancipated American girl faced with the traditional civilizations and cosmopolitan societies of Europe. And whereas Emma's moral and emotional problems are those which easily allow an outcome of comedy, Isabel's quest is altogether deeper and wider. Though the mainspring of her character, like that of Emma's, is "an unquenchable desire to think well of herself," it involves a high abstract idealism of moral behavior and romantic dream which would seem strange indeed to an inhabitant of Highbury. Isabel's quest is ultimately a spiritual one—the pursuit of freedom to live fully. She sets out with everything seemingly in her favor. True, she is innocent and ignorant, but she is young, attractive, intelligent, independent in spirit, sensitive and sympathetic. She has no family responsibilities. To all this is added her unexpected inheritance. Yet the story is that of the defeat of her aspirations, as actuality proves much stronger than dream, and as her theoretical idealisms are shattered at the first clash with the harsh realities of common greed and skillful intrigue.

James's technical problem in the first part of the novel is to create in the reader a sympathy and liking for Isabel's enthusiasm, fresh curiosity of mind and quick wits, while at the same time he is made aware of her dangerous immaturity and her mixture of overconfidence and uncertainty. She is the product of transcendental idealism, of her father's indulgence and of her provincial upbringing. James's method of revealing this is to set her first in the English surroundings of Gardencourt and Lockleigh, among the Touchetts and the Warburtons. Her favorite room in her old home in Albany had an unused door on to the street, whose sidelights were covered with green paper. Here Isabel would lose herself in her reading, and "had never assured herself that the vulgar street lay beyond." She knew, in fact, as little about the actualities of life in America as elsewhere. Carrying on the architectural images as suggestive of the attitudes and lives lived among them, James makes Gardencourt a beautiful Tudor house, bought twenty years before by Mr. Touchett, an American banker; bought "with much grumbling at its ugliness, its antiquity, its incommodity," but now appreciated by him with "a real aesthetic passion" for its history and its setting. Many scenes take place in its garden, with its age-old smooth lawns, its fine trees and its formal flower beds; while Lockleigh, nearby, the seat of Lord Warburton, seems to Isabel like "a castle in a legend."

During her visit to England we see Isabel in her relations with the three men whom she rejects as life companions: Ralph Touchett, whose sickness sets him apart from the active world, but whose fineness of nature and clarity of insight could have brought her own potentialities to true fulfillment; Lord Warburton, symbol of the cultivated English aristocracy; and Caspar Goodwood, the young American who represents the best of the new world. Isabel herself hardly knows why she is so sure she cannot marry Warburton, but what it comes down to is her fear of losing her chance of "the free exploration of life." He rightly senses that this is an abstraction, and tells her: "I never saw a person judge things on such theoretical grounds." Yet she continues to be convinced that the marriage would impose on her an alien "system," separating her "from life—from the usual chances and changes, from what most people know and suffer."

She sees Goodwood as a danger to her plans in a different way. It is his energy, his self-reliance, his virility that repel her. She senses that "he was naturally plated and steeled, armed essentially for aggression"; his eyes seem to shine at her through the vizard of a helmet. In refusing him, she is rejecting her own young militant country, again in favor of a fancied romantic freedom: "I don't wish to marry till I've seen Europe."

Europe appears first in the figure of Madame Merle. James regarded the scene where Isabel first meets her, playing the piano in the drawing room at Gardencourt, as one of the highlights of the book, producing "the maximum of intensity with the minimum of strain." Yet though Mrs. Touchett's acid remark about Madame Merle's fondness for mystery, and James's own description of her eyes as "incapable of stupidity—incapable, according to some people, even of tears," are slightly sinister, and though Isabel is immediately attracted to her uncritically as a person of "large experience," the scene hardly registers as an intense sequence, compared with many later in the book. It is in the following chapter, where James infuses a good deal of ironic analysis of his own, as well as recording Isabel's innocent reactions to Madame Merle's clever tactics, that we recognize her as the serpent in the garden. When we find that Isabel is convinced that Madame Merle is "aristocratic"; that she has "a sort of greatness about her"; that she feels she can make a close friend of this worldly, polished parasite, so "round and smooth," we know that she is to meet qualities of which so far she has been completely ignorant—cold calculation, self-interest, hypocrisy.

The early part of the story is full of ironic revelations about Isabel which we remember later. We are told that in her daydreams (like Lord Jim) "sometimes she went so far as to wish that she might find herself some day in a difficult position, so that she should have the pleasure of being as heroic as the occasion demanded." When Mrs. Touchett does not allow her to sit up alone with the men in the evening at Gardencourt, Isabel protests that she is fond of her own way:

> "But I always want to know the things one shouldn't do."
> "So as to do them?" asked her aunt.
> "So as to choose," said Isabel.

She emphasizes this need for liberty of choice when she dismisses Goodwood in London:

> "If there's a thing in the world I'm fond of, it's my personal independence . . . I can do what I choose . . . I wish to choose my fate."
> "One would think you were going to commit some atrocity!" said Caspar Goodwood.
> "Perhaps I am. I wish to be free even to do that if the fancy takes me."

And as Caspar insists that he will come back in two years to propose to her again, her reply is: "And remember too that I shall not be an easy victim."

The supreme irony in the book, however, is that Ralph Touchett, whose judgment is so sure in other matters, and who loves Isabel with a selfless devotion, should persuade his father (who sees its dangers) to leave Isabel the fortune which causes her ruin. Ralph is convinced that the money will make her free, and it shackles her forever.

He has said that he looks forward to her giving them some grand examples of the unexpected, and Isabel herself has visions of "the fine things to be done by a rich, independent, generous girl who took a large human view of occasions and obligations." But before we meet her again, six months later, we have overheard the chilling conversation about her attractions between Madame Merle and Gilbert Osmond, and can guess the unsuspected hidden trap ahead:

"What do you want to do with her?" he asked at length.

"What you see. Put her in your way."

"Isn't she meant for something better than that?"

"I don't pretend to know what people are meant for," said Madame Merle, "I only know what I can do with them."

In spite of Isabel's confident remark to Caspar earlier, she proves the easiest of victims. No one else, however limited in perception, is taken in by Osmond. Mrs. Touchett knows immediately that Madame Merle has been the driving force behind his pursuit of Isabel. As for himself, she sums him up tersely. "An obscure American dilettante ... There's nothing *of* him ... He has no money, he has no name, he has no importance." Indeed it is Osmond's nonentity which impresses everyone. His own sister, the Countess, snorts: "Who is he, if you please? What has he ever done?" Ralph first dismisses him with a gibe: "He has a great dread of vulgarity; that's his special line! he hasn't any other that I know of." To Lord Warburton, a little later, Touchett adds more. After he has first repeated that Osmond is "Nothing at all," Lord Warburton asks:

"Is he awfully clever?"

"Awfully," said Ralph.

His companion thought. "And what else?"

"What more do you want?" Ralph groaned.

We realize the truth of this comment when to Caspar's bitter query "Who and what is this Mr. Gilbert Osmond?" Isabel answers: "Nobody and nothing but a very good and very honorable man." In her ignorance and trustfulness she is the complete dupe of his skillful play-acting. Ralph refuses at first to believe in her blindness. "She's making fools of us all," he tells his mother. But Isabel is the only one who is fooled.

James suggests Osmond's negation of any of the flesh-

and-blood humanity that Isabel's infatuation endows him with, by describing him in terms of inanimate works of art. He likens Osmond's face to that of "a fine old coin," and makes Isabel's first impression of his head as "fine as one of the drawings in the long gallery above the bridge of the Uffizi," while his voice seems like the clear vibration of glass. She feels that "she had never met a person of so fine a grain," and is sure that to him "life was a matter of connoisseurship." As he shows her his collection and describes his pretended renunciation of all ambition except the pursuit of beauty, poor Isabel's only fear is that she will expose "her possible grossness of perception." To Osmond, Isabel herself does not appear as a beautiful and generous woman, but as a valuable acquisition, "a young lady who had qualified herself to figure in his collection of choice objects." In the same way he regards his daughter Pansy as a rare piece to be sold to the highest bidder in the marriage market.

During her courtship, both Lord Warburton and Caspar Goodwood come to Italy, and James makes Isabel subconsciously recognize their healthy masculinity. She looks at Warburton, "with his pleasant steady eyes, his bronzed complexion . . . his manly figure," and at Caspar, "straight, strong and hard," possessing within him "a splendid force." Yet consciously she makes no comparison between them and the effete Osmond, and when Ralph bursts out that he is nothing but "a sterile dilettante," the infatuated Isabel snubs him "with majesty":

> In everything that makes one care for people Mr. Osmond is pre-eminent. There may be nobler natures, but I've never had the pleasure of meeting one.

In Chapter 36, the focus of the narrative changes abruptly as Ned Rosier visits Madame Merle in Rome to beg her support for his marrying Pansy. We have left Isabel three years before in that "charmed and possessed condition" against which all rational argument is futile. Our first hint of the change is when Rosier suggests that

Isabel might favor his suit. Madame Merle replies:

> "Very likely—if her husband doesn't."
> He raised his eyebrows. "Does she take the opposite
> line from him?"
> "In everything. They think quite differently."

We have seen before how James uses architectural imagery to suggest different human attitudes and atmos-
pheres. Just as the home at Albany, and Gardencourt and
Lockleigh told us much about the states of mind of their
inhabitants, so Osmond's romantic Florentine villa and
garden had formed a suitable background for Isabel's
dreams. We hear now that they have moved to an old
palace, "a dark and massive structure" in the heart of
Rome. To young Rosier it appears like a dungeon: "It
seemed to him of evil omen that the young lady he wished
to marry ... should be immured in a kind of domestic
fortress." It is not a dungeon for Pansy only, as we realize
from a little exchange between Ned and Isabel that evening. She has seemed cold to his plea for her intervention.

> "Ah, you're offended, and now you'll never help me."
> She was silent an instant, and then, with a change
> of tone: "It's not that I won't; I simply can't!"
> Her manner was almost passionate.

In the next few chapters we are made aware of the
change in Isabel through the mind of Ralph, and through
her conversation with her husband on the arrival of Lord
Warburton and his attraction to Pansy, which Osmond
naturally is determined to foster. We witness too a little
scene where for the first time Isabel suspects some secret
understanding between her husband and Madame Merle.
But it is not until Chapter 42, through the device of the
internal monologue, that Isabel reveals the full consciousness of her situation. Some critics see this reverie as the
germ of the "stream of consciousness" technique developed later by Joyce and Virginia Woolf. But it is more an
extension and deepening of the method Jane Austen had

practiced when she made Emma examine her own conduct and confront her own mistakes and self-deceptions. It employs no "free association" of ideas and images; it is a logically controlled soliloquy designed to forward the action and communicate events and emotions more economically than could be done by direct comment or narrative.

Osmond's insistence in the scene before that it is in her hands to make or mar his ambitions for Pansy leads Isabel to an examination of her relations with Warburton and from that into an attempt to analyze the whole disaster of her marriage. We hear that Osmond has the "faculty for making everything wither that he touched, spoiling everything for her that he looked at," and of the gulf of mistrust that now separates them. She cannot accept any fault in herself, "she had practised no deception; she had only admired and believed . . . then she had suddenly found the infinite vista of a multiplied life to be a dark, narrow alley with a dead wall at the end." It is as if Osmond "deliberately, almost malignantly, had put the lights out one by one." She had followed him blindly, and

> he had led her into the mansion of his own habitation, then, *then* she had seen where she really was. . . . Between those four walls she had lived ever since; they were to surround her for the rest of her life. It was the house of darkness, the house of dumbness, the house of suffocation.

At last she sees what Ralph had noted so much earlier, that while pretending to despise the world, Osmond's only standards have been those approved by the world; "he was unable to live without it." She, who had refused to marry Lord Warburton for fear of being drawn into an alien "system," has seen Osmond's "rigid system" close about her; her real offense in his eyes "was her having a mind of her own at all." She has awakened from her dream to see him as he really is—dominating, hypocritical, snob-

bish, vain—and to the knowledge that he hates her. With
the revelation of the corruption of Osmond comes the
companion revelation of the wisdom and generosity of
Ralph. But she is not yet humble enough to confess any
of this to him, and decides that it will be "an act of devotion to conceal her misery from him." For a moment we
then slide into Ralph's consciousness of this self-delusion
of hers, and sense how much more clearly he sees into
her than she sees into him.

This "meditative vigil," says James, "was designed to
have all the vivacity of incident and all the economy of
picture," and he declares that though "it is obviously the
best thing in the book . . . it is only a supreme illustration
of the general plan."

It has not been noticeably the general plan up to this
point in the story. James himself saw "a want of action
in the earlier part," though he praised its "sense of ampli-
tude and leisurely accretion." But now incident and picture follow swiftly, with all the vivacity and economy that
was absent before. It is all the most adroit and delicate
blending of scene, imagery, dramatic dialogue and inner
analysis. The series of revelations to individuals about
one another, and the reversals of attitudes held in the
past, bring heightened tension and movement. Lord
Warburton, fully intending to press his suit for Pansy,
sees both that she is in love with Rosier and, in one
truthful look "straight at each other" between him and
Isabel, that there would be danger for both of them in
the marriage. Ralph sees that Osmond will inevitably believe the match fell through because Isabel was jealous
of Pansy. When he accuses her of disloyalty, and she
counters, "How much you must want to make sure of
him," we see a new Isabel as "a momentary exultation
took possession of her—a horrible delight in having
wounded him." But to Henrietta's direct question "Why
don't you leave him?" She states her puritan creed:

One must accept one's deeds. I married him before all
the world; I was perfectly free; it was impossible to do
anything more deliberate. One can't change that way.

To Casper she seems completely changed, "so still, so
smooth, so hard." She will not tell him the truth, but as
we see them say good-bye in Rome, so much tragedy is
packed into the picture and the little exchange. He asks
"one sole satisfaction"—that she tell him if he may pity
her:

> "That at least would be doing something. I'd give my
> life to it."
> She raised her fan to her face, which it covered all
> except her eyes. . . . "Don't give your life to it; but give
> a thought to it every now and then."

The next sequence of incidents, pictures and revelations
of consciousness is that between Isabel, Madame Merle
and Osmond. When Isabel finds how ardently Madame
Merle is supporting Osmond in the matter of Pansy's marriage, she gets the first shattering glimpse of the truth.

> "Who are you . . . What have you to do with me?"
> Madame Merle got up, stroking her muff, but not re-
> moving her eyes from Isabel's face.
> "Everything!" she answered.

For the first time Isabel knows that Mrs. Touchett had
been right: "Madame Merle had married her."
She drives out of the city to look over the Campagna,
"for in a world of ruins the ruin of her happiness seemed
a less unnatural catastrophe," and she "rested her weari-
ness upon things that had crumbled for centuries and yet
still were upright." It is a shock, however, to the reader to
discover that to the former high-spirited, independent
Isabel, being "upright" means the passive acceptance of
her fate.
The crisis comes when, in response to a telegram from

her aunt, saying that Ralph is dying, she tells Osmond that she must go to Gardencourt. Osmond declares that to do so will be "a piece of the most deliberate, the most calculated opposition." Isabel, for the first time, openly gives her opinion of her husband: "It's your own opposition that's calculated. It's malignant." Osmond calls the proposed visit dishonorable and indecent and argues the sanctity of marriage: "What I value most in life is the honor of the thing." In spite of her sense of her husband's "blasphemous sophistry," and the knowledge that "they attached different ideals to the same formula," she too believes in "the observance of a magnificent form." However, to Osmond's insistence on the importance of "living decently together," she flashes out: "We don't live decently together." It is while she is weeping with misery and indecision that the Countess finds her and tells her the whole story of Osmond and Madame Merle and that Pansy is Madame Merle's daughter. She leaves her with the sensible advice:

> "Be a little easy and natural and nasty; feel a little wicked, for the comfort of it, once in your life! . . . You don't take it as I should have thought."
> "How should I take it?" Isabel asked.
> "Well, I should say as a woman who has been made use of."

Isabel decides to go to England, but her conflict is further complicated by poor Pansy, who has been sent back to the convent to remove her from Rosier. It is there that Isabel confronts Madame Merle and makes her aware that her secret is known, but the most moving scene is that between Isabel and Pansy. It is clear that Pansy, in her loyalty to her father, is to be as helpless a victim of Osmond's sadistic domination as Madame Merle has been in the past and as Isabel herself is too. Pansy, however, pleads desperately that Isabel will return, and she gets the promise, "I won't desert you."

So Isabel journeys back to Gardencourt while "the truth of things, their mutual relations, their meaning, and for the most part, their horror, rose before her with a kind of architectural vastness." She puts all regrets behind her, except "that Madame Merle had been so—well, so unimaginable." The scene with Ralph is perfect in its poignancy. All barriers are down between them; "it brought them supremely together." Indeed it is perhaps the only scene in the book where two individuals speak what is truly in their hearts. Yet it is only because Ralph is dying that Isabel can be truthful, and when at the end she cries through her tears "Oh my brother!" the sensation is that she identifies the spiritual death of her own youth and happiness with his physical one.

And what of the conclusion? To the criticism that he had not seen Isabel "to the end of her situation," James replied: "The whole of anything is never told, you can only take what groups together. It is complete in itself—and the rest may be taken up or not later." Thus, though the dying Ralph has said: "I don't believe such a generous mistake as yours can hurt you for more than a little," it is idle to speculate what Isabel may do finally. She exists only in the pattern created for her in a work of art. The only question is whether or not we feel that the conclusion completes satisfactorily the relationships as revealed through the rest of the book.

She rejects Caspar Goodwood's plea that they are free to do as they please, "the world's all before us." His kiss is like white lightning,

> But when darkness returned she was free. . . . She had not known where to turn; but she knew now. There was a very straight path.

It is the strait and narrow path of moral "rightness." When Ralph has said that she must stay at Gardencourt, she has replied: "I should like to stay as long as seems right." He repeats her words in the form of a question:

"As seems right? . . . Yes, you think a great deal about that." Isabel has said several times, in the face of emotional decisions, "I am afraid of myself," and it is always a stern moral code that triumphs, as it does here. She goes back to fulfill her promise to Pansy, though we know she cannot help her, and to support what the base and worthless Osmond has cynically called "the honour of the thing," in the "house of darkness, the house of dumbness, the house of suffocation."

The conclusion, however, is consistent with what has gone before and makes the story "complete in itself." For is it not true that Isabel's career in the novel, in spite of her moral idealism, has been throughout a series of self-deceptions and imperfect insights, from which she never does emerge. Does James perhaps intend us to see her final renunciation as her last mistake and delusion rather than as any positive moral triumph? Her suffering has not brought her any growth or spiritual fulfillment, but simply a negative acceptance and resignation.

James says elsewhere: "I have called the most general state of one's most exposed and assaulted figures *the state of bewilderment*," and is it not that state which he creates so brilliantly in the figure of Isabel? We are told at the beginning that she has "an immense curiosity about life," and also that "she carried within herself a great fund of life." But does it ever appear? Is not Lord Warburton's early remark profoundly true, that she acts from theoretical positions only? Though insisting on the importance of freedom, she is always fearful of committing herself to any natural impulse even before her marriage. After it, by the time we see her again she has lost all spirit of her own, has accepted her matrimonial slavery and puts on a social mask to her friends. She even vacillates about the "rightness" of going to the dying Ralph, until the Countess tells her the truth about her husband and Madame Merle. She does indeed awaken in the reader tenderness rather than criticism, for she is the innocent

victim of unscrupulous trickery, and she is so well-inten-
tioned, so considerate of others, so dignified. But does anyone with "a great fund of life" in her meet such a situation so passively, and accept suffering without action as
her final fate?

We must not, of course, apply contemporary social
standards to a book written in 1881, or think of Isabel as
a modern girl. The conventions of his day shackled
James as much as they did other Victorian writers. But
apart from that, his vision of life is in essence a tragic
one. He says in a letter: "I have the imagination of disaster—and see life indeed as ferocious and sinister."
"Ferocious" hardly seems the word for the atmosphere he
creates, if we compare it with that of Hardy or Conrad
or Dickens, but it is disastrous and sinister enough. The
tragic irony in *The Portrait of a Lady,* as elsewhere in
James's work, is that the sensitive and aspiring characters are so easily defeated by the callous, the corrupt and
the second-rate; and that Isabel, in her "bewilderment," is
incapable of mature intelligent judgment, either of her
own mistakes or of the value of her friends, or of any
creative plans for the future. The "amount of felt life"
James endows her with does not allow for any passionate
impulse, any animal vitality or any full-blooded assertion.
Those qualities in Caspar Goodwood must go to waste, as
unfulfilled as Isabel's quest for freedom, or Pansy's gentle
sweetness, or Lord Warburton's honest manliness, or
Ralph's idealistic generosity.

However sad we may find this vision, we have the
aesthetic joy of watching a great artist in fiction creating
a masterpiece; of observing how that intense sensibility,
moral, emotional and sensuous, translates it into a pattern of formal beauty through the variety and mastery of
his technical means; of how he plays "the game of art"
whereby the "huge spider-web of fine silken threads suspended in the chamber of consciousness" catches its "subject," and fashions it into a perfect symmetry of design.

"Form alone *takes,* and holds and preserves substance," wrote James, in a letter to Hugh Walpole:

> There is nothing so deplorable as a work of art with a *leak* in its interest, and there is no such leak of interest as through commonness of form. Its opposite, the *found* (because the sought for) form is the absolute citadel and tabernacle of interest.

Whatever disappointment we may find in James's human conclusions, there is no "leak" or commonness of interest in *The Portrait of a Lady.*

JAMES JOYCE
1882–1941

A Portrait of the Artist as a Young Man

At the end of *A Portrait,* Joyce dated the book: Dublin, 1904; Trieste, 1914. It was the result, therefore, of ten years' gestation and creation before it satisfied him that it was completed in final form. Richard Ellmann tells us in his biography of Joyce that he wrote the first sketch for it when he was twenty-one, then extended it under the title *Stephen Hero* to over a thousand pages. This was completed in 1907 and immediately Joyce decided to scrap the whole thing and recast and concentrate it into a third of its length, with its present title. Joyce had his usual troubles over publication, and when it finally appeared in America in 1916 and in England the following year, its reception was very mixed. One reviewer called it "a study in garbage" and another "a brilliant and nasty variety of pseudo-realism." But it was also hailed as "one of the most remarkable confessions outside Russian and French literature"; Ezra Pound said it contained the best prose of the decade and was one of the few works that showed creative invention; while the English magazine *The Nation* called Joyce "a new writer with a new form."

Joyce himself had characterized this "new form" in his description of his original sketch. He pointed out that the past has no "iron memorial aspect" but implies "a fluid succession of presents." What we are to look for is not a fixed character but an "individuating rhythm." In its final design, however, he changed the whole focus of this rhythm. The change in title points to a change in perspective. From the fragment of *Stephen Hero* that survives we see that the development centered in the individ-

uality of the protagonist as a *man*. In *A Portrait* the accent
falls on the *artist*. The material is similarly slanted. In
the early version the treatment of Stephen in his unhappy
relations with family, church and society is much fuller
and more direct, and illustrated with much more narrative
action. In *The Portrait* the Dublin environment is not attacked so much frontally, as wrecking the *individual;* it is
revealed as the deadly enemy that threatens the free development of the *artist,* and undermines the primary need
of the artist to be loyal to his calling.

We must not read the book as straight autobiography.
Some critics, indeed, argue that Stephen Dedalus is not
James Joyce at all. While that seems most improbable,
nevertheless the book is a work of art, not a slice of
life, and the materials of the life it creates have been se-
lected, arranged, altered, dramatized and fictionized to
support the central theme. They are probably all true to
the spirit of Joyce's development, but not necessarily to
the facts. The result is an evocation of the growing conscience and consciousness of a dedicated writer and of
the warping and uncongenial environment that surrounds
him; the story of how a gifted imaginative and intellectual
misfit frees himself from the shackling influence of family,
church and society and sets out as an exile to fulfill his
vocation.

Stephen has been a spiritual exile from his social surroundings since early childhood. The description of him
in the football game at Clongowes might be a metaphor
for all his participation in the life of his fellows: "He
crept about from point to point on the fringe of his line,
making little runs now and then." When he is at Belvedere
College he champions Byron and Shelley and Ibsen, feels
in his schoolmates "a vague general malignant joy" when
he is accused of heresy in an essay, and sees himself
"proud **and sensitive and suspicious,** battling against the
squalor **of his life** and the riot of his mind." At the University the students distrust his "intellectual crankery."
He feels equally isolated from the church and knows that

he could never train for the priesthood: "His destiny was
to be elusive of social and religious orders. . . . He was destined to learn his own wisdom apart from others or to
learn the wisdom of others himself wandering among the
snares of the world." In his own family he is equally
apart. He realizes it when he has spent his prize money on
trying to restore some order and elegance into the home:

> He saw clearly his own futile isolation. He had not
> gone one step nearer the lives he had sought to ap-
> proach. . . . He felt that he was hardly of one blood with
> them but stood to them rather in the mystical kinship
> of fosterage, foster child and foster brother.

Again, in his phase of religious devotion, he finds it impossible to combine his pious practices with any human
charity toward others: "To merge his life in the common
tide of other lives was harder for him than any fasting or
prayer."

In spite of "little runs now and then" he remains always
on the "fringe" of any corporate life and an exile within
his own country. To fulfill himself he must leave Ireland,
and he tells his friend Davin why. Davin urges him to be
"one of us," that is, a dedicated Irishman. Stephen replies bitterly that Ireland has always rewarded devotion
to her cause by betrayal; she is "the old sow who eats her
farrow," and he continues:

> When the soul of a man is born in this country there
> are nets flung at it to hold it back from flight. You talk
> to me of nationality, language, religion. I shall try to
> fly by those nets.

The book is the story of the nets and the escape from
them to freedom, and the name of the hero is full of symbolic significance. Stephen is the name of the first Christian martyr. He protested that God's message to the people had been misinterpreted: "which of the prophets have
your fathers not persecuted?" But the synagogue said he
spoke blasphemy and "they cast him out of the city and

stoned him." That Joyce meant this analogy to be drawn
is clear when he makes Stephen think of St. Stephen's
Green in Dublin as *his* green. Indeed the later treatment
of Joyce by Dublin—over the publication of *Dubliners,*
and in the banning of his later books—has borne out the
parallel. But the surname Dedalus is far more important,
since the symbolism surrounding that encloses the whole
story from start to finish. It has a double significance for
Joyce. The mythical Dedalus was imprisoned in a labyrinth on the island of Crete, and escaped by inventing
wings. He is a symbol, therefore, not only of the rebel who
breaks out of his prison, but of the inventor who creates
the instrument of his escape. He is both man and artist.
Etymologically the name means "the cunning one," and
the epigraph of the book is a line from Ovid's *Metamor-
phoses* which tells of Dedalus making his plans: "And
he gave up his mind to obscure arts."

The full force of the analogy reveals itself in the crucial scene of the book, at the end of the fourth chapter.
Stephen, having decided flatly against entering the priesthood, in spite of the temptation to power it provides,
goes out on the seashore and has a vision of his true vocation. He watches the clouds drifting westward, bound
for Europe, and seems to hear "a confused music within
him as of memories and names which he was almost conscious of but could not capture even for an instant"—the
voices of his tradition. The music recedes and he hears
some of his schoolmates calling: "Hello, Stephanos! . . .
Here comes The Dedalus!" The boys are bantering him,
giving him the title "Stephanos"—"one crowned with
wreaths"—and that of the cunning inventor. He recognizes
their mockery, but it flatters him:

> Now, as never before, his strange name seemed to him
> a prophecy. . . . Now, at the name of the fabulous artif-
> icer, he seemed to hear the noise of dim waves and to
> see a winged form flying above the waves and slowly
> climbing the air. What did it mean? Was it a quaint de-

vice opening a page of some medieval book of proph-
ecies and symbols, a hawklike man flying sunward
above the sea, a prophecy of the end he had been born
to serve and had been following through the mists of
childhood and boyhood, a symbol of the artist forging
anew in his workshop out of the sluggish matter of the
earth a new soaring impalpable imperishable being?

His heart trembled ... and a wild spirit passed over
his limbs as though he were soaring sunward. ... His
soul was soaring in an air beyond the world and the
body he knew was purified in a breath and delivered of
incertitude and made radiant ... An ecstasy of flight
made radiant his eyes and wild his breath and tremulous and wild and radiant his windswept limbs.

The words "soaring" and "radiant" repeat themselves
ryhthmically throughout, and this image of flight, of soaring on wings fashioned out of "the sluggish matter of the
earth," carrying a body made radiant by spirit, reborn
into a new dimension of being—this is the symbol
throughout for the identity of the artist. It is echoed in a
different key in the scene later on the steps of the library.
He watches the wheeling swallows and wonders if they
augur good or evil for him, and fear of the unknown
seizes him: "a fear of symbols and portents, of the hawklike man whose name he bore ... of Thoth, the god of
writers." Quickly, though, the cry of the birds, the moving
patterns of their flight and the words of a poem all melt
together in his consciousness. The thought of escape
from Ireland and escape into language flow together into
a sense of profound release.

In direct opposition to all the images of flight, of the
open sky and the open sea of freedom of movement and
warm creative zest, "the call of life to his soul," are a
whole series of contrasting symbols to suggest the forces
of captivity which imprison the young Stephen. Hints of
the labyrinth appear in the school corridors, the "maze of
narrow and dirty streets," the playground at Clongowes,

the racetrack in the park, while later he is to find himself
caught in the labyrinth of sin; and his mind "wound itself
in and out" as he tries "to grope in the darkness of his
own state." In opposition to the images of soaring sunward flight over the sea are many of impeded flight or
earthbound heaviness. The greasy football in the game at
Clongowes "flew like a heavy bird through the grey light"
and the "call of life" is that of the shouting boys and the
prefects urging them on. Another vivid scene is where the
director of the Jesuits offers Stephen the "secret knowledge and secret power" of the priestly office. Stephen recognizes another "call of life," of which he had often
dreamed, but as he imagines himself in the novitiate "his
lungs dilated and sank as if he were inhaling a warm
moist unsustaining air," and he smelled again the atmosphere of the "sluggish turfcoloured water" in the bath at
Clongowes. As a child this produced "a vague fear" and it
becomes symbolic of the *stagnation* he feels around him.
It is associated with the dark pool of the dripping jar in
his sordid home, "scooped out like a boghole." Again,
Stephen's mind quickens as he walks with Lynch, discussing the rhythm and vitality of art, but when they come
to the canal "a crude grey light, mirrored in the sluggish
water, and a smell of wet branches over their heads
seemed to war against the course of Stephen's thought."
When he looks in at the windows of a smart hotel he wonders how he could arouse the conscience and imagination
of the "patricians of Ireland" so that "they might breed a
race less ignoble than their own."

> And under the deepened dusk he felt the thoughts and
> desires of the race to which he belonged flitting like
> bats across the dark country lanes, under trees by the
> edges of streams and near the poolmottled bogs.

Five times in the book the soul of Ireland is described as
batlike: blind, verminous, haunting the dark, "flitting"
instead of "soaring."

The Dedalus symbol, then, is rich and many-faceted. Dedalus is a rebel escaping from the labyrinths and nets of authority; he escapes through his own ingenuity; he is maker, artificer. He escapes by flight, in a double sense— in the meaning of "liberation" and of "soaring above." The wings on which he rises are those of the maker, fashioned from "the sluggish matter of the earth" which appears to hold him down. The wings belong to the sense world, though through them the sense world is transcended, and becomes "a new soaring impalpable imperishable being."

These elements in the symbol are all paralleled in Stephen's story. He has to rebel from the actualities of contemporary Ireland; the captivity of family, nationality and religion. As he says: "I will not serve that in which I no longer believe, whether it call itself my home, my fatherland or my church." All these are obstructions to his flight. Stephen creates his "wings," as it were, in two ways. On the personal level his intellectual and emotional development fit him finally to assert his own freedom by leaving Ireland; as future artist, he is learning all the time to use *language,* his medium of ingenuity. The new "being" which he finally does create is the book itself, completed ten years after the last events it describes.

The structure of the novel, as critics have pointed out, is in the form of a series of trial flights. At the end of each chapter, Stephen makes some assertion of his own identity which frees him for a time from the particular outer and inner pressures of confusion and despair which constrict him. The diary form at the end of the book, in spite of much of its "flip" tone of cynicism, hints of doubts and wavering distrust. Stephen comments on the story of an old peasant who evidently represents Ireland: "I fear him. . . . It is with him I must struggle all through this night till day come." Torn with conflicting emotions about the girl, who also typifies Ireland, he dismisses them: "O, give it up, old chap! Sleep it off!" To his mother's prayer that in his self-banishment he may learn "what the heart is and what it feels," he acquiesces indifferently: "Amen. So be it." But the final words are exultant:

> Welcome, O life! I go to encounter for the millionth time the reality of experience and to forge in the smithy of my soul the uncreated conscience of my race.

Then the simple invocation:

> Old father, old artificer, stand me now and ever in good stead.

The "conscience of his race" as it appears in the world of his own childhood and adolescence and youth is uniformly corrupt and brutal. Even in the little prelude giving impressionistic glimpses of his earliest memories, *fear* of authority is one element in the atmosphere—"He hid under the table"—and the only way to escape cruel punishment is to submit: "Pull out his eyes,/Apologise." The little boy is surrounded by adults with rigid ready-made standards of all conduct and values, and he must conform. At Clongowes external reality shapes itself into a world of unintelligible and confusing codes, of secret guilt and vague sins, of a mob of shouting, pushing fellow creatures, "the whirl of the scrimmage," of snobbish values —your father must be a magistrate—and of gross injustice whereby you are shouldered into a slimy ditch if you won't consent to swap a little snuffbox for a chestnut. Stephen, however, triumphs over all this in the final sequence, where he is unjustly beaten by the sadistic Father Dolan. His shame and rage drive him to report the cruelty to the rector. He is exonerated; his schoolmates applaud his rebellion and he feels "happy and free."

This is all over very soon. The second chapter telescopes his career to the age of sixteen. Again, in the environment of an uncomprehending family, of casuistical priests, of vulgar, insensitive, tormenting schoolboys, Stephen struggles to keep his identity. He finds himself bombarded with exhortations urging him to be athletic and patriotic, a good son, a "decent fellow" and "a good catholic above all things." His only escape is in daydream. Meanwhile, the demands of his growing body subdue everything else. The experience with the harlot which ends the chapter, though so different from his dreams of romance, is again expressed as a triumph. It is an initiation. The yellow gas flames burn "as if before an altar," the groups of women in the street appear "arrayed as for some rite." With a sense of "joy and relief" he surrenders body and mind to the experience and feels suddenly "strong and fearless and sure of himself."

The natural man reaches a temporary fulfillment here, and in the next chapter the spiritual man—or adolescent rather—prevails. The mature Joyce, who is writing the book, reports with deadpan irony the methods of the church to produce repentance. The sermons, addressed by the Jesuit father to his "dear little brothers in Christ," are the crudest appeal to fear. They describe the physical and mental tortures devised by the infinite love of God for his erring children. Stephen, however, perceives no irony. Under the direct emotional onslaught he feels "a terror of spirit as the hoarse voice of the speaker blew death into his soul." In an agony of self-abasement he seeks confession, and then goes home "holy and happy," assured that this was "not a dream from which he would awake. The past was past."

Stephen throws himself into schemes for spiritual regeneration which are heroic in their aspirations. Joyce is openly ironic as he looks back on his young self and describes some of the absurd disciplines he practiced. At the same time he knows very well that the mysteries of religion and its rituals are akin to those of art. He is not ironic when he speaks of Stephen's awe before "the divine gloom and silence wherein dwelt the unseen Paraclete, whose symbols were a dove and a mighty wind . . . the eternal, mysterious secret Being to whom as God, the priests offered up mass once a year, robed in the scarlet of the tongues of fire." The flying figure of the hawklike

man and his own "deliverance to the winds" while his
soul is "soaring sunward" is the secular parallel to the
worship of the Holy Ghost. Yet the priest who suggests he
may have a religious vocation is part of the evil "conscience of his race" that threatens him. Hugh Kenner has
pointed out how the details of this scene are an unspoken
comment on the church. The priest stands with his back
to the light and the light itself is fading, which makes his
head look like a skull. His hands are "slowly dangling and
looping the cord of the blind" (making a noose for
Stephen's neck). As he goes out, the priest's face seems
"a mirthless mask reflecting a sunken day." Only when
Stephen has put that vision of the future behind him and
has asserted his right to go to the University does the
vision of his true vocation come, with its sense of exultant ecstasy.

The long last chapter repeats again all the elements in
his environment which inspire his rebellion. The feckless,
poverty-stricken family, where he is still treated like a
child by his mother, while mentally and spiritually he is
a complete stranger. As he passes from his home to the
waterlogged streets, stumbling through wet rubbish and
moldering offal, he is conscious only of "the sloth of body
and soul" which paralyzes Dublin and "the corruption
arising from its earth." His blanket condemnations exclude
any political or literary hope for his country, and his descriptions of his fellow students at the University are uniformly unfavorable. They are of a different breed from
himself. They have unpleasant looks and unpleasant
voices; they use the coarsest and most limited vocabulary:
they have no intellectual capacity or curiosity, and are
utterly without sensibility or dignity. The teachers are no
better. As Stephen sits in the classroom "an odour assailed
him of cheerless cellar damp and decay," and a "dull
torpor of the soul" looks out from "the pale loveless eyes"
of the dean of studies. The religion which dominates everything is now dead to him; he gibes at the Irish church as
"the scullery maid of Christendom."

It is difficult to know just what Joyce means us to think of Stephen in this chapter. He completed the book when he was a mature man of thirty-two, yet there is little to suggest that he does not regard the priggish and egocentric Stephen with full approval. No doubt by the time he was writing the end of the book, he had *Ulysses* in mind, and knew that Stephen's next appearance would reveal the emptiness of his prideful self-complacency, and that there he would appear as Icarus, "sea-bedabbled, fallen, weltering." But this final chapter gives no hint of that double vision, so well illustrated in *The Mill on the Floss*, by which maturity can create youth in all its rawness and yet suggest a further adult standard of judgment. Stephen emerges as a most unattractive figure. We sympathize deeply with him in his despair at his temporal conditions: "the life of his body, ill-clad, ill-fed, louse-eaten," and all the humiliations of his miserable poverty and lonely ambitions. We understand that his defensive arrogance springs from inner insecurity. At the same time, except for the one little scene where he pities his brothers and sisters, Stephen has no humility, no generosity, no warmth of heart. He is simply the innocent victim of a hostile environment. He has nothing but scorn for all his fellows; the only person he approves of is himself.

Yet perhaps Joyce's intention may be to suggest that these unpleasant, self-centered qualities in his young self are what made it *possible* for him to take the necessary step toward exile. To all Cranly's moving pleas of human ties and responsibilities he answers stubbornly, "I have to go." His calling as artist demands it and he must serve that vocation.

All through the book Stephen's struggles with his external conventional environment is fused with the development of his own inner life. Toward his surroundings (except at the time of his religious conversion) he is first in unconscious, then in fully conscious, revolt. At the same time, however, he has been shaping a positive identity of his own in "silence, exile and cunning." From the first he possesses the artist's abnormal acuteness to sense impressions. At Clongowes the sensations of cold and wet and darkness particularly assail him, or the "no-coloured" cruel eyes of Father Dolan and the terrible *sound* of the pandybat as it descends. At the same time the memory of colored flowers blots out the misery of doing sums, peasants have a lovely smell of "air and rain and turf and corduroy," and the sound of the cricket bats is "like drops of water in a fountain falling softly in a brimming bowl." Besides all the bombardment of his external senses, he learns one all-important fact: that if he closes the flaps of his ears he can shut out the noise of the refectory and listen to what is going on in his own head. More important still is the discovery that *words* are as full of mystery as experience in the actual world and are inextricably bound up with it. The same word "belt" can mean different things; the expression "a toe in the rump" is not "nice" and must not be repeated; some words, like "suck," have an ugly sound, but others are "sad and beautiful, like music"; others, like "wine," are full of suggestions, of purple grapes growing outside houses in Greece like white temples.

As he grows older the worlds of reality and dream clash more openly. He continues to learn words avidly, even if he does not yet understand their meaning, or assigns wrong meanings to them. He weaves a romantic ambiance by identifying himself with the hero of *The Count of Monte Cristo,* but is jolted out of that when he finds he is too timid to kiss the willing E—— C—— on the tram. Next day, however, as he tries to write a poem to her, he becomes imaginative artist: ". . . by dint of brooding on the incident, he thought himself into confidence," while "all those elements which he deemed common and insignificant fell out of the scene." Several years later, when he writes his villanelle, the same "enchantment of the heart" pervades him. A "rose and ardent light" glows around, sending forth rays of rhyme and rhythm. On his table is a dirty soup plate and the candle "with its tendrils of tallow"; on his bed his lumpy pillow; outside, life will awaken to "common noises, hoarse voices, sleepy prayers." But he, cowled in his blanket, inhabits the world of creative memory and reverie, while "the liquid letters of speech, symbols of the element of mystery, flowed forth over his brain."

Throughout, the language he hears around him offends his mind and his ear: the "drawling jargon" exchanged by the whores; "a heavy lumpish phrase" used by Cranly, which sinks "like a stone through a quagmire" and depresses his heart as he compares its quality with either "rare phrases of Elizabethan England" or quaintly turned Irish peasant idioms. As he roams the Dublin streets, musing on Newman's prose or the poetry of Guido Cavalcanti or Ben Jonson and reading "shop legends," he feels he is walking "among heaps of dead language." They are part of the labyrinths he must escape from.

In the last chapter Stephen propounds an aesthetic theory which has been much written about. It seems unnecessary to take most of this very seriously. It is Stephen's adolescent theory and is therefore dramatically appropriate, but much of it has, as his friend Lynch remarks coarsely, "the true scholastic stink." Passages read more like a textbook of aesthetics than the living creed of a revolutionary writer. Moreover, Stephen himself repudiates it, saying: "When we come to the phenomena of artistic conception, artistic gestation and artistic reproduction, I require a new terminology and a new personal experience."

The clues to these really vital personal practices, as apart from a set of precepts, are in the writing of the book itself and concern the innovations Joyce himself created.

Much traditional method is used, some good, some bad. The scene of the Christmas party is a brilliant piece of dramatic narrative, but the later chapters have a good deal of rather lush, repetitive overwriting (the influence of Pater and the eighteen nineties). The sermons in the

third chapter become tedious and some of the conversations in the last chapter heavy and boring. *The Portrait*
is, however, so far as I know, the first novel which is enclosed in a sustained symbolic pattern. Recurrent imagery
is a feature of the writing of Hawthorne, of Henry James,
of Conrad and D. H. Lawrence, but Joyce extends this to
pattern the whole theme on the Dedalus myth, and to
create its form into a series of "flights" and failures. At
the same time he avoids making the outline in any way
abstract. The symbolic theme is absorbed into biographical
narrative, which includes abrupt transitions from description to dialogue to reverie to diary. In this way Stephen's
outer and inner life are presented simultaneously, and
we are kept vividly in the immediate, concrete, realistic
present, while we watch the growth of inner consciousness
and thought processes. Though the story is told in the
third person, the author never interrupts with comments
of his own, which distinguishes the Joycean method from
that of any earlier novelist, even Henry James.

This objective mingling of outer and inner consciousness, especially the revelation of the inner *through* the
outer, is the most outstanding feature of Joyce's writing.
To him the creative process in man is a perpetual reenact-
ment of the miraculous union in himself of the worlds of
sense and spirit. The conviction of the simultaneous presence of these two worlds is of course behind all religious
systems, and their union is commemorated perpetually in
sacramental rituals by which objects in the sense world
symbolize unseen spiritual forces; they become "the outward and visible signs of an inward and spiritual grace."
Joyce was saturated in Catholic thought and symbolism,
and when his religion became the dedication to art, it was
very natural that he should transfer the concepts of one
to the other. As Stephen describes the making of his villanelle he cries: "O! in the virgin womb of the imagination the word was made flesh." Inspiration is an annunci-
ation; the conception and creation of the work of art is
an incarnation in which "the sluggish matter of the earth"

is united with spirit to produce the miracle of "the word." Again, using what he calls "the radiant image of the Eucharist," Stephen describes himself as "a priest of eternal imagination, transmuting the daily bread of experience into the radiant body of everlasting life."

This "radiance" is the quality Joyce particularly stresses in his theory of art. He translates Aquinas' definition of beauty—*integritas, consonantia, claritas*—as "wholeness, harmony and radiance." *Integritas*, the unity of the work, and *consonantia*, the relationship of its parts, are defined in traditional terms, but his interpretation of *claritas* as "radiance" and his further definition of it as "the scholastic *quidditas*, the *whatness* of a thing," its essence, is his own. In *Stephen Hero* he elaborates it as the faculty by which the soul of a scene "leaps to use from the vestment of its appearance."

Joyce critics usually call this faculty the making of "epiphanies," an epiphany being a showing forth, a revealing of the inner through the outer. It is another example of Joyce's use of a religious vocabulary for his artistic concepts. But he does not use the word in *The Portrait*. He used it in *Stephen Hero*, but discarded it deliberately, and refers to it in *Ulysses* only to mock his early use. It seems unnecessary, therefore, to perpepuate the term as if it were a device peculiar to Joyce. For this quality he calls "radiance" is what we have met before in Henry James, in Conrad and in Lawrence, in scenes such as the deathbed of Ralph Touchett, the description of the *Patna* before the accident, or the rabbit episode in *Women in Love*, incidents where the external scene and its psychic content are perfectly fused. "Radiance" is an excellent word for it, since it suggests its artistic value in two ways. First, it *lights up* the external action or object so that its inner emotion is revealed; and then it extends the meaning so that it *radiates* from the words and images and rhythms. The concluding scenes of the first three chapters are good examples, but it is behind the intensity which Joyce injects throughout into quite minor episodes, such

as the child Stephen's discovery of the word *Foetus* cut
in the desk of some forgotten medical student at Cork, or
the conversation with the Jesuit dean of studies as he is
lighting the fire, or the flight of the birds outside the library, or the vision when he sees all his teachers transformed into buffoons.

More complex than any other is the description of the
figure of the girl on the beach after the vision of "the
hawklike man flying sunward above the sea," and the suggestion of all the emotional associations which radiate
from the glimpse of her.

> A girl stood before him in midstream: alone and still,
> gazing out to sea. She seemed like one whom magic
> had changed into the likeness of a strange and beautiful
> seabird. Her long slender bare legs were delicate as a
> crane's and pure save where an emerald trail of sea-
> weed had fashioned itself as a sign upon the flesh. . . .
> Her slateblue skirts were kilted boldly about her waist
> and dovetailed behind her. Her bosom was as a bird's,
> soft and slight, slight and soft as the breast of some
> dark-plumaged dove. But her long fair hair was girlish:
> and girlish, and touched with the wonder of mortal
> beauty, her face.

Stephen has just experienced the certitude of his vocation
as artist, and this strange and beautiful figure is a symbol
of this. She is Stephen's Muse, as it were. She is mysterious, for all such spiritual revelations rest on mystery. She
is birdlike, for the message has come to him from the
sky in the symbol of flight. She is a seabird, standing in
the flowing waters of life. She is also associated with the
dove, bringing to mind the Christian stories of the Annun-
ciation, and the descent of the Holy Ghost—the gift of
tongues. Her blue skirts are Mary's color: she is the mother
of the Word. But Venus, goddess of beauty, had her doves
too, and the pagan symbolism of Venus rising from the sea
and being welcomed from the air is there too. (We think
of Botticelli's famous painting.) The seaweed, though,

making its sign on her flesh, is emerald: she is also Ireland, the emerald isle. She is Stephen's own race, whose uncreated conscience he will forge. She is also Woman, "mortal beauty," for it is from the mortal matter of the earth that the artist creates the immortal word which shall not die.

> Her image had passed into his soul for ever and no word had broken the holy silence of his ecstasy. Her eyes had called him and his soul had leaped at the call. To live, to err, to fall, to triumph, to recreate life out of life! . . . On and on and on and on!

This is the radiant image of his inspiration as it appeared to young Stephen as a romantic adolescent, and it is written in the language of romantic ecstasy. But basically it remains the same, though he creates a bitter parody of this scene in *Ulysses*. The whole atmosphere of Joyce's later books is very different, but all that this figure evokes is in everything he ever wrote: the mingling of Christian and pagan tradition; Ireland; Woman; the flow of river and sea as symbols of the waters of time and life. These are always the primal matters to which he gives a "new and radiant body" in language.

VIRGINIA WOOLF
1882–1941

To the Lighthouse

Virginia Woolf wrote criticism on almost all the great
Victorian writers. She appreciated them deeply and owns
that they have given her more delight than she can measure. But in an essay "On Re-Reading Novels," she asks
her readers to examine some basic assumptions: "Let us
consider a few of the questions which the prospect of re-
reading a long Victorian novel at once arouses in us."
She has some harsh things to say. First, the boredom of it.
The novels last so long and are so loosely written. They
"pour to waste" and lose shape. Then the subject matter
itself; they are so much concerned with the mere externals
of living and "one has enough life on one's hands already
without living it all over again in prose." She concludes:
"The genius of Victorian fiction seems to be making its
magnificent best of an essentially bad job," and that no
one before Henry James can be called an artistically mature novelist. They are all amateurs, he is the first professional: "The novel is his job."

Nothing could point more clearly than these remarks
to the rift between the writers of the nineteenth and twentieth centuries. For it is evident that when Virginia Woolf
addresses her imaginary readers here, she is not identifying herself—as Dickens or George Eliot would be—with
the general reading public. That public has always enjoyed
long realistic novels ever since the novel was invented, and
it continues to enjoy them. She is addressing a small mi-
nority group within the general social community. She is
speaking as an artist in a society where the artist has lost
his public function. She speaks as an experimenter in an

age of literary revolution, to those who are interested in experiment and revolution. The world of the serious artist is no longer the same world as the world of the reader. He inhabits a new world, or a transformed world rather, seen in the light of fresh ideas about life and therefore about its communication in art.

While Virginia Woolf had none of the social rebellion of Joyce or D. H. Lawrence, she shared their rebellion against the conventional naturalistic novel form as an adequate expression. "Is life like this?" she challenges, as she guys the structure of traditional fiction. She answers firmly that it is not. Life is a shower of ever-falling atoms of experience, not a narrative line. It is "a luminous halo, a semi-transparent envelope surrounding us from the beginning of consciousness to the end." In this essay, "Modern Fiction," written in 1919, she points to *A Portrait of the Artist* and to the early chapters of *Ulysses,* then appearing serially, as the hope for the future. There she finds the new psychological vision and the new method which shall replace the narrative structure of the past. Joyce, she says, "is concerned at all costs to reveal the flickering of that innermost flame which flashes its messages to the brain . . . If we want life itself, here surely we have it."

Henry James had shifted the main interest of the novel to the inner consciousness of his central characters, but their thought processes are always firmly anchored to the logic of the external events they are living through. It was his brother William James, in his *Principles of Psychology,* published in 1890, who pointed out that the true characteristic of consciousness is its "teeming multiplicity of objects and relations"; that it is not clear and logical, it is a continuous flow of images, sensations and thoughts into one another, so that a river or stream is its natural metaphor. "Let us call it a stream of thought, of consciousness or of subjective life."

Sterne had built *Tristram Shandy* on this wealth of inner experience and had contrasted "clock time" with "psy-

chic time," so that volumes of speculation and memory
take place between the birth and baptism of the hero. In
Tristram Shandy, however, outer and inner experience
both move horizontally, in parallel lines. When Joyce saw
the creative literary possibilities in the new psychological
visions and invented the "stream of consciousness" as a
literary technique, it had a double movement, horizontal
and vertical. The inescapable forward movement of temporal progression is counterpointed against the inward and
downward exploration of the psychic time of memory, introspection, association, sensation, daydream, where hours
or years can be collapsed to moments, events from past
and present, or far apart in place, can be telescoped and
folded into one another. In the first chapters of *Ulysses,*
during a few morning hours marked by a small scattering
of external happenings, the characters and circumstances
of Stephen Dedalus and Mr. Bloom are revealed to us entirely by the revelation of the multiple contents of their
two minds as they live from moment to moment.

The characters in *To the Lighthouse* reveal themselves
in the same way, but Virginia Woolf's method differs from
that of Joyce. She imposes the same limitations of mathe-
matical time. The action, such as it is, takes place in a
few hours of two days, ten years apart. She does not, however, put us directly into the minds of her people. While
she very seldom slips in comments of her own, she, the
controlling intelligence, is always present. She speaks in
the third person, she is the narrator, telling us what is
going on in the various minds. But these minds all speak
in the same language, the prose of Virginia Woolf. In the
central section of the book, "Time Passes," we see a great
deal of it through her own vision and general comment.

What kind of experience did her own supersensitive consciousness develop from? Virginia Woolf's world is as
limited in external scope as that of Henry James. She was
the product of the same kind of civilized, sophisticated
mentality. From her childhood and all through her life,
she was surrounded by writers, artists, men of learning

and exceptional women. Her father, Sir Leslie Stephen, after having been ordained a priest of the Anglican Church, left it and became an avowed agnostic, and she too remained so. She never knew real poverty and could develop all her potentialities without material cares. Her marriage to Leonard Woolf, a writer on political science, was ideally happy. Her sister Vanessa was a well-known artist, married to a well-known art critic, Clive Bell. Her brother was one of the earliest disciples of Freud. She and her husband ran a successful publishing house, the Hogarth Press, and their home in Bloomsbury was a center of the cultural life of the time. Her novels never move out of this environment. They never concern themselves with "society" in any real way. Their problems are those of the relationships of individuals of her own cultural kind; the problems of the value of these relationships; and the problems of communication between them. She is concerned with *personality*, in fact, with the relations of personalities to one another in moment-to-moment living, and to the universal background of life, death and time against which all personality must function.

Her vision is more metaphysical than that of Henry James or Joyce in *A Portrait*. James's standard is a code of personal and social ethics, and Joyce's imagination is centered in the image of the artist escaping from bondage. But Virginia Woolf had an almost mystic assurance of a "reality" behind and within the façade of the temporal. "I want to put practically everything in . . . but made transparent," she explains, and we cannot doubt that she is speaking of her own writing when she describes Lily Briscoe's ambitions in paint: "Beautiful and bright it should be on the surface, feathery and evanescent . . . but beneath the fabric must be clamped together with bolts of iron." When the critics praised her for all her subtleties and her delicate sensibilities and colorful prose, she confided to her diary: "What I want is to be told that it is solid and means something." Her aim in *To the Lighthouse* is to present what she feels as a central truth about human experience through the form of her art and in the contents of the individual minds that it creates.

In her diary she says she feels "reality" as "something abstract beside which nothing else matters: in which I exist and shall continue to exist," but she concludes: "How difficult not to go making 'reality' this or that, whereas it is one thing." Elsewhere she defines it as "what is left in us of past times and of our loves and hates," and tells us: "Whatever it touches, it fixes and makes permanent." These are desultory comments in her own person, but how does she create "reality" in the book, where, as it is the central theme, it must emerge from the whole structure, as well as from the supporting experience of individual characters?

This leads us into the complex and subtle symbolism of the book. In her diary, Virginia Woolf says she believes in tossing aside *prepared* symbols and using them simply as images, "never making them work out; only suggest." The symbolic design controls everything, but it has no firm outline. It is rather like the "great scroll of smoke" from the steamer that Lily looks at, "which stayed there curving and circling decoratively, as if the air were a fine gauze which held things together and kept them softly in its mesh . . ." The chief things "held together" in what she speaks of elsewhere as "an invisible elastic net" are four main symbols which pervade the book: the sea; the light-house; the personality of Mrs. Ramsay in life and in death; Lily Briscoe's picture. These are all woven together into a central meaning, a revelation of what Virginia Woolf sees as the nature of life.

"The sea is to be heard all through it" she said, and the sea is the eternal flux of life and time in the midst of which we all exist. It constantly changes its character. To Mrs. Ramsay at one moment it sounds soothing and consoling like a cradle song, at others, "like a ghostly roll of drums remorsely beating a warning of death," it brings terror. Sometimes its power, "sweeping savagely in," seems to reduce the individual to nothingness, at others it sends up "a fountain of bright water" which seems to match the sudden springs of vitality in the human spirit.

The sea surrounds the island on which the action takes place, which suggests both the human race in general and the individual personality. The sea also surrounds the Lighthouse as it stands solitary, sending out its intermittent beams. The Lighthouse holds a whole cluster of suggestions. To James Ramsay as a child it had seemed "a silvery, misty-looking tower with a yellow eye, that opened suddenly and softly in the evening." When he nears it in the boat at the end it is a stark, straight tower, with windows in it and wash spread on the rocks to dry: "So that was the Lighthouse, was it? No, the other was also the Lighthouse. For nothing was simply one thing." The Lighthouse is a mystery, but it also concerns day-to-day living. It is at once distant and close at hand. It is man-made; something permanent and enduring that man has built in the flux of time, to guide and control those at the mercy of its destructive forces. From this aspect it seems related to the human tradition and its values, which last from generation to generation and tell of both the unity and the continuity of man. Man tends its light, which sends its beams out over the dark waters to those on the island and so establishes communication with them and illumines them. To Mrs. Ramsay, as she sits knitting in the window, it seems at one moment the light of truth, stern, searching and beautiful, with which she can unite her own personality; at another, steady, pitiless, remorseless, an enemy of any peace of mind; or again a reminder of past ecstasy, thus bringing it into the present. But it always illumines and clarifies the human condition in some way.

The title of the book is *To the Lighthouse*. It is a quest for the values the Lighthouse suggests. The tower is frequently shadowed in mist, its beams are intermittent in

the darkness, the moments of assurance they bring are
momentary, but upon these assurances "reality" rests. The
book opens with a sentence hinting at two basic limitations
to human fulfillment: "Yes, of course, if it's fine tomorrow." "If" points to the uncertainty and insecurity of human fate, "tomorrow" to its imprisonment in time. The
final sentence, however, is: "I have had my vision." *Something* stable has been revealed as a flash in the general
doubt, something which seems to triumph over the eternal
cycle of change. To the six-year-old James, his mother's
words hold no qualifications; they convey an extraordinary
joy: "As if it were settled, the expedition were bound to
take place, and the wonder to which he had looked forward, for years and years it seemed, was, after a night's
darkness and a day's sail, within touch." The next moment, all this is dashed by the father he hates: "But it
won't be fine." The longing to kill his father which then
sweeps over James remains embedded in his nature until
ten years later, when, most unwillingly and sulkily, he
sails to the Lighthouse with him. As he skillfully steers
the boat toward the tower on the rock, hating his father
for his egotistical tyranny, Mr. Ramsay watches him and
suddenly says triumphantly, "Well done!" The world is
transformed for James by this warming praise, the separation between himself and his father falls away in a sense
of union and outgoing understanding. He wants his father
to ask for something so that he may give it. Mr. Ramsay's
response is left uncertain: ". . . he might be thinking, we
perished, each alone, or he might be thinking, I have
reached it. I have found it; but he said nothing." At the
same moment, however, Lily Briscoe, on the island, struggling with the aesthetic relationships in her picture, has
the illusion of the loving presence of Mrs. Ramsay, who is
dead, and the compulsion to share her emotion with Mr.
Ramsay, whom she has always feared and disliked. That
very morning she had denied him sympathy, though
hating herself for her poverty of spirit. Looking now to-

ward the Lighthouse, she knows that "Whatever she had wanted to give him, when he left her that morning, she had given him at last." To reach the Lighthouse is to establish a creative relationship.

It is the assurance of the continued presence of the creative spirit of Mrs. Ramsay in their lives which gives Lily her final "vision," and in directly personal terms, as well as her importance as symbol, Mrs. Ramsay pervades the whole book. She is above all the creator of fertile human relationships, symbolized by her love of matchmaking and her ubiquitous knitting; and of warm comfort, symbolized by her green shawl. Draped first over the frame of a picture of the Madonna and Child, it is then put over her shoulders when she strolls with her husband, and later used to cover up the skull in the children's bedroom. Left behind in the deserted house, it loosens, fold by fold, and falls to pieces. But these qualities are illustrated concretely in the scenes with her children, her husband, her friends and guests, or anyone in trouble or pain. As Lily recalls, after her death: "It was her instinct to go, an instinct like the swallows for the south, the artichokes for the sun, turning her infallibly to the human race, making her nest in its heart." Even the cynical and self-centered Charles Tansley has a vision of her "stepping through fields and flowers and taking to her breast buds that had broken and lambs that had fallen." When her husband craves sympathy and reassurance, James feels her spirit rise "in a rosy-flowered fruit tree laid with leaves and dancing boughs." At the end of that scene, when as "fountain and spray of life" she has refreshed "the beak of brass, barren and bare" of her husband, and he has gone "like a child who drops off satisfied," though she is exhausted by the life-giving effort, she experiences "the rapture of successful creation."

At the beginning of the dinner party, again, she is in a mood of spiritual depletion: "She had a sense of being past everything, through everything, out of everything."

As they sit at the table "nothing seemed to have merged.
They all sat separate. And the whole of the effort of merg-
ing and flowing and creating rested on her." But as her
personality warms to her task, the party, which has been
a collection of resentful egos, sheathing their true feelings in empty social insincerities, becomes a harmony of
good fellowship. Then the sense of "reality" visits her, in
what is perhaps the most memorable and characteristic
passage in the book.

> Just now (but this cannot last, she thought, dissociat-
> ing herself from the moment while they were all talk-
> ing about boots) just now she had reached security;
> she hovered like a hawk suspended; like a flag floated in
> an element of joy which filled every nerve of her body
> fully and sweetly, not noisily, solemnly rather, for it
> arose, she thought, looking at them all eating there,
> from husband and children and friends; all of which
> rising in this profound stillness (she was helping Wil-
> liam Bankes to one very small piece more . . .) seemed
> now for no special reason to stay there like a smoke,
> like a fume rising upward, holding them safe together.
> . . . There it was, all round them. It partook, she felt,
> carefully helping Mr. Bankes to a specially tender piece,
> of eternity; as she had already felt about something
> different once before that afternoon; there is a coherence
> in things, a stability; something, she meant, is immune
> from change, and shines out (she glanced at the win-
> dow with its ripple of reflected lights) in the face of
> the flowing, the fleeting, the spectral, like a ruby . . .
> Of such moments, she thought, the thing is made that
> endures.
> "Yes," she assured William Bankes, "there is plenty
> for everybody."
> "Andrew," she said, "hold your plate lower, or I shall
> spill it." . . . Here, she felt, putting the spoon down, was
> the still space that lies about the heart of things,
> where one could move or rest; could wait now . . . lis-

tening . . . resting her whole weight upon what . . . her husband was saying about the square root of one thousand two hundred and fifty-three. That was the number, it seemed, on his watch.

This moment, when Mrs. Ramsay experiences the sense of assurance and joy is inextricably interwoven with the most commonplace surface moments. It occurs in the midst of talking about boots, reproving one of the children, serving the meat, listening to her husband on square roots. The timeless and time coexist. We pass from the assurance of permanence to Mr. Ramsay's watch; from helping Mr. Bankes to a specially tender piece of beef, to eternity—where even the syntax of the sentence encloses the concrete action within the universal significance. Mrs. Ramsay feels above everything, in a different element, transcending the mundane, communicated in the images of the hawk, the flag, the smoke; and yet she is in the center of husband, children, friends, food and general conversation, and "the whole is held together."

When the party is over Lily feels: "directly she [Mrs. Ramsay] went a sort of disintegration set in; they wavered about, went different ways. . . ." And when Mrs. Ramsay is dead and Lily comes back, she has the same sensation: "how aimless, how chaotic, how unreal it was . . . a house full of unrelated passions." As she sets to work on her picture she remembers a scene from the past of herself and Charles Tansley on the beach squabbling and making friends again and Mrs. Ramsay's presence.

But what a power was in the human soul! she thought. That woman sitting there . . . resolved everything into simplicity; made these angers, irritations fall off like old rags; she brought together this and that and then this and so made . . . this moment of friendship and liking—which survived, after all these years complete . . . and there it stayed in the mind affecting one almost like a work of art.

She pauses a moment while the old unanswerable question: What is the meaning of life? darkens over her. But this time she finds the answer.

The great revelation perhaps never did come. Instead there were little daily miracles, illuminations, matches struck unexpectedly in the dark; here was one . . . herself and Charles Tansley and the breaking wave; Mrs. Ramsey bringing them together; Mrs. Ramsay saying, "Life stand still here"; Mrs. Ramsay making of the moment something permanent (as in another sphere Lily herself tried to make of the moment something permanent)—this was something in the nature of a revelation. In the midst of chaos there was shape; this eternal passing and flowing . . . was struck into stability.

Lily sees that Mrs. Ramsay's gift of harmonizing human relationships into memorable moments is "almost like a work of art," and in the book art is the ultimate symbol for the enduring "reality." In life, as Mrs. Ramsay herself well knows, relationships are doomed to imperfection, and are the sport of time and change; but in art the temporal and the eternal unite in an unchanging form— though, as in Lily's picture, the form may be very inadequate. We cannot doubt that Lily's struggles with the composition and texture of her painting are a counterpart of Virginia Woolf's tussles and triumphs in her own medium, but she chooses poetry as the image that reminds mankind that the ever-changing can yet become immortal. Just before the dinner party breaks up Mr. Ramsay starts quoting a poem (*Luriana Lurilee* by a forgotten nineteenth-century poet, Charles Elton). It seems to crown the harmony of the evening; everyone feels the same "relief and pleasure"; the poet seems the voice of mankind giving the words for what men feel. Later that evening, as her husband reads Sir Walter Scott, Mrs. Ramsay reads poetry. It arouses in her the sensuous impressions of lights and flowers, the sensation of climbing and rhythmical swinging out of and above her life of doing; it creates the sense of wholeness that has come to her only in fugitive moments.

> "Nor praise the deep vermilion in the rose," she read, and so reading she was ascending, she felt . . . on to the summit. How satisfying! How restful! . . . And then there it was, suddenly entire; she held it in her hands, beautiful and reasonable, clear and complete, the essence sucked out of life and held rounded here—the sonnet.

In a way, Mr. Carmichael, the poet, really rounds out the book better than the rather unconvincing completion of Lily's picture. He is a symbolic figure; his is the only mind we never enter. When Lily has her impulse of compassion toward Mr. Ramsay, and we have seen the scene at the Lighthouse itself between him and the children, Mr. Carmichael comes puffing up to join Lily. By simply saying, "They will have landed," it seems to her that he has somehow brought together and answered all that she has been feeling about the quest for meaning, for permanence, for harmony. He is, as it were, poetry itself.

> He stood there as if he were spreading his hands over all the weakness and suffering of mankind; she thought he was surveying, tolerantly and compassionately, their final destiny. Now he has crowned the occasion, she thought, when his hand slowly fell, as if she had seen him let fall from his great height a wreath of violets and asphodel which, fluttering slowly, lay at length upon the earth.

In the first and last sections of the book, the "bolts of iron" which, to Virginia Woolf, are the permanent and enduring things are revealed solely through the feathery and evanescent surface of the immediate moment of living. Between them, to bridge the ten-year gap, is the section "Time Passes." Some of this is a tour de force of lyrical evocation; beautiful writing, but almost too mannered in its elaborately cadenced and image-strewn passages. Its "meaning," however, supports the rest of the book, though the whole perspective of vision changes. From the immediate process of living in the outer and inner experiences of a group, we are removed to a distance, contemplating the sea, the island and the house as time relentlessly passes. From this view, the individual shrinks. The death of Mrs. Ramsay, in one way the most important event in the book, becomes a parenthesis. Man, dwarfed into insignificance, asks his questions of meaning in the presence of the vast cyclical moods of physical nature. He finds himself baffled by the universal oppositions of creation and destruction, light and darkness, clarity and confusion. Trying to relate himself to these forces, he swings from an assurance of some purpose, to the conviction of complete alienation, or of a mindless chaos totally indifferent to his existence. Coming closer then to the island, we watch the house and garden falling into ruin, the flowers choked with weeds and briars, rats gnawing the woodwork, swallows nesting in the drawing room and plaster falling from the ceilings, while the Lighthouse beam connects with nothing as it stares over the beds and walls.

But as the house, "sinking, falling," seems doomed, it is saved: "There was a force working." A message has come that the family are coming back. The force that sets to work is the human instinct to arrest corruption and decay, to make the disordered fertility of nature obey its disciplines, to direct its energies toward a purpose. It is traditional civilizaton. Its first representatives here are not very highly developed specimens of the human race— Mrs. McNab and Mrs. Bast, the cleaning women. Yet the description of Mrs. McNab, in spite of her clumsiness and crudity, contains the ideas of *light* and directed action: "Mrs. McNab, when she broke in and lurched about, dusting, sweeping, looked like a tropical fish oaring its way through sun-lanced waters." Hobbling and toothless, she sings as she works, seeming "persistency itself, trodden down but springing up again." She is a part of the unquenchable spirit of man. She and Mrs. Bast stay Time's corruption and rot; they reinstate the traditions of creative civilization, of social community, of technical achievement: "fetched up from oblivion all the Waverly novels and a tea-set one morning; in the afternoon restored to sun and air a brass fender and a set of steel fire-irons," and won "a magnificent conquest over taps and bath." As they mop and scour "some rusty laborious birth seemed to be taking place."

Mrs. McNab, being human, also possesses memory, which keeps the past alive in the present. She comes into the house, which has stood all these years "without a soul in it," and the sight of Mrs. Ramsay's clothes and possessions bring back to her vivid pictures of Mrs. Ramsay's warmth and good fellowhip. Soon *relationship* establishes itself again between past and present, between men and women and between man and nature. Mrs. McNab and Mrs. Bast are joined by Mrs. Bast's son, who catches the rats and scythes the grass. When they have left, things seem "mysteriously related . . . somehow belonging." The human story has been reborn.

Since "reality" is the sense of harmonious relation, its most insidious enemy is the human lack of relation, and the seeming impossibility of establishing it satisfactorily. This inescapable fact permeates every consciousness we enter. For one thing, so much of personality is submerged, dwelling in "that loneliness which is the truth about things" and never attaining overt expression: "Who knows what we are, what we feel? Who knows even at the moment of intimacy?" thinks Lily. Then personality can never be a fixed, objective thing; it lives in shifting emotions, sensations, daydreams, and in clashes with the personalities of others. Each consciousness is subtly changed by the company it keeps, each is at the mercy of mood, each seeks to supply its own psychological needs by its attitude to others. Lily, for instance, knows she uses Charles Tansley as a whipping boy:

Her own idea of him was grotesque . . . Half one's notions of other people were, after all, grotesque. They served private purposes of one's own.

Lily sees how Mrs. Ramsay, with all her good intentions, is blind to some things in Lily herself, and in Mr. Carmichael and Mr. Bankes, giving them all the wrong kind of pity: "it was one of those misjudgments of hers that seemed to be instinctive and to arise from some need of her own rather than of other people."

For Mrs. Ramsay, besides being a symbol for outgoing emotion, is a very real human being, with the inevitable self-deceptions and psychic compulsions. She tries to be honest, even to questioning if there is a taint of selfishness in her own selflessness: "For her own satisfaction was it that she wished so instinctively to help, to give, that people might say of her, 'O Mrs. Ramsay! dear Mrs. Ramsay . . .' and need her and send for her and admire her?" And she is thus "made aware of the pettiness of some part of her, and of human relations, how flawed they are, how despicable, how self-seeking, at their best." In the same way she is forced to face the imperfections of her relations with her husband. She needs to venerate the male intellect and judgment, yet while she longs to rest contentedly on her husband's strength, she has to recognize repeatedly that he is really dependent on her. She tries to shut out the facts of his vanity and insecurity and that she must constantly supply flattery and assurance; that he tyrannizes over the children and that "children never forget"; and that she feels, "without hostility, the sterility of men." As a result she hates her own insincerity, but knows it is inescapable. Indeed no relationship in the book escapes that taint. Everyone, too, at one time or another—justifiably or unjustifiably—feels resentful toward others; feels wounded or snubbed or guilty or hostile, or just hopeless about any real communication. Everyone, too, suffers the human dissatisfaction with his own lot, or the anguish of frustration and longing, feeling with Lily: "to want and not to have—to want and want—how that wrung the heart, and wrung it again and again."

Just as Mrs. Ramsay, in spite of her flaws—and the flaws others invent for her to satisfy their own subjective needs—remains the symbol of creative vitality, so Mr. Ramsay stands as the symbol of the sterile, destructive barriers to relationship. Virginia Woolf must allow him some saving grace, but we are seldom allowed to see what has made Mrs. Ramsay give him her devotion, and the moments of real communion between them are very few. In general, just as Mrs. Ramsay is described in images of fertility and the warmth and comfort of love and of harmony with others, Mr. Ramsay is evoked in images of sterility, hardness and cruelty and of deliberate isolation. He stands at the window "lean as a knife, narrow as the blade of one," full of the "twang and twitter" of nervous tension; he is "the beak of brass, barren and bare . . . the arid scimitar of the male," which plunges into Mrs. Ramsay's "fountain and spray of life"; he is the wagon wheel that James imagines going blindly over a person's foot, leaving it purple, crushed. He continually dramatizes himself as an heroic lonely figure, the leader of a lost expedition in the mountains or the Arctic or the desert. While he is valiantly struggling to the death on a lonely quest, he quotes suitable tags of verse, visualizing himself in the Light Brigade at Balaklava, "stormed at by shot and shell" because "someone had blundered," or perishing alone like Cowper's Castaway. Only he can never keep up the pose; always in actuality or in imagination, with his insatiable craving for sympathy, he flies to women to be soothed and reassured. Mrs. Ramsay reveres his intellect, but to Virginia Woolf that too is barren. She makes him envisage knowledge as an alphabet of single letters which can be toiled through by plodding perseverance. He knows, though, that this is not the way of genius, the inspired, "who, miraculously, lump all the letters together in a flash." Knowledge is fragmented, wisdom and vision are wholeness and harmony.

To the Lighthouse was published in 1927, the fifth of
Virginia Woolf's eight novels, and is generally considered
the finest; the one in which she brought her method to its
delicate perfection. It is indeed a wonderful piece of
workmanship. Her foundation of ideas is "clamped together" in the symbolic structure she chose to suggest it.
At the same time the "feathery, evanescent" nature of
consciousness—the permeation of the present by the past,
the outer by the inner, the currents uniting personalities
and dividing them, the moments when things come together and fall apart, the intermingling of the emotions
and the senses, all the mazy motions of reverie—all this
is vividly revealed. Her characters all come to life, as we
see into their own minds and into their images in the
minds of others. We constantly recognize the truth of her
psychological insights. Her mastery of her medium and
her riches of concrete metaphorical suggestion are everywhere. Unquestionably she was a "professional," evolving
a new form of fiction and creating a masterpiece in it.

Any criticism must center on how much of "felt life"
this form of fiction is capable of holding. "I want to put
practically everything in . . . but made transparent." What
does Virginia Woolf *not* put in? In one of her reveries
Mrs. Ramsay meditates on some of the terrible aspects of
life:

> There is no reason, order, justice: but suffering, death,
> the poor. There was no treachery too base for the
> world to commit; she knew that. No happiness lasted;
> she knew that.

None of these things enters the book; but then Jane Austen
also excluded all powerful emotion. Virginia Woolf provides no comprehensive social structure to acquiesce in
or rebel from; but Emily Brontë excluded that too. No,
the one thing we really miss is the lack of any progressive
action involving moral and emotional choices and decisions; any pattern of relationships being shaped and directed by such action. In all the other books we have

discussed, we watch the characters *making* their lives; in *To the Lighthouse* we see very clearly what they *have made* of them, but they are forced to remain static; it is all expansion without progression.

This, however, is how Virginia Woolf sees life. James, in the boat going to the Lighthouse, "began to search among the infinite series of impressions which time had laid down, leaf upon leaf, fold upon fold, softly, incessantly upon his brain." To Virginia Woolf it is this ceaseless fall of the atoms upon the consciousness that creates human identity. In the book we live among these myriad impressions, from the past and in the immediate present, which have patterned personality and from which the texture of experience is woven. Our insights are sharpened, our senses delighted. The moral values are there too; we look through the transparent "luminous halo" and know in a general way what Virginia Woolf sees as the springs of human good and human evil. We believe in the moments of heightened consciousness which seem to transcend time, and accept, again in a general way, the analogy with the "wholeness, harmony and radiance" of a work of art. But what we are shown lacks substance and particularity. We miss the conflict of wills and the dynamic movement which the method forbids; reactions can never be as powerful as actions, or impressions as events. In *The Portrait of a Lady* or *A Portrait of the Artist* we live a great deal in the inner world of consciousness, and important themes are embodied in recurrent imagery and symbolic structure. But these are reinforced by an interplay of action creating character, and character originating action, and are carried forward with seeming inevitability toward a resolution. The pure "stream of consciousness" method excludes this, and that is probably why it has not survived. It founders on that bedrock necessity which E. M. Forster laments though accepts: "The novel must tell a story."

Epilogue

No work of literary art is written to be an event in social history; it is not created as a symptom of a social climate. It is a vision of experience as seen by a particular individual, and it is an assertion of that personal vision and identity. At the same time, no writer lives in isolation. He is a unique personality, but like everyone else, he is a personality alive in a particular place, in a particular period of time, and part of a particular social, political, economic, moral and intellectual background. He is the product of an environment; of his upbringing, of the institutions under which he lives, of the quality of the times into which he has been pitched, of the character of the people who have influenced him—parents, teachers, colleagues, friends, lovers. He is the center of a huge web of relationships, personal and impersonal, and his development as an entity is a result of his conscious and unconscious reactions to these relationships. He may feel in harmony with his society or he may be in violent rebellion against it or he may try to escape from it, but any of these attitudes implies its importance to him. Indeed, as Virginia Woolf says: "The transaction between a writer and the spirit of the age is one of infinite delicacy, and upon a nice arrangement between the two the whole future of his work depends."

In certain ages this "arrangement" seems particularly happy and literature becomes suffused with a communal vitality. The nineteenth century was such a time. An extraordinary creative zest seems to have been in the air, which expressed itself particularly in the novel. All the

social strata of the day appear in it and the books are full
of living human creatures of great richness and variety,
whose names have passed into the common cultural tradition. The French and Russian novelists were freer in
scope, since they were not limited by the English and
American sexual taboos, but all shared in the vigor with
which they could create a multiplicity of vivid human
relationships and the problems arising from such relationships. Much searching satire on social injustice and
human inadequacies colored even the most hopeful of
these writers, but even if their visions were uniformly
dark—it would be hard to find any more deeply cynical
than that of Balzac or more despairing than that of
Hardy—they all had the same magical creative energy.

It is a commonplace to assert that the twentieth century
has little of this. Two cartoons by the English artist and
writer Max Beerbohm, published in 1918, sum up the
change in spirit. The titles of the drawings are: "The
Future as Seen by the Nineteenth Century" and "The Future as Seen by the Twentieth Century." In the first a
substantial John Bullish-looking middle-class figure, cheerful, well-fed and self-satisfied, is contemplating with
complacency an enlarged vision of himself. The second
shows a lanky, nervous, anxious-looking young man, with
a black band on his arm, and his vision of the future is
simply a large question mark on a dim and cloudy background.

The cartoons were published at the conclusion of World
War I, and the general impact of that war on the outlook
and spirit of the intelligentsia is felt in a speech by the
French poet Paul Valéry at the opening of a Writers' Con-
ference in Zurich in 1922.

> The storm has died away, and still we are uneasy as
> if the storm were about to break. Almost all the affairs
> of men remain in a terrible uncertainty ... We do not
> know what will be born and we fear the future not
> without reason ... Doubt and disorder are in us and

with us. There is no thinking man who can hope to
dominate this anxiety, to escape from the impression
of darkness, to measure the probable duration of this
period when the vital relations of humanity are profoundly disturbed.

Like the cartoons, this suggests the disruptive changes of
which the war itself had been the concrete symbol; the
loss of the stability and security of the old European
world; the collapse of the integrating elements which make
a unified cultural structure—traditional intellectual, moral
and social assumptions, peaceful international relations,
stable economic systems.

Valéry felt that it was impossible to measure the probable duration of the period of uncertainty when "Doubt
and disorder are in us and with us" and "the vital relations of humanity are profoundly disturbed." In the forty
years since he wrote, all he and his fellow writers dreaded
has been confirmed a hundredfold. The writer today, like
everyone else, faces a civilization split and darkened with
ideological, political and economic conflicts, and their resulting violence and bloodshed; a whole new world of
science and technology has transformed the old patterns
of knowledge; a revolution in conceptual thinking has
shaken traditional philosophy; a vast new mass materialism makes the old-fashioned liberal ideal seem more
and more alien and obsolete.

The age of rebellion against the nineteenth-century
novel, however, started before the war. The old traditional
forms had been challenged by Henry James, Conrad,
Marcel Proust, and Joyce, and a new rebellious attitude of
the young against the conventional moral pattern of their
elders was in the air. The discovery by the adolescent of
the hypocrisy, falsity and stupidity of his family and of
the adult world, and the consequent misery of his own
personal conflicts, has been revealed in a steady stream
of novels since the turn of the century. Generations of
young people since then have successively identified them-

selves with the heroes of *The Way of All Flesh, Of Human Bondage, A Portrait of the Artist as a Young Man, Look Homeward, Angel,* and *The Catcher in the Rye.* Victorian assumptions and conventions about the nature of reality and the place of the individual in society were steadily undermined. Many writers were in rebellion against what they were supposed to feel and do by training and habit reaction, and were bent on exploring what they did in fact feel. This led to all the psychological exploration in the nineteen twenties and the resulting new visions and new techniques. In the contemporary world, however, no new great names have yet supplanted those of Joyce, D. H. Lawrence and Virginia Woolf in England, or Hemingway and Faulkner in America, and perhaps this is not surprising. The novel has always been the result of the interrelationship set up between the subjective artist and the objective reality of the society around him, and it is just this interrelationship which is now so precarious.

In the past, novelists had always attacked the evils of their societies. They showed them to be riddled with individuals subject to every common human vice. Nevertheless they still felt that they belonged to such societies; they wrote from the inside, so to speak. Now the sensitive artist so often feels that he and his society are separate and hostile. He is an exile, a talented outsider. His heroes are apt to be in the same condition of frustrated, disillusioned bewilderment, adrift in a fractured culture, with no common ethos and no larger organic social structure into which they can build themselves and within which they can meet a wide diversity of experience.

Perhaps the novel must wait for a rebirth until the "two cultures" and the other disruptive forces in our civilization have shaken down into some new general synthesis of knowledge and perspective. Certainly it is not the business of the novelist to supply solutions to the problems of his age, but only to explore them through a personal vision which is exciting and illuminating. There are many talented writers doing this today, in many different moods and in many different directions: the historical novel; the regional novel; the myth or fable; the picaresque adventure. But there is no one who has produced a succession of memorable characters or a body of work which matches either the creative energy of the nineteenth-century traditionalists or that of the early-twentieth-century innovators. The literary artists themselves are the first to admit that the "transaction" between them and the spirit of their age is an unhappy one. Not every generation can hope to produce great novels any more than it produces great poetry or great drama. Great works cannot be written to order by either the artists or the public. They will come, for the form is much too sturdy not to renew itself constantly with fresh vigor. Henry James gave novelists their creed in an essay on "The Future of the Novel," published in 1889, which sounds as if it might have been written today. After deploring man's faculty for mutilating and disfiguring his own creations, he declares nevertheless that so long as life retains the power of projecting itself upon man's imagination, the novel will remain the best mirror for his impressions.

Anything better for the purpose has assuredly yet to be discovered. He will give it up only when life itself too thoroughly disagrees with him. Even then, indeed, may fiction not find a second wind, or a fiftieth, in the very portrayal of that collapse? Till the world is an unpeopled void there will be an image in the mirror. What need more immediately concern us, therefore, is the care of seeing that the image shall continue various and vivid.

Suggestions for Further Reading

Almost all the critics mentioned in the text are represented in this selection of books. The starred items are available in paperback editions.

* ALLEN, WALTER. *The English Novel.* New York: Dutton, 1955. A short critical survey.

BAGEHOT, WALTER. *Literary Studies.* 2 vols. New York: Dutton (Everyman's Library), 1916. Victorian essays on Sterne, Thackeray and Dickens.

BEACH, JOSEPH WARREN. *The Twentieth Century Novel: Studies in Technique.* New York: Appleton Century, 1932. Material on Conrad, Joyce and Woolf, with much background and comparison with earlier novelists.

BOOTH, WAYNE C. *The Rhetoric of Fiction.* Chicago: University of Chicago Press, 1961. "Aims to free both critics and novelists from the constraints of abstract rules about what novelists must do, by reminding them in a systematic way of what good novelists have in fact done." Full of stimulating insights.

* CECIL, DAVID. *Victorian Novelists: Essays in Revolution.* Chicago: University of Chicago Press, 1958. Essays on Dickens, Thackeray, Emily Brontë and George Eliot.

DAICHES, DAVID. *The Novel and the Modern World.* Rev. ed. Chicago: University of Chicago Press, 1960. Deals exclusively with Conrad, Lawrence, Joyce and Woolf.

EDEL, LEON. *The Psychological Novel 1900–1950.* Philadelphia and New York: Lippincott, 1955. A general discussion and survey, with much material on James, Joyce and Woolf.

* FORSTER, E. M. *Aspects of the Novel.* New York: Harcourt Brace, 1927. Lively and always interesting if at times prejudiced!

JAMES, HENRY. *The House of Fiction,* ed. Leon Edel. London: Rupert Hart-Davis, 1957. General essays on fiction, and a review of *Far from the Madding Crowd.*

* KETTLE, ARNOLD. *An Introduction to the English Novel.* 2 vols. New York: Hutchinson's University Library, 1951–53. The best short history (the volumes are small), with individual discussions of *Emma, Wuthering Heights, Vanity Fair, The Portrait of a Lady, To the Lighthouse.*

LEAVIS, F. R. *The Great Tradition.* New York: George W. Stewart, 1948. George Eliot, Henry James and Conrad are treated at length, but many other novelists either praised or dismissed. Mr. Leavis is always provocative.

* LUBBOCK, PERCY. *The Craft of Fiction.* New York: Scribner, 1955. "The whole intricate method . . . I take to be governed by the question of the point of view—the question of the relation in which the narrator stands to the story." Many interesting criticisms of technique, with Henry James getting the highest grades.

MCKILLOP, ALAN D. *The Early Masters of English Fiction.* Lawrence, Kans.: University of Kansas Press, 1956. Full treatment of the eighteenth-century figures.

MENDILOW, A. A. *Time and the Novel.* London: Peter Nevill, 1952. Particular discussions of *Tristram Shandy* and *To the Lighthouse,* and much interesting material on the whole subject of the title.

* O'CONNOR, WILLIAM VAN (ed.). *Forms of Modern Fiction.* Bloomington, Ind.: Indiana University Press, 1959. Almost all the novels discussed are mentioned in this

stimulating collection of essays by leading contemporary critics.

STEPHEN, LESLIE. *Hours in a Library*. New York: G. P. Putnam, 1904. Chapters on Defoe, Richardson, Fielding, George Eliot.

* VAN GHENT, DOROTHY. *The English Novel: Form and Function*. New York: Rinehart, 1953. An analysis of eighteen individual novels, ten of which form chapters in the present work. A most valuable and perceptive book.

* WATT, IAN. *The Rise of the Novel: Studies in Defoe, Richardson, and Fielding*. Berkeley: University of California Press, 1957.

* WOOLF, VIRGINIA. *The Common Reader*. New York: Harcourt Brace, 1925.

* ———. *The Second Common Reader*. New York: Harcourt Brace, 1932.

———. *Granite and Rainbow*. New York: Harcourt Brace, 1958. Essays or comments on all the English novelists.